Adobe® Scripting

Your visual blueprint™ for
scripting in Photoshop® and Illustrator®

by Chandler McWilliams

Visual

From

maranGraphics®

&

WILEY

Wiley Publishing, Inc.

Adobe® Scripting: Your visual blueprint™
for scripting in Photoshop® and Illustrator®

Published by
Wiley Publishing, Inc.
909 Third Avenue
New York, NY 10022

Published simultaneously in Canada

Library of Congress Control Number: 2003101790

ISBN: 0-7645-2455-0

Manufactured in the United States of America

10 9 8 7 6 5 4 3 2 1

1V/RV/QU/QT/IN

Trademark Acknowledgements

Important Numbers

For U.S. corporate orders, please call maranGraphics at 800-469-6616 or fax 905-890-9434.

For general information on our other products and services or to obtain technical support please contact our Customer Care Department within the U.S. at 800-762-2974, outside the U.S. at 317-572-3993 or fax 317-572-4002.

Permissions

maranGraphics

Built during a 17-year period from 1869 to 1886, the lavishly romantic Neuschwanstein Castle stands as a monument to the "Mad" King of Bavaria, Ludwig II. Unfortunately, the king died before his faux medieval fairy-tale castle was finished, causing all work on the project to cease. Although part of the interior remained incomplete, the structure is still a festival of banner-fluttering towers and battlements, making this Disney-like castle the most photographed in Germany. Learn more about German castles in *Frommer's Germany,* available wherever books are sold or at www.frommers.com.

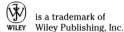
is a trademark of
WILEY   Wiley Publishing, Inc.

U.S. Corporate Sales	**U.S. Trade Sales**
Contact maranGraphics at (800) 469-6616 or fax (905) 890-9434.	Contact Wiley at (800) 762-2974 or fax (317) 572-4002.

PRAISE FOR VISUAL BOOKS...

This is absolutely the best computer-related book I have ever bought. Thank you so much for this fantastic text. Simply the best computer book series I have ever seen. I will look for, recommend, and purchase more of the same.

—*David E. Prince (NeoNome.com)*

I have always enjoyed your Visual books, as they provide a quick overview of functions. Visual books are helpful even for technically inclined individuals who don't have the time to read thick books in order to get the job done. As a frequent traveler, I am extremely grateful to you for providing a pdf version of each book on a companion CD-ROM. I can easily refer to your book while on the road without much additional weight.

—*Kin C. Wong (Calgary, Alberta, Canada)*

I just want to let you know that I really enjoy all your books. I'm a strong visual learner. You really know how to get people addicted to learning! I'm a very satisfied Visual customer. Keep up the excellent work!

—*Helen Lee (Calgary, Alberta, Canada)*

These Visual Blueprints are great books! I just purchased ASP 3.0 — it could not have introduced programming with ASP any easier!

—*Joseph Moglia (St. Louis, MO)*

This book is PERFECT for me - it's highly visual and gets right to the point. What I like most about it is that each page presents a new task that you can try verbatim or, alternatively, take the ideas and build your own examples. Also, this book isn't bogged down with trying to "tell all" — it gets right to the point. This is an EXCELLENT, EXCELLENT, EXCELLENT book and I look forward purchasing other books in the series.

—*Tom Dierickx (Malta, IL)*

I have quite a few of your Visual books and have been very pleased with all of them. I love the way the lessons are presented!

—*Mary Jane Newman (Yorba Linda, CA)*

I am an avid fan of your Visual books. If I need to learn anything, I just buy one of your books and learn the topic in no time. Wonders! I have even trained my friends to give me Visual books as gifts.

—*Illona Bergstrom (Aventura, FL)*

I just had to let you and your company know how great I think your books are. I just purchased my third Visual book (my first two are dog-eared now!) and, once again, your product has surpassed my expectations. The expertise, thought, and effort that go into each book are obvious, and I sincerely appreciate your efforts.

—*Tracey Moore (Memphis, TN)*

Compliments to the chef!! Your books are extraordinary! Or, simply put, extra-ordinary, meaning way above the rest! THANK YOU THANK YOU THANK YOU! I buy them for friends, family, and colleagues.

—*Christine J. Manfrin (Castle Rock, CO)*

I write to extend my thanks and appreciation for your books. They are clear, easy to follow, and straight to the point. Keep up the good work! I bought several of your books and they are just right! No regrets! I will always buy your books because they are the best.

—*Seward Kollie (Dakar, Senegal)*

Thank you for making it clear. Keep up the good work.

—*Kirk Santoro (Burbank, CA)*

maranGraphics is a family-run business
located near Toronto, Canada.

At **maranGraphics**, we believe in producing great computer books — one book at a time.

maranGraphics has been producing high-technology products for over 25 years, which enables us to offer the computer book community a unique communication process.

Our computer books use an integrated communication process, which is very different from the approach used in other computer books. Each spread is, in essence, a flow chart — the text and screen shots are totally incorporated into the layout of the spread. Introductory text and helpful tips complete the learning experience.

maranGraphics' approach encourages the left and right sides of the brain to work together — resulting in faster orientation and greater memory retention.

Above all, we are very proud of the handcrafted nature of our books. Our carefully-chosen writers are experts in their fields, and spend countless hours researching and organizing the content for each topic. Our artists

rebuild every screen shot to provide the best clarity possible, making our screen shots the most precise and easiest to read in the industry. We strive for perfection, and believe that the time spent handcrafting each element results in the best computer books money can buy.

Thank you for purchasing this book. We hope you enjoy it!

Sincerely,

Robert Maran

President
maranGraphics
Rob@maran.com
www.maran.com

CREDITS

Project Editor
Maureen Spears

Acquisitions Editors
Jen Dorsey
Tom Heine
Jody Kennen

Product Development Manager
Lindsay Sandman

Copy Editor
Jill Mazurczyk

Technical Editor
Toby Boudreaux

Editorial Manager
Rev Mengle

Media Development Specialist
Megan Decraene

Senior Permissions Editor
Carmen Krikorian

Production Coordinator
Nancee Reeves

Screen Artists
Ronda David-Burroughs
Jill A. Proll

Book Design
maranGraphics®

Layout
Sean Decker
LeAndra Johnson
Kristin McMullan

Cover Illustration
David E. Gregory

Proofreaders
John Tyler Connoley
Andy Hollandbeck
Susan Moritz
Carl W. Pierce
Ethel M. Winslow

Indexer
Johnna VanHoose

Special Help
Cricket Krengel

**Vice President and Executive
Group Publisher**
Richard Swadley

Vice President and Publisher
Barry Pruett

Composition Director
Debbie Stailey

ABOUT THE AUTHOR

Chandler McWilliams received his first Apple IIc when he was in third grade and has been hooked ever since. He attended Columbia College in Chicago where he studied Photography and Film and later graduated from the University of Illinois at Chicago in 1998 with a degree in Political Science. In 2002, he earned an MA from the Graduate Faculty at the New School for Social Research.

Taking leave of academia, he started working at The Chopping Block as a Design Technologist creating award-winning Web sites. He has taught at the School of Visual Arts and The Cooper Union. He currently lives in New York City.

AUTHOR'S ACKNOWLEDGMENTS

Writing a book is not as easy as it sounds. I wouldn't have been able to do it without the help of the wonderful people at Wiley including Jen Dorsey, Tom Heine, and Jill Mazurczyk. And of course my Project Editor Maureen Spears who helped me work through some tough spots and pushed me just enough to keep at it, without running myself ragged.

I'd like to thank some of the people at Adobe for their support and assistance: Ted Alspach who recommended me, and John Nack and Mordy Golding for all their great support and encouragement. Also Jesper Bache and Tom Burbage for all their help.

Finally, thanks to all the great people in my life for all of their support and love: Mom, Pat, Dad, Michelle, and Jacky. Toby, you are invaluable as friend as well as a technical editor. Thanks also to Dan, Jon, and everyone at The Chopping Block, Mike, Mihow, Ann, Spencer, the 90 Day Men, and all the folks in Chicago.

TABLE OF CONTENTS

Adobe Scripting:
Your visual blueprint for scripting
in Photoshop and Illustrator

3) WORKING WITH DOCUMENTS

4) WORKING WITH LAYERS

TABLE OF CONTENTS

5) WORKING WITH PATH ITEMS IN ILLUSTRATOR

6) TEXT IN PHOTOSHOP

Adobe Scripting:
Your visual blueprint for scripting
in Photoshop and Illustrator

7) TEXT IN ILLUSTRATOR

8) WORKING WITH THE FILE SYSTEM IN PHOTOSHOP AND ILLUSTRATOR

TABLE OF CONTENTS

9) WORKING WITH VARIABLES AND DATASETS IN ILLUSTRATOR

10) EXPORTING AND PRINTING

11) BATCH PROCESSING IN PHOTOSHOP AND ILLUSTRATOR

Adobe Scripting:
Your visual blueprint for scripting
in Photoshop and Illustrator

12) DEBUGGING SCRIPTS IN PHOTOSHOP AND ILLUSTRATOR

HOW TO USE THIS BOOK

Adobe Scripting: Your visual blueprint for scripting in Photoshop and Illustrator uses simple, straightforward examples to teach you how to create powerful and dynamic programs.

To get the most out of this book, you should read each chapter in order, from beginning to end. Each chapter introduces new ideas and builds on the knowledge learned in previous chapters. When you become familiar with *Adobe Scripting: Your visual blueprint for scripting in Photoshop and Illustrator,* you can use this book as an informative desktop reference.

Who This Book Is For

If you are interested in creating powerful scripts that extend the functionality and usability of Photoshop and Illustrator and help you automate repetitive tasks, *Adobe Scripting: Your visual blueprint for scripting in Photoshop and Illustrator* is the book for you.

This book is geared toward someone who is experienced at using Photoshop or Illustrator and has an understanding of the basic elements of working in these applications. It is also perfect for someone who is familiar with JavaScript or Flash ActionScript and has an interest is expanding the functionality of these applications.

What You Need to Use This Book

The tasks in this book require a computer running Windows or Mac OS and Photoshop or Illustrator. A text editor is also needed to write the scripts.

The Conventions in This Book

A number of typographic and layout styles have been used throughout *Adobe Scripting: Your visual blueprint for scripting in Photoshop and Illustrator* to distinguish different types of information.

Courier Font

Indicates the use of Visual Basic for Applications (VBA) code such as tags or attributes; scripting language code such as statements, operators, or functions; and Excel Object Model code such as objects, methods, or properties.

Bold

Indicates information that you must type.

Italics

Indicates a new term.

Apply It

An Apply It section usually contains a segment of code that takes the lesson you just learned one step further. Apply It sections offer inside information and pointers that you can use to enhance the functionality of your code.

Extra

An Extra section provides additional information about the task you just accomplished. Extra sections often contain interesting tips and useful tricks to make working with Excel macros easier and more efficient.

The Organization of This Book

Adobe Scripting: Your visual blueprint for scripting in Photoshop and Illustrator contains 12 chapters and 3 appendices.

Adobe Scripting:
Your visual blueprint for scripting
in Photoshop and Illustrator

The first chapter, "An Introduction to Scripting," discusses the basic ideas behind scripting Photoshop and Illustrator. You learn how to install scripting support for Photoshop and become familiar with some of the types of tasks scripting can accomplish.

The second chapter, "Programming with JavaScript," lays the foundation for a basic understanding of creating scripts in JavaScript and introduces the basic syntax and concepts of the language.

Chapter 3, "Working with Documents," shows you how to begin applying JavaScripting techniques to manipulate documents in Photoshop and Illustrator. You learn how to create and size documents, work with document meta-data, and understand selections in Photoshop.

In Chapter 4, "Working with Layers," you learn the basics of interacting with layers in Photoshop and Illustrator documents. This chapter also discusses how to apply filters to layers in Photoshop.

The fifth chapter, "Working with Path Items in Illustrator," teaches you the ins and outs of creating and transforming vector artwork in Illustrator. You also learn how to create symbols from artwork, group items together, and work with selections.

Chapters 6 and 7 discuss how to create and modify text in Photoshop and Illustrator, including changing the font, size, and alignment of text, and wrapping text around other objects.

Chapter 8, "Working with the File System in Photoshop and Illustrator," introduces how you can work with files and folders using JavaScript.

Chapter 9, "Working with Variables and Datasets in Illustrator," explains the basics of working with document variables in Illustrator, and teaches you how to use JavaScript to access datasets and variables to create dynamic documents.

Chapter 10, "Exporting and Printing," teaches you how to use JavaScript to export and print documents in both Photoshop and Illustrator.

In Chapter 11, "Batch Processing in Photoshop and Illustrator," the basic concepts of working with repetitive tasks are introduced. Many common tasks, such as exporting and sizing a large number of documents, and packaging files for delivery, are discussed.

The last chapter, "Debugging Scripts in Photoshop and Illustrator," helps you learn basic techniques for locating and dealing with errors in your scripts.

The three appendices include quick references for many of the objects and methods used in JavaScript for Photoshop and Illustrator.

What's on the CD-ROM

The CD-ROM included in this book contains the sample files for the book as well as the Photoshop scripting support installer and trial versions of BBEdit, UltraEdit, and Illustrator that you can use to work with *Adobe Scripting: Your visual blueprint for scripting in Photoshop and Illustrator*. An e-version of the book is also available on the disc.

SCRIPTING WITH PHOTOSHOP AND ILLUSTRATOR

You can use scripting to control the behavior of Photoshop and Illustrator. A *script* is a series of commands that tell Photoshop or Illustrator what to do. With scripting, you can streamline your workflow by consolidating repetitive tasks into a single script.

As you become more comfortable with scripting, you can start to build a library of scripts and functions that make it easy to solve a wide variety of problems in a short amount of time. If you can define ahead of time the steps required for a specific task, chances are you can quickly write a script that can do the work for you; and after you write the script, you can use it again and again to solve similar problems.

WHY USE SCRIPTING

A script can perform a wide variety of automation tasks. You can do everything from creating a new document with a specified size to automating the application of filters and effects on an entire directory tree. You can also create and manipulate the many types of layers and layer sets in Photoshop and Illustrator. You can even use scripting to create path items, symbols, and other art in Illustrator. See Chapter 3 for more on working with documents, Chapter 4 for more on working with layers, and Chapter 5 for more on creating paths, symbols and art in Illustrator.

Scripting also allows you to create and manipulate text and text items in both Photoshop and Illustrator. You can create functions to apply commonly used styles to a number of text items, or to quickly change the font, size, justification, or any number of properties. You can then easily make changes to all text items in a document or even an entire folder of documents. See Chapter 6 for more information on working with text in Photoshop and Chapter 7 for how to use text in Illustrator.

By using variables and datasets with Illustrator, and opening and reading text files, you can use scripting to separate form and content. You can import and change text and images easily. Using information you find in a text file, a simple script can change all the text in a document and swap images. See Chapter 9 for more on using variables and datasets, and Chapter 8 for more on file systems in Illustrator and Photoshop.

Automating complex and repetitive tasks is one of the most powerful uses of scripting. You can take care of the small, repetitive day-to-day tasks that often interfere with the creative process by using scripting and save time and frustration. You can create scripts to operate on open documents, create new documents, or process all the files in an entire directory tree. When coupled with the ability to export documents to a wide range of formats, scripting opens up a world of ways to save time and get jobs done quickly. See Chapter 11, for more on batch processing and the foundational skills you need to automate your workflow. See Chapter 10 for more on exporting and printing your document.

Scripting for Photoshop and Illustrator uses files that are separate from the applications themselves. This makes it easy to trade and distribute your scripts to others. There is a young community developing on the Internet of people using scripting for Photoshop and Illustrator. Photoshop 7 and Illustrator 10 are the first versions of these applications to support scripting, but as more people become familiar with its uses, this community will surely grow. You might want to look through the Adobe forums at: www.adobe.com/support/forums/main.html.

ACTIONS VS. SCRIPTS

Photoshop and Illustrator both support two different models of automation: actions, and scripting. The traditional way to automate a task is using a recorded *action*. An *action* is sort of macro that runs a recorded action. You begin recording and step through the task step-by-step, and after you finish recording, you can use the action. One advantage actions have over scripting is recordability. Writing a script is sometimes more of an intense task than pressing Record and creating an action. You can quickly achieve many short, simple tasks with actions.

However, actions are severely limited in the type of operations they can perform. Most importantly, actions cannot have conditional logic. This means they do the same thing every time and cannot make decisions based on the current situation.

Automating Photoshop and Illustrator with scripting allows you to incorporate logic in your automated tasks. Scripts can use logic to make decisions at key points, changing their behavior in response to the conditions they encounter. You can even implement complex decision trees when using scripts for automation. For example, a script can make decisions about how to handle files based on the name of their directory. You can have a directory of full-size images and a directory called thumbnails, and the script can apply a different set of filters, effects, and sizes to the contents of the thumbnails directory. You can also use actions and scripts together to easily automate complex and powerful operations.

SUPPORTED SCRIPTING LANGUAGES

You can script Photoshop and Illustrator using three different scripting languages: AppleScript on the Mac; Visual Basic for Windows; and JavaScript for cross-platform compatibility. Scripting is only supported as of Photoshop 7.0 and Illustrator 10.0 and all three languages work with both applications. Both AppleScript and Visual Basic allow scripts to communicate with multiple applications and a variety of Web services and other data sources.

Although JavaScript is somewhat limited in these respects, it does have the advantage of being cross-platform. A

script you write on a Mac continues to work on Windows. Keeping your scripts platform independent makes them easier to distribute and reduces the likelihood of rewriting an old script to work on a new computer.

JavaScript is also an easy to learn and widely applicable language. The core syntax for scripting Photoshop and Illustrator in JavaScript is identical to the syntax you use in JavaScript on the Web. If you are familiar with using JavaScript on the Web, or even ActionScripting for Flash, you can quickly learn Photoshop and Illustrator scripting.

DIFFERENCES BETWEEN PHOTOSHOP AND ILLUSTRATOR SCRIPTING

The fundamental features for scripting Photoshop and Illustrator are the same; there are, however, some slight differences in the execution of specific commands. Many of the differences are simply a result of the different features and purposes of each application. For example, both use the `documents.add()` method to

create a new document. But the parameters this method takes vary between the two applications; Photoshop offers different color modes and fill types, while Illustrator has a choice of color spaces. Despite these specific differences, the basic concepts still hold and you can apply them to both applications.

INSTALL SCRIPTING SUPPORT FOR PHOTOSHOP

As of Photoshop 7, scripting support is not included out-of-the-box. To allow Photoshop to be scriptable using AppleScript, Visual Basic, and JavaScript, you must download and install the Scripting Support Plug-In from Adobe. Installation is easy and allows you to utilize the power of scripting. Future versions of Photoshop may include support for scripting without the need to perform this installation. Check the Photoshop documentation or the Adobe Web site for more information.

To enable scripting for Photoshop 7, you must download the scripting plug-in from Adobe. The Web site for is this: www.adobe.com/support/downloads/detail.jsp?ftpID=1535 for Macintosh users, and www.adobe.com/support/downloads/detail.jsp?ftpID=1536 for Windows users. A copy of the plug-in for both platforms is also included on the CD-ROM included with this book.

On the Macintosh, the installer package comes as a disk image. Simply mount the image by double-clicking it, and then run the Photoshop Scripting Support installer. For Windows, the installer is a self-extracting archive that, when launched, creates a folder. After the expander finishes, double-click the Photoshop Scripting Support installer. On both platforms, make sure Photoshop is not running when you start the installer.

The installer comes with release notes, sample scripts, documentation, and utilities. Keep a copy of the documentation, sample scripts, and utilities for later reference. The Utilities folder contains the Scripting Listener plug-in, which allows you to record complex actions and translates these actions into JavaScript, and Visual Basic on Windows, that you can use in your scripts. Make sure not to install the plug-in right away. It is difficult to use and severely slows down the speed of Photoshop. Just keep it somewhere handy for use later on. See Chapter 11 for more on using this plug-in.

INSTALL SCRIPTING SUPPORT FOR PHOTOSHOP

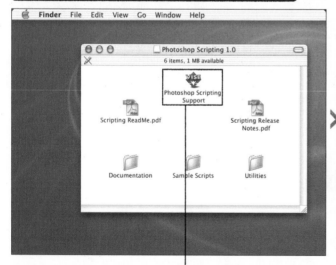

1 Download the installer from the Adobe site, or copy it from the CD.

2 Double-click the Photoshop Scripting Support installer.

■ The Adobe Photoshop 7.0 Scripting Support start screen appears.

3 Click Continue.

Extra

Occasionally Adobe releases a new version of scripting support for Photoshop. These newer versions may include expanded functionality and fix issues that may have cropped up in older versions. A great resource for finding the latest version of the Scripting Support installer is www.versiontracker.com.

Illustrator comes with scripting support enabled with the application. You do not need to install anything for AppleScript, Visual Basic, and JavaScript to work with Illustrator. There are, however, a few extras on the Illustrator CD-ROM that are not copied to your hard drive when you install Illustrator. Insert the CD-ROM and open the Illustrator Extras folder. A scripting folder contains sample scripts and documentation. You should copy this folder to your hard drive for later reference. One of the best ways to learn any programming language is to look closely at the work of others and try to understand the way their code works. Once you feel more comfortable with JavaScript, you should take a look at the sample scripts. There are different types of sample scripts included depending on your platform; make sure that you are looking at the JavaScript examples.

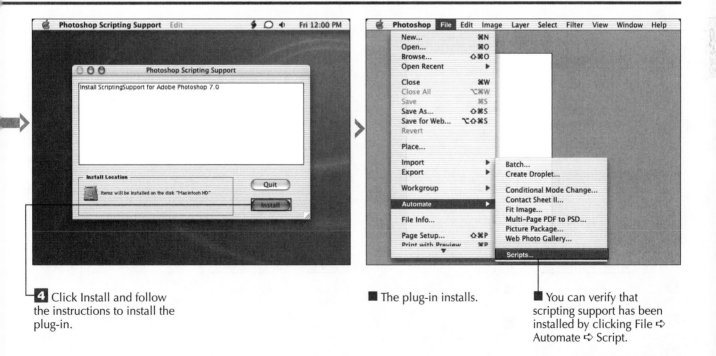

■ Click Install and follow the instructions to install the plug-in.

■ The plug-in installs.

■ You can verify that scripting support has been installed by clicking File ➪ Automate ➪ Script.

RUN A SAMPLE SCRIPT IN PHOTOSHOP AND ILLUSTRATOR

You can run a JavaScript from inside Photoshop and Illustrator. Running a script lets the application know that it should execute the steps defined in the script. Before you can use your own scripts, you need to familiarize yourself with how to execute scripts in Photoshop and Illustrator.

There are minor differences in the steps required to run a script in Photoshop and Illustrator. In Photoshop, you access the Scripts option via the File ⇨ Automate menu path. You then select and execute your sample script from a dialog box that appears. Photoshop does not allow you to run scripts if you select text or if you are currently entering text with the Text tool. Make sure that you are not in text mode before running any scripts. In Illustrator, you access scripts via the File ⇨ Scripts menu path. Instead of a dialog box, Illustrator lists all scripts in the menu that appears. Selecting a script for the menu runs the script. For both

Photoshop and Illustrator, you can also browse to find a script in another location. In Photoshop, you use the Browse button on the dialog box. In Illustrator, you use the Browse menu option.

The Photoshop scripting support installer installs some sample scripts to get you started and Illustrator come packaged with a number of sample scripts as well. Take a look at some of the sample scripts by opening them in a text editor. Looking at other people's scripts helps you learn and helps you discover new and better solutions to problems you may encounter.

See the section "Storing Scripts" for more on adding scripts to the Scripts menu in Illustrator and dialog box in Photoshop. Please note that the results shown in the steps of this section may differ from your results depending on the script that you run.

RUN A SAMPLE SCRIPT IN PHOTOSHOP AND ILLUSTRATOR

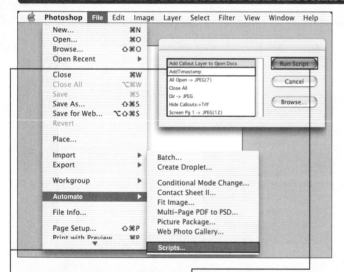

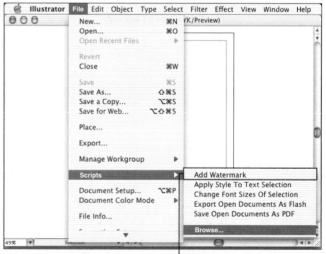

RUN A SCRIPT IN PHOTOSHOP

1 Open a document in Photoshop.

2 Click File ⇨ Automate ⇨ Scripts.

3 In the Scripts dialog box, click the script name.

4 Click Run Script.

■ You can also double-click a script name to run it.

■ The script runs and modifies the document.

RUN A SCRIPT IN ILLUSTRATOR

1 Open a document in Illustrator.

2 Click File ⇨ Scripts and select a script to run.

■ The script runs and modifies the document.

STORING SCRIPTS

You can keep your scripts organized in Photoshop and Illustrator. You can easily access your scripts from inside Photoshop and Illustrator to save you time and automate common tasks. Keeping your scripts organized is a good way to make them easier to find, modify, and use. They can also help you develop a library of reusable code. It is much easier to write a function that serves a particular task once and then to reuse that function whenever a similar task turns up. For example, you may need to add a piece of text or label to every open document. By writing this script in a general way, you can easily modify it to add a watermark image to all open documents.

The scripts that appear in the Photoshop Script menu are located next to the Photoshop application in the Presets/Scripts folder. Any scripts that you place in this folder are visible in the Run Script dialog box. If you want to keep your scripts in another location, you can always use the Browse button to browse your hard drive to find the script.

In Illustrator, all scripts are stored in the analogous location, the Presets/Scripts folder next to the Illustrator application. Any scripts you place in this location appear in the Scripts menu in Illustrator. Illustrator has the added advantage of allowing you to store your scripts in folders. The menu includes all folders, and you can navigate to them from within Illustrator. The Scripts menu also contains a Browse item to let you locate scripts kept in another location. The Script menu in Illustrator is limited to displaying only four levels of folders.

STORING SCRIPTS

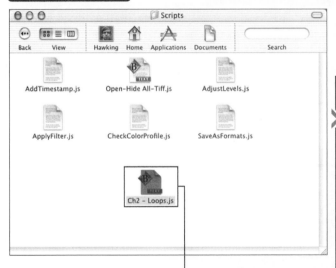

1 Open the Scripts folder located in the Presets folder next to either the Photoshop or Illustrator application.

2 Choose a script from the CD-ROM and copy it to the folder.

3 Launch the application.

■ The script appears in the Script menu.

Note: If you choose to use Photoshop, the Scripts dialog box appears and displays the newly added script.

UNDERSTANDING JAVASCRIPT SYNTAX

I f you are unfamiliar with JavaScript, the information in this section gives you some background as to the language's origins, helping you gain a foothold and get a better idea about where to look for help. This page also compares JavaScript to other popular programming languages. Becoming familiar with the similarities and differences between languages is a great way to begin learning any programming language because you can apply the knowledge gained from other languages in new ways.

THE HISTORY OF JAVASCRIPT

Netscape originally developed JavaScript to add interactivity to previously static HTML Web pages. JavaScript is not a relative of Java and was originally named LiveScript, but the name was changed to associate it with the hot topic of the time, Java.

As JavaScript grew in popularity, the ECMA (European Computer Manufacturers Association) made it a standard and called it ECMAScript. Because of the enormous popularity of JavaScript, many companies use the core language as the foundation for new and exciting scripting languages. As of version 5, Macromedia's Flash ActionScript is based on ECMAScript, and many of the new Adobe products include support for creating cross-platform scripts using a language based on ECMAScript.

SIMILARITIES AND DIFFERENCES WITH OTHER PROGRAMMING LANGUAGES

Much like C, C++, and Java, JavaScript employs programming constructs such as brackets [], braces (or curly brackets) {}, if statements, and functions. However, there is little similarity beyond syntax. Unlike C, C++, and Java, JavaScript is an *untyped* language, which means that you do not have to associate variables with a specific data type. JavaScript allows you to change the type of the variable midway through a script. Also, depending on the type of operations you try to perform, JavaScript converts a variable's type on the fly. See the section "Using Operators" for more on type conversions.

JAVASCRIPT OPERATIONS

To see the results of some of the operations in this chapter, you must make heavy use of the alert() function. Functions are discussed later in the chapter, but for now remember that whenever you type alert(), an alert box appears and displays whatever you place between the parentheses. To display a box with the text "Hello!" you type **alert("Hello!")** and then run the script in Photoshop or Illustrator.

USE OF TABS IN JAVASCRIPT

Another formatting issue to be aware of is the use of tabs to indicate structure within a script. When creating functions, conditions, loops, and so on, you often indent the body of the structure. This makes it easier to read code at a glance and understand the relationships between the different parts of the script.

UNDERSTANDING PROGRAMMING STYLE

You can make your scripts easier to write and modify by developing good coding habits. A large part of writing a successful script is debugging and modifying existing code. Some good habits to get into are designing your scripts ahead of time using comments, documenting your code with comments, writing code to become part of a reusable library, and keeping your code simple. Keep in mind that the code is not only for a machine, but also for you and other programmers.

DESIGN SCRIPTS USING COMMENTS

The first step in writing good code is to think through what you want to happen. Begin with the big steps, or major points, along the way. Then go back and fill in the smaller tasks between them. After you type out all the steps for your script, getting a feel for the whole thing is easier. This helps you spot potential errors before you start coding.

One way to start this process is to design scripts using comments and Pseudo Code. *Pseudo code* is a programming term for writing out the basic structure of a program in plain text. Describing what it is you want your script to do in plain language helps you clarify your thoughts and hammer out what you need to do.

You can translate your pseudo code into comments; this starts the processes of commenting your script and provides a useful outline. After you have your pseudo code comments in place, you can go back and fill in the blanks with real code. As you write the script, the comments provide an anchor and keep you on track.

DOCUMENT CODE WITH COMMENTS

As your script develops, make sure to leave notes to yourself along the way so that you can easily return to the script and understand how it works. You may find it very helpful to add a comment for major variables in the script; that way the role and importance of different variables is easy to spot at a glance.

Remember that most of the time you spend scripting is not focused on writing new code, but on reworking old code to serve new purposes. Writing comments can make this process easier and more productive.

SET UP A REUSABLE CODE LIBRARY

When writing your scripts, try to think of ways in which you or other users may reuse the script as a whole in the future. For example, if your script requires the creation of a stroked circle in Illustrator, it might make sense to create a function to do this so you save time later. Because creating a circle is such a common task, it makes sense to write the code for reuse to avoid reinventing the wheel every time. Instead of using variable, function, and array names that you tie to their specific role in the script you are developing, try to think of names that refer to the role it plays in the script, abstracted from the task at hand.

DECLARE VARIABLES

You can use variables to store values generated in a script. You can think of variables as buckets — empty containers ready to fill with some content or value. As in algebra, you assign a variable a value, and then you use it in place of the value. If you change the value of the variable, the result of the operation also changes. In JavaScript, however, you can make values more than just numbers.

The first step in declaring, or creating, a variable is to decide on its name. You can make the name almost anything you want, but there are a few simple rules. The variable name can only contain alphanumeric characters, and underscore (_). Also, the name cannot contain any spaces and must begin with a letter or underscore. In JavaScript, all variables are case sensitive.

Creating a variable is as easy as typing the JavaScript keyword var, and then the name of the variable, followed by an equal sign, and then the value you want to assign it. There are three main types of variables you use in your everyday work. *Strings* are pieces of text, *numbers* are numerical values, and *Booleans* are true/false values. Each of the three types performs a different task and allows different sorts of manipulations. See the section "Understanding JavaScript Syntax" for more information on variable types and the *untyped* nature of JavaScript.

When declaring a new string variable, you must enclose the value in quotes. You can make them single (') or double (") quotes, but they must always appear in pairs, one opening and one closing the string. A Boolean variable can have only two values, true or false, and the value appears without quotation marks. Likewise, setting the variable equal to a number without quotation marks creates a number variable.

DECLARE VARIABLES

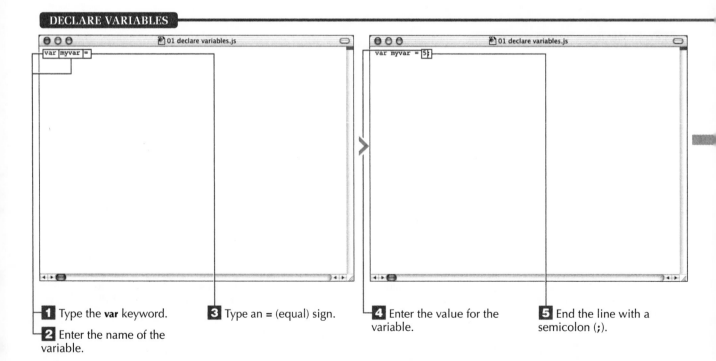

1 Type the **var** keyword.
2 Enter the name of the variable.
3 Type an = (equal) sign.
4 Enter the value for the variable.
5 End the line with a semicolon (;).

10

Extra

JavaScript provides a special comma (,) operator that allows you to declare several variables at the same time. You may find this useful when initializing scripts and keeping similar values together. For example, if you create a number of counter variables, you can declare them all at once and keep them together on a single line.

Example:
```
var i=0, j=1, k=2;
```
Is equivalent to:
```
var i=0;
var j=1;
var k=2;
```

You can use the `typeof` operator to find the type of a variable by typing **typeof**, followed by the variable name. The result is a string describing the type, string, number, object, function, undefined, null, or Boolean. Although JavaScript is an untyped language, every variable always has a type at a given time depending on the value of the variable. The untyped nature simply means that you can give the variable a different type of value without causing an error.

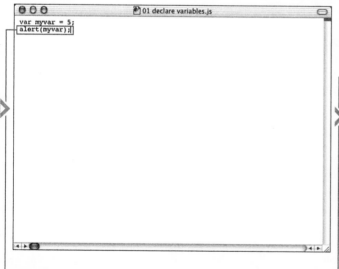

6 Type **alert();**, placing your variable name between the ().

Note: For more on running a sample script, see Chapter 1.

7 Execute the script in Photoshop or Illustrator.

■ A dialog box appears showing the value of the variable.

USING OPERATORS

You can manipulate variables in JavaScript using a set of operators. JavaScript's operators allow you to concatenate strings, execute arithmetic operations on numbers, and even perform Boolean operations.

The most common operators are the arithmetic operators: + (addition), – (subtraction), * (multiplication), and / (division). You perform any of these operations by placing the operator between the two values:

2 + 8

You can also use operators to manipulate the value of variables. As in the example above, you add two variables by placing the operator between the two variables, `firstnumber + secondnumber`. Also, you can make one value a variable and one a number as in: `x * 3`. You read this as "x times 3."

In JavaScript, the plus (+) operator behaves differently depending on the type of the values involved. If the values are both numbers, the plus executes a numerical addition. However, if one or both of the values is a string, the plus performs a concatenation and appends the second value to the end of the first.

When the values you use with an operator are different, the untyped nature of JavaScript becomes apparent. See the section "Understanding JavaScript Syntax" for more information. For example, when using the plus operator with a string as one value and a number as the second, the number temporarily converts into a string in order to concatenate the values together. Type conversion also works the other way. If a variable has a string value that can convert into a number, as in: `x = '3'`, and you try to perform a numerical operation that uses an operator other than +, the string converts to a number and the result is a number. In ambiguous situations, JavaScript converts the values to strings.

USING OPERATORS

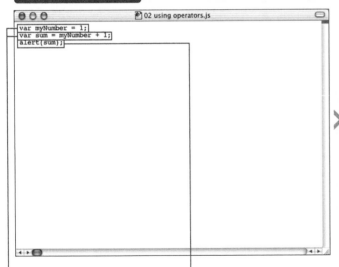

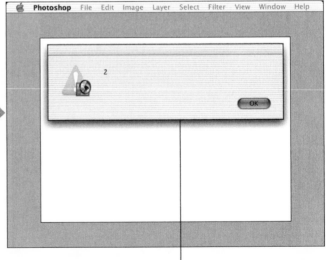

1 Create a new variable with a value, in this example a value of 1.

2 Create another variable and set it equal to the variable from step 1 plus 1.

3 Type **alert()** and place the variable name in the parentheses to display the value of the variable.

4 Execute the script in Photoshop or Illustrator.

■ A dialog box shows the resulting value of the variable, in this case 2.

The plus (+) operator has different effects on both strings and numbers. The other mathematical operators, however, apply only to numbers. When JavaScript encounters code that attempts to perform a mathematical operation on a string, it first tries to convert the string to a number. If this is unsuccessful, normally because the string contains more than only numerical values, JavaScript returns the NaN value, which stands for "Not a Number." No error generates, but the script cannot use the value of the operation. You can only test the NaN value to verify the success or failure of an arithmetic operation. The value of result in the following code is NaN.

Example:
```
var myString = "a string";
var result = myString * 5;
```

When performing addition operations on variables, you can use the Number() function to force JavaScript to interpret the variable in the parentheses as a number. In the following code, the value of result1 is 12, because the two values were treated as strings. The value of result2 is 3, because JavaScript interprets each value as a number and adds them together.

Example:
```
var one = "1";
var two = "2";
var result1 = one + two;
var result2 = Number(one) + Number(two);
```

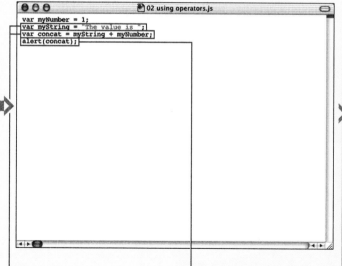

```
var myNumber = 1;
var myString = "The value is ";
var concat = myString + myNumber;
alert(concat);
```

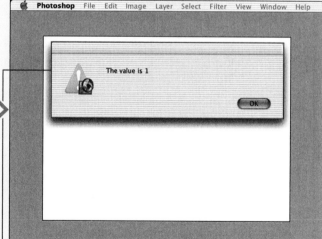

The value is 1

■5 Create another variable, giving it a string value such as "The value is ", and name the variable myString.

■6 Set a fourth variable equal to the result of the variable from step 1 plus the one you created in step 5.

■7 Type alert() and place the variable name in the parentheses to display the value of the variable.

■8 Execute the script in Photoshop or Illustrator.

■ A dialog box appears showing the value of the concat variable.

INCREMENT AND DECREMENT A VARIABLE

In addition to the standard operators, JavaScript provides special shortcut operators to handle common incrementing and decrementing of variables. These operators help keep your code clean while saving time and typing.

The most common of the special operators is ++. If you have a variable x with a value of 3, and you want to add 1 to it, the long-hand way of achieving this task is to write x = x + 1. Rather than write this out every time, you can use the ++ operator to increment a variable by a value of 1. You can then rewrite the code above as x++.

Likewise, the – operator decrements a variable by 1. So instead of writing x = x −1, you can write x−−. These shorthand operators not only save time, but also help make your code cleaner and easier to read.

JavaScript also provides operators for incrementing and decrementing a variable by an arbitrary amount. You can accomplish this by using the += and −= operators. For example, += allows you to add 5 to a variable by typing x += 5. This reads "Add 5 to the value of x." Unlike the increment and decrement operators, the assignment operators require two operands, first the variable to modify, then the value of the modification. As you might expect, the += operator also works on strings by setting the variable to its value and the value of the second operand appended to the end.

The assignment operators are not limited to plus and minus. In addition, there is an assignment operator for * (multiplication) and / (division).

INCREMENT AND DECREMENT A VARIABLE

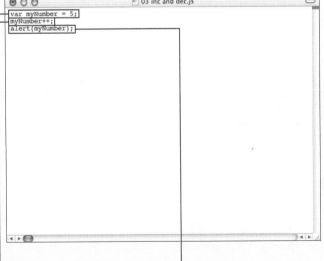

1 Create a variable and give it a value, in this example 5.

2 Increment the variable by 1 by typing the name of the variable and then **++**.

3 Type **alert()** and place the name of the variable in the parentheses.

4 Execute the script in Photoshop or Illustrator.

■ The alert box shows the value of the variable as 6.

Extra

You do not always need to place the ++ and −− operators after the variable name. When you use them in conjunction with the assignment (=) and comparison (==) operators, the order makes a subtle difference in the results. In these cases, if the variable is first, JavaScript determines the value of the variable before it increments them. If the operator comes first, JavaScript increments the variable before it determines the value. In the following example, the number2 variable equals 5, while the number3 variable equals 6.

Example:
```
var myNumber = 5;
var number2 = myNumber++;
var otherNumber = 5;
var number3 = ++otherNumber;
```

Also, keep in mind that the += operator behaves exactly like the + operator with respect to strings. It appends the value on the right side to the end of the value of the variable on the left. For example, in the following code, the value of the myString variable is "The value is 5".

Example:
```
var myString = "The value is ";
myString += 5;
```

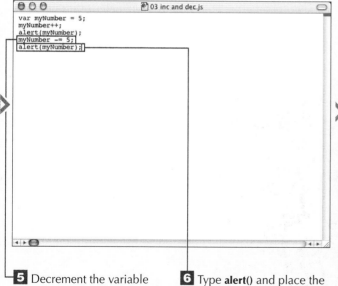

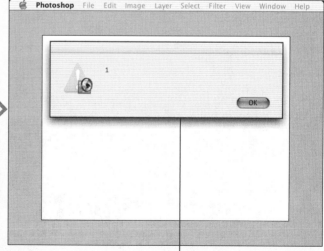

5 Decrement the variable by typing the name of the variable, **-=**, and then the desired amount.

■ In this case, the code **-=** 5 calls for a decrement of 5.

6 Type **alert()** and place the name of the variable in the parentheses.

7 Execute the script in Photoshop or Illustrator.

■ A dialog box shows the value of the variable.

CONTROL PROGRAM FLOW USING CONDITIONALS

You can use JavaScript to make decisions based on the value of variables. Using the `if` control statement and JavaScript's comparison operators, you can develop more advanced programs to respond to different situations.

The most basic form of an `if` statement simply tests a Boolean variable for a `true` or `false` value. If the variable is `true`, then the condition is met, and an action takes place; otherwise the script skips the action.

You can create more advanced program flow using the `else` statement. The `else` statement allows you to specify that an action occurs if the condition is `false`, rather than simply skipping actions. You can also combine `else` and `if` statements to specify further conditions.

JavaScript provides a set of comparison operators to perform more complex evaluations for use in `if` statements. The `==` operator allows you to test if two values are equal. The syntax may appear rather odd, but it distinguishes a comparison from an assignment. For example, `x == 6` reads as "X is equal to 6" and is `true` if and only if the value of x is the number 6, or is a string that can convert to the number 6. There is also a `!=` operator which reads "Not equal to" so the code `x != 3` reads "X is not equal to 3." Four other comparison operators allow you to compare numbers: > (greater than), < (less than), >= (greater than or equal to), and <= (less than or equal to).

You can also use the comparison operators in conjunction with the logical operators to create complex conditions. The logical operators are `&&` (and), `||` (or), `!` (not). For example, the expression `(x > 1) && (x != 5)` is `true` if x is greater than 1, but not equal to 5.

CONTROL PROGRAM FLOW USING CONDITIONALS

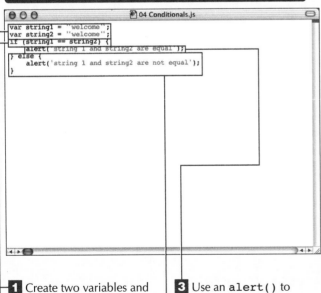

1 Create two variables and assign the same string value to each.

2 Create an `if` statement comparing the value of the two variables.

3 Use an `alert()` to display a message if the two values are equal.

4 Create an `else` statement, and use `alert()` to display a message if the values are different.

5 Execute the script in Photoshop or Illustrator.

■ The condition is met and an alert is displayed.

■ You can change the value of the variables to change the outcome of the condition and run the script again.

Note: The text in the alert box may differ, depending on the value of the variables in the condition.

Apply It

It is a bit counter-intuitive and difficult to remember to use two equal signs to test for equality. Many beginning programmers have trouble getting in the habit of using == to test for equality and mistakenly use the assignment operator (=). This is especially frustrating for new programmers because using the wrong operator does not often cause an error. If you notice that your scripts do not behave as expected at conditionals, go back and make sure that you are using the correct operator. Here is an example of this sort of error.

TYPE THIS:

```
x = 3;
if (x = 5) {
    alert ('x is equal to 5');
}
```

RESULT:

An alert displays because the value of x is set to 5 instead of being compared to 5. Because the assignment is successful, the expression is true and the statement executes. This should read:

```
x = 3;
if (x == 5) {
    alert ('x is equal to 5');
}
```

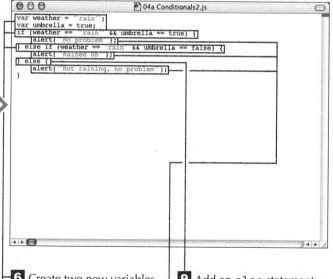

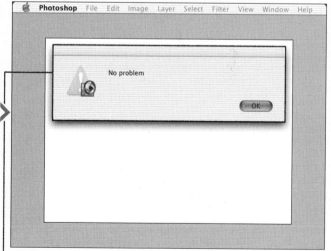

6 Create two new variables and assign them values.

7 Create an if condition to test the values of each variable.

8 Add an else if statement to test for a different condition.

9 Add an else statement for when neither condition is met.

10 Use an alert() statement to display a message for each outcome.

11 Execute the script in Photoshop or Illustrator.

■ An alert box displays a message depending upon the outcome of the conditional.

Note: The text in the alert box may differ, depending on the values of the variables in the condition.

■ You can alter the values of the variables to change the outcome of the condition and run the script again.

USING ARRAYS

JavaScript lets you organize data into Arrays. An *array* is a numbered list of values organized as a single object. Arrays are a great way to keep related data organized. For example, it makes more sense to keep a list of ages together as an array, rather than creating a new variable for each age. Many of Photoshop and Illustrator's fundamental objects, such as layers, documents, and path items, are organized as arrays.

In an array, each value has an index that JavaScript uses to access that value. For example, one way to keep track of three names is to create three variables — name1, name2, and name3. But by using arrays, you can create a single names array and store as many names as you need in a single object.

To create an array, use the new Array() constructor. You can optionally set an initial size of the array by passing in a number between the parentheses, although this is not necessary.

Arrays in JavaScript, like C, C++, and Java, are 0 indexed. This means that the numbering of items in the array begins with 0. When an array is created, the elements are automatically given an index in the array. Using the index and the [] operator, you can access and modify individual elements in the array. To retrieve a specific value in an array, type the name of the array and then the [] operator, placing the index between the brackets. For example, you access the first element in an array with the name "people" by typing **people[0]**.

You can also define an entire array using the [] operator. By separating each value in the brackets with a comma, you can quickly define an entire array.

USING ARRAYS

```
var myArray = new Array(3);
myArray[0] = "first";
myArray[1] = "second";
myArray[2] = "third";

alert(myArray[0]);
alert(myArray[1]);
alert(myArray[2]);
```

1 Create a new array using new Array() with the size of the array in the parentheses.

2 Assign a string value to each element in the array.

3 Display the value of each element using alert().

4 Execute the script in Photoshop or Illustrator.

■ An alert box displays the elements in the array.

Apply It

You can easily determine how many items are currently in an array. Every array has a built-in property called `length`. You can access this property by typing the name of the array followed by **.length**. See the section "Using Objects, Properties, and Methods" for more on using properties.

TYPE THIS:

```
var myArray = new Array();
myArray[0] = "first value";
myArray[1] = "second value";
myLength = myArray.length;
alert("The length of the array
is " + myLength);
```

RESULT:

An alert appears with the text: "The length of the array is 2."

When an array is passed to `alert()`, JavaScript automatically converts it to a string using the `toString()` method of the array. This causes the array to be converted to a string, with each value separated by a comma.

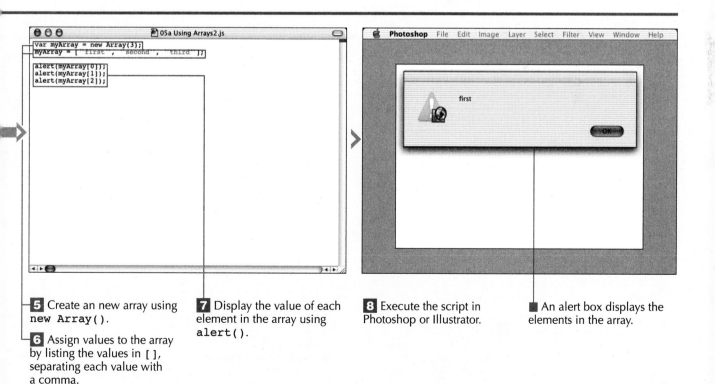

5 Create an new array using `new Array()`.

6 Assign values to the array by listing the values in [ ], separating each value with a comma.

7 Display the value of each element in the array using `alert()`.

8 Execute the script in Photoshop or Illustrator.

■ An alert box displays the elements in the array.

USING WHILE LOOPS

You can create loops to cycle through data and perform repetitive actions. Loops allow you to write simpler code that is easier to understand and works in a wider variety of situations. JavaScript has many different types of looping structures. The simplest type is the while loop.

The while loop syntax begins by defining a condition that must be met for the loop to continue looping. As long as this condition evaluates to true, the loop continues. In this way, while loops are similar to an if condition. See the section "Control Program Flow Using Conditionals" for more on if conditions.

After you define the condition, the code for execution in the loop follows. Much like the if statement, you enclose the code in curly braces {}. When looping, it is common to use a variable to count and restrict the number of times the loop runs. For example, your condition might read while

(x < 5). If x has a value less than 5 when the script encounters this statement, JavaScript executes the code in the loop body. At the end of the loop body, JavaScript evaluates the condition and determines if the loop should run again.

To make sure the code in the loop body only executes a specified number of times, the last line of code in a while loop is commonly where a variable increments. For example, you may increment your counter variable using x++. This way, the value of the x variable increments by 1 before JavaScript evaluates the condition. Once the value is greater than 5, the loop stops and the script continues.

You can use any expression that JavaScript can evaluate to a true or false condition with a while loop. You can even place the true value as the condition, which causes the loop to continue indefinitely.

USING WHILE LOOPS

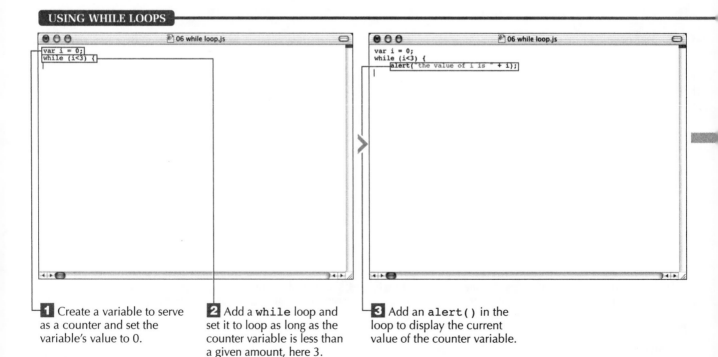

1 Create a variable to serve as a counter and set the variable's value to 0.

2 Add a while loop and set it to loop as long as the counter variable is less than a given amount, here 3.

3 Add an alert() in the loop to display the current value of the counter variable.

Extra

It is programming tradition to use i as the counter variable in for loops where possible; doing so makes it easier for other programmers to understand your scripts.

JavaScript provides two ways to alter the behavior of a loop. The break statement exits the current loop and allows the script to continue. For example, if you want to search for a particular value in an array, you can exit the loop as soon as the script finds the value, rather than looping through the entire thing. In the following example, the loop exits after i takes on the value of 3 instead of looping five times.

```
Example:
var i = 0;
while (i<5) {
  if (i==3) {
    break;
  }
  i++;
}
```

The other way to alter the behavior of a loop is to use a continue statement, which does not exit the loop but tells the script to skip to the end of the loop. In the case of a for loop, this means that the counter variable increments and JavaScript tests the condition again, as if the loop had completed its cycle normally. See the section "Using For Loops" for more on the for loop.

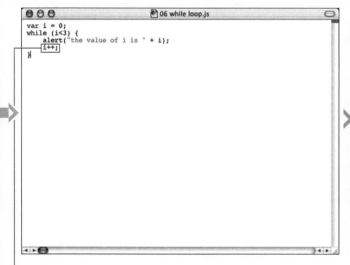

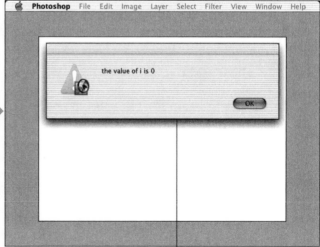

4 Increment the value of the counter variable.

Note: See the section "Increment and Decrement a Variable" for more information.

5 Execute the script in Photoshop or Illustrator.

■ In this example, the script causes three alerts to appear successively, one for each cycle in the loop.

USING FOR LOOPS

The most common type of looping structure in JavaScript is the `for` loop, which you can use to consolidate looping structures and perform repetitive actions. JavaScript's `for` loops are particularly useful for performing a series of actions on the elements of an array.

The `while` loop, which is covered in greater detail in the section "Using While Loops," has three common features: a counter; a test condition, which the script tests before each loop cycle to determine if the loop should run; and a command to increment the counter. The `for` loop condenses these three common features into a single structure.

When creating a `for` loop, the first step involves initializing the counter variable. This is a simple variable declaration; see "Declare Variables" for more information. The second part is the condition. The condition takes the same form as

in an `if` statement or `while` loop. See the section "Control Program Flow Using Conditionals" for more information about `if` statements. The final element of the `for` loop is to specify how JavaScript increments the counter variable at the end of each loop. Counter variables are most commonly incremented by one using the `++` operator. See the section "Increment and Decrement a Variable" for more information.

You place each of the three elements in parentheses and separate them with a semicolon. For example, a loop that cycles 5 times and uses `i` as the counter variable looks like: `for (var i=0; i<5; i++)`.

You often use loops with arrays. You can set the condition to loop for each item in the array using the `length` property of the array. Because arrays are zero-indexed, you often start the counter variable with a value of 0. For more on arrays, see the section "Using Arrays."

USING FOR LOOPS

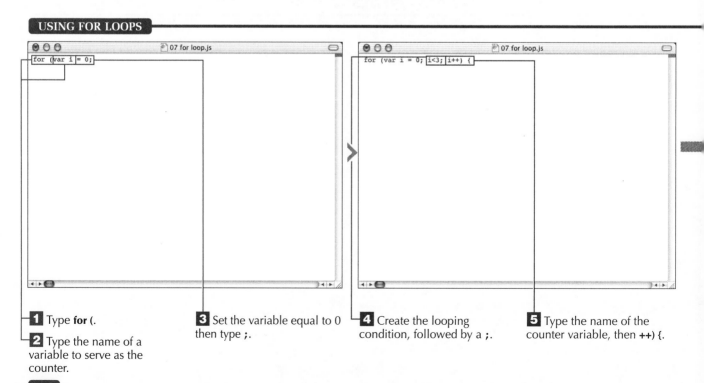

1 Type **for (**.

2 Type the name of a variable to serve as the counter.

3 Set the variable equal to 0 then type **;**.

4 Create the looping condition, followed by a **;**.

5 Type the name of the counter variable, then **++) {**.

Apply It

You can use arrays and loops together to quickly and easily perform an action on every item in an array. You access the values in an array using a numerical index, and you can determine the number of items in an array using the `Array.length` property. See the sections "Using Arrays" and "Using Objects, Properties, and Methods" for more information on arrays and properties.

By creating a loop that continues as long as the counter variable's value is less than the length of the array, you can quickly access every item in the array. For example, the following code displays an alert showing the index and value for each item in the array.

TYPE THIS:

```javascript
var pets = ["cooper", "pooshka", "oscar"];
for (i=0; i<pets.length; i++) {
  alert("Item " + i + " of the array is: " + pets[i]);
}
```

RESULT:

An alert displays for each item in the array. The counter variable's current value, as well as the value of the current item is in the array, displays in the alert box. For example, the first alert reads "Item 0 of the array is: cooper."

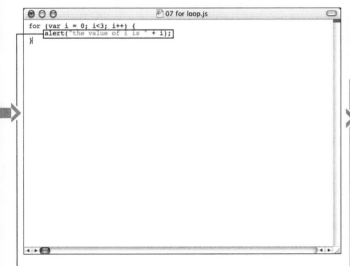

6 Add an `alert()` to the loop body to display the value of the counter variable.

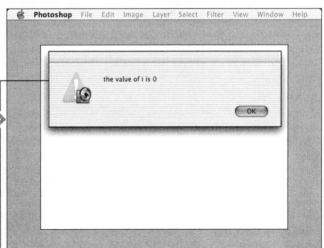

7 Execute the script in Photoshop or Illustrator.

■ The script loops per your specifications.

■ In this example, the script causes three alerts to appear successively, one for each cycle in the loop.

CREATE A FUNCTION

You can organize often-reused code into functions. *Functions* are a way to keep complex actions together, and to allow your script to execute them repeatedly without retyping code. JavaScript provides a set of predefined functions that you can call to perform certain operations. For example, `alert()` is a built-in function you can use to display information in an alert box.

You use the `function` statement to create a new function. After the function statement, you type the name of the function; the naming of functions follows the same conventions that apply to naming a variable. You follow the name with a set of `()` parentheses, and then a curly brace (`{`).

After the curly brace, you can define the body of the code for the function. Much like when you create an `if` statement, you usually indent the body of a function to make it easier to read. After you define the code for the function, you end the function declaration with a closing `}`.

When you run the script, the statements in the function body do not execute, but are stored inside the definition of the function. You have no limit to the code that can appear inside a function definition. Functions can, and often do, contain loops, conditionals, arrays, and many other scripting constructs.

After you create a function, you can call it using the `()` operator. By typing the name of the function followed by two parentheses, you instruct JavaScript to execute the code in the body of the function. For example, if you define a function called `myFunc`, the code of the function executes when you type **myFunc()** . As soon as the function is called and its code executes, the script continues normally.

CREATE A FUNCTION

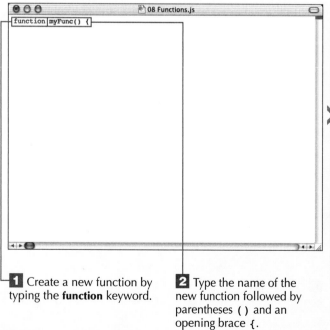

1 Create a new function by typing the **function** keyword.

2 Type the name of the new function followed by parentheses **( )** and an opening brace **{**.

3 Enter some JavaScript code to define the function body.

4 End the function body with a closing brace **}**.

Apply It

Variables in JavaScript have what is called a *scope*, which is the different places in the script where variables are available. The method of creating variables, described in the section "Declare Variables," creates *global* variables, meaning they are accessible from anywhere within the script. All variables declared in the main body of the script are global variables. When working with functions, however, you can define *local* variables, which are variables that are available only while the function executes. To define a variable in a function as local, declare it normally using the `var` keyword. To create a global variable, declare the variable *without* the `var` keyword. JavaScript destroys local variables as soon as the function completes its execution, so creating local variables helps keep memory clear of unnecessary information. Global variables, however, are still available after the function executes. The following script creates a local variable and attempts to display its value after the function executes.

TYPE THIS:

```
function scopeTest() {
   var theVariable = "Hello World";
}
scopeTest();
alert(theVariable);
```

RESULT:

The alert box shows a value of `undefined`. If you remove the `var` keyword from the variable declaration, so the line reads `theVariable = "Hello World";`, the alert displays the contents of the variable.

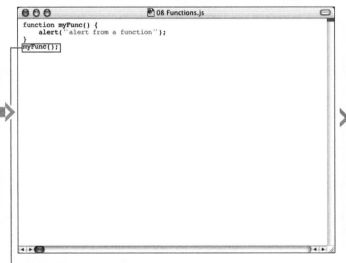

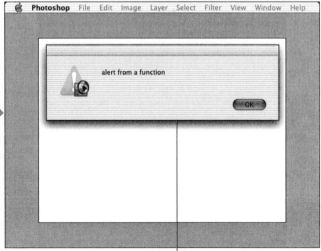

5 Call the function by typing the function name followed by parentheses ( ).

Note: The parentheses are required to tell JavaScript to execute the function.

6 Execute the script in Photoshop or Illustrator.

■ The code in the function executes.

PASS PARAMETERS TO A FUNCTION

Functions allow you to organize code for easy reuse. You can make even more dynamic functions by creating functions that accept passed values. You can create functions to accept *parameters*, also called *arguments*. Parameters allow you to pass values to a function to control the behavior of the function. The `alert` function in the other sections of this chapter takes a single parameter, which is the message that appears in the alert box.

Creating a function that accepts parameters is similar to the process described in the section "Create a Function." You begin with the `function` statement, and follow it with the name of the function you want to create. Next, name the parameters you want to create and place them between the (). You can have as many as needed, separating them using a comma.

When you define parameter names, you create temporary variables that only exist inside the body of the function. The body of the function can reference these variables and act accordingly. For example, you can write a function that adds text to a passed string and displays an alert of the new string.

Unlike other languages, JavaScript does not require you to declare the types of the parameters when you create the function. Also, you can make parameters of different types. For example, a function can accept a string message, an array of names, and an array of job titles, and then in the function body you can combine and manipulate the information to create a message showing the name and title of everyone in the arrays.

To call a function and pass parameters, type the name of the function followed by parentheses, placing the value that you want to pass to the function between the parentheses. Separate each value using a comma.

PASS PARAMETERS TO A FUNCTION

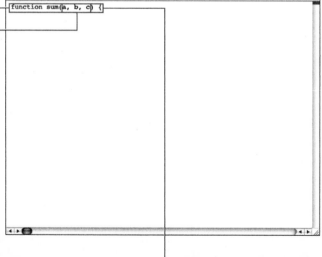

1 Type the **function** keyword and give the function a name, followed by an open parenthesis (.

2 Add parameters by typing names for the variables to hold the passed values.

■ This example uses three variables.

3 Type a closing parenthesis) and an opening brace {.

4 Create a local variable to hold the sum of the parameters.

5 Add an `alert()` statement to display the value of each parameter and their sum.

Extra

When a function is called, you can make the parameters that you pass to the function a *value*, such as 3 or 'adobe'; a *variable*, in which case the value of the variable at the time of the function call is passed; or an *expression*. When passing an expression, such as x*3, JavaScript first evaluates the expression and then passes the result to the function. Placing expressions in parentheses when passing them as a parameter is a good idea, as this helps keep your code clear and easy to read.

Functions can also accept any number of parameters. Unlike other languages, JavaScript does not require that you pass a value for every parameter. If a function is called and no value is passed for a parameter, JavaScript gives the parameter the undefined value.

When you define a function, you specify the parameters in order. Although you are not required to pass a value for every parameter, you cannot skip a parameter. When JavaScript executes the function, it interprets the passed values in order and assigns them to the appropriate parameter.

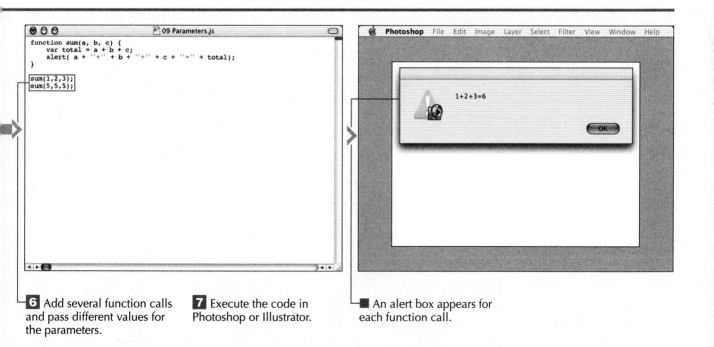

```
09 Parameters.js
function sum(a, b, c) {
    var total = a + b + c;
    alert( a + "+" + b + "+" + c + "=" + total);
}
sum(1,2,3);
sum(5,5,5);
```

Photoshop   File   Edit   Image   Layer   Select   Filter   View   Window   Help

1+2+3=6

OK

6 Add several function calls and pass different values for the parameters.

7 Execute the code in Photoshop or Illustrator.

■ An alert box appears for each function call.

RETURN A VALUE FROM A FUNCTION

You can return a value from a function using the return keyword. The return keyword allows the function to send a value back to the context from which the function was called. Creating functions with return values allows you to organize common actions, such as computations, without retyping your code.

The simplest example is a function that adds two numbers together. If your function contains a variable named results to hold the results of the addition, you can return this value by adding return results at the end of the function body.

There are two ways you can call a function with a return value. First, you can call the function normally and use the returned value *inline*, as if it were a variable containing that value. The other, and most common, way to call a function with a return value is to create a variable to hold the

returned value. Using the above example, mytotal = sumFunc(2,2) sets the mytotal variable equal to the returned value, in this case 4.

When JavaScript encounters the return keyword, the function execution ends immediately. Be sure that all of the code that you want to execute occurs before a return statement.

Functions can return any type of value. Functions with return values are great way to build a personal library of often used actions. For example, you can create a function that finds the distance between two points. Rather than type out the equation every time, you can use a function that returns the value. Whenever you create a new script that requires this functionality, you have a function ready to solve the problem.

RETURN A VALUE FROM A FUNCTION

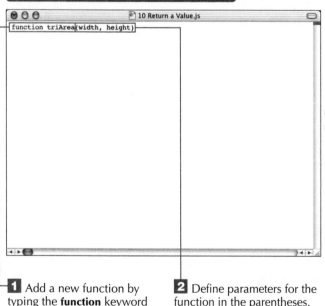

1 Add a new function by typing the **function** keyword followed by the name of the function.

2 Define parameters for the function in the parentheses.

■ This example, which returns the area of a triangle, defines two parameters.

3 Define the function body by adding code to manipulate the parameters, using parentheses to set the order of operations.

■ In this example, the area of a triangle is the result of the width times the height divided by 2.

4 Return the result of step 3 using the **return** keyword and close the function body.

Apply It

Return statements are useful for creating *recursive* functions, or functions that call themselves. The most common example of a recursive function is a function that calculates the value of a factorial for a given number. The factorial of a number is equal to the number multiplied by every number smaller than it, but greater than 0. So the factorial of 4 (written 4!) is equal to 4*3*2*1. You can also see this as the number (n) multiplied by the factorial of n-1. Using this definition, you can create a function to calculate a factorial.

TYPE THIS:

```
function factorial(n) {
  if (n <= 1) {
    return 1;
  } else {
    return n * factorial (n-1);
  }
}
```

RESULT:

When this function is called, if the number is larger than 1, the function calls itself to get the value of the current number –1.

You may find recursive functions very useful when creating directory trees and navigating files. See Chapter 8 for more information on working with files.

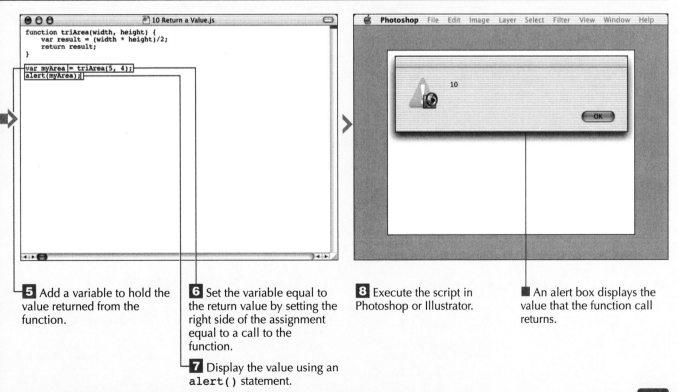

5 Add a variable to hold the value returned from the function.

6 Set the variable equal to the return value by setting the right side of the assignment equal to a call to the function.

7 Display the value using an **alert()** statement.

8 Execute the script in Photoshop or Illustrator.

■ An alert box displays the value that the function call returns.

USING OBJECTS, PROPERTIES, AND METHODS

You can create more powerful code by using objects in JavaScript. JavaScript uses objects to store and organize data and actions. Each *object* is an abstract container made up of named pieces of data, much like an array consists of numbered pieces of data. JavaScript has a large number of built-in objects that allow you to access and modify documents and files in Illustrator and Photoshop.

The named pieces of data in an object are called *properties*. Named properties take the place of the numbered indexes used in arrays. To access and modify a property of an object, type the name of the object followed by a . (period), and then the name of the property. For example, if an object named myObject contained a property named title, you can access the property with myObject.title. Properties behave just like variables and can contain any type of data.

Objects can also have *methods*, which are functions that exist inside the object. Methods often perform functions specific to the object of which they are members. You reference methods just like properties; myObject.addValues() calls the addValues method of the myObject object. As properties behave like variables, methods behave like functions and can return values and accept parameters.

In addition to the built-in objects provided by JavaScript, you can create your own objects using the new Object() constructor. The syntax, myObj = new Object(), is similar to the syntax you use to create an array; see the section "Using Arrays" for more information on arrays. To add properties to the object, type the name of the object, followed by a dot (.) and then the name of the property. To add a property named title to the object, type **myObj.title = "My First Object";**. This creates a title property with a value of "My First Object."

USING OBJECTS, PROPERTIES, AND METHODS

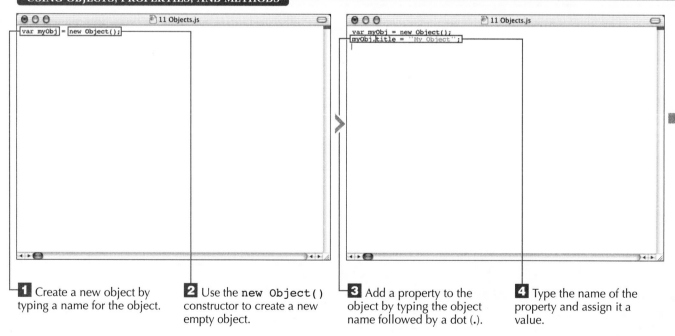

1 Create a new object by typing a name for the object.

2 Use the `new Object()` constructor to create a new empty object.

3 Add a property to the object by typing the object name followed by a dot (.).

4 Type the name of the property and assign it a value.

Apply It

When using objects, JavaScript provides a special keyword, `this`, to refer to the current object. When adding methods to an object, you can use the `this` keyword to refer to other methods and properties of the same object. The `this` keyword is important for making the scope of the variable clear to JavaScript. You should always include the `this` keyword when writing methods to access other properties and methods of the same object.

Without the `this` keyword, JavaScript attempts to locate the variable or function in the global scope. The following code illustrates the use of the `this` keyword to access a property of an object.

TYPE THIS:

```
var title = "Global Title";
var myobj = new Object();
myobj.title = "My First Object";
myobj.showName = function() {
    alert(this.title);
}
myobj.showName();
```

RESULT:

The alert box displays the value of the title property of the object.

Try removing the `this` keyword and running the script again. Without the keyword, JavaScript displays an alert containing the contents of the global `title` variable.

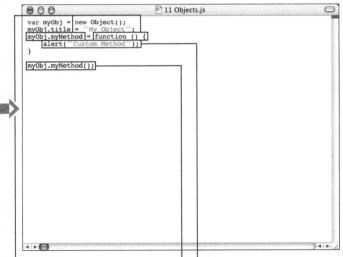

5 Add a method to the object by typing the name of the object followed by a dot (.) and the name of the new method.

6 Assign the method the value of a function by typing the **function** keyword followed by parentheses.

7 Add code to the body of the method.

8 Call the method by typing the name of the object followed by a dot (.), and the name of the new method followed by parentheses.

Note: Adding methods in this way takes advantage of another way to use the function constructor.

9 Execute the script in Photoshop or Illustrator.

■ The results of the objects, properties, and methods display.

RETRIEVE A RANGE OF CHARACTERS FROM A STRING

You can perform complex manipulations on a string using JavaScript's built-in string methods. For example, you can extract a portion of a string and change its value.

All of the data types discussed in the section "Declare Variables" are associated with an object type. Each type of object, string, number, and Boolean, has a different set of methods and properties associated with it. In JavaScript, every string is an instance of the built-in String object. This means that you can use all of the methods of the String object whenever JavaScript creates a string variable.

Two of the most useful string methods are String.slice() and String.substr(). The slice method requires the first parameter to specify the starting point in the string, *start*, and an optional second parameter indicating the ending point, *end*. If you do not specify the

second parameter, the returned slice includes all characters through the end of the string. Much like arrays, strings in JavaScript are *zero-indexed*, meaning the first character is 0. To extract the first through third characters in a string named mystr, you type **mystr.slice(0, 3)**. One confusing thing to remember is that the slice contains every character of the string from and including the start and up to but not including the end.

Another way to extract part of a string is to use the String. substr() method. Much like slice, substr can take two parameters. The first is required and specifies the start position of the string to extract. The second is optional; if it is specified, it defines the *length* of the returned string. If you omit it, the string contains all characters through the end of the string. For example, mystr.substr(0, 5); returns the first five characters of mystr.

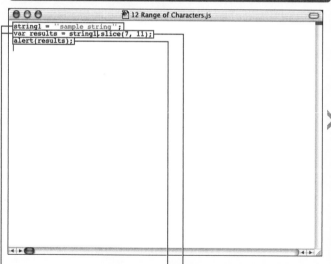

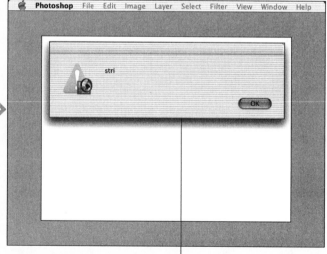

USING THE SLICE METHOD

1 Create a new variable and assign it a string value.

2 Create a variable and set it equal to the variable from step 1.

3 Type a dot (.), and then call the **slice** method by typing **slice()**, passing the starting and ending points of the portion of the string to extract.

4 Add an **alert()** to display the results variable.

5 Run the script in Photoshop or Illustrator.

■ The alert box shows the characters from the start point up to but not including the end point.

Apply It

The `String.slice()` method allows you to pass negative numbers as parameters. Negative numbers allow you to specify character locations relative to the end of the string. For example, the number –1 represents the last character of the string, –2 the second to last, and so on. Both the start and end parameter can have a negative value. You can think of the result of a negative parameter as being the same as subtracting the value from the length of characters in the string. This very useful when working with files because it allows an easy way to retrieve a filename without the extension.

TYPE THIS:

```
var myStr = 'SourceFile.txt';
var filename = myStr.slice(0,-4);
```

RESULT:

The filename variable has the value 'SourceFile' without the .txt extension.

Negative parameters do not work with the `substr` method. JavaScript interprets a negative value for the first parameter as 0. Because the second parameter is the length of the string, a negative value does not make sense.

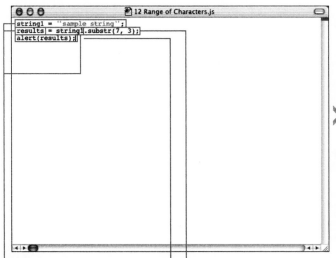

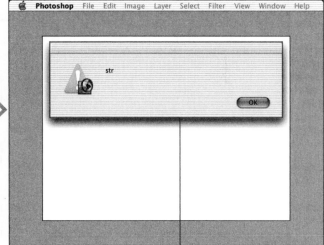

USING THE SUBSTR METHOD

1 Create a new variable and assign it a string value.

2 Create a variable to hold the results of the **substr** operation.

3 Type = followed by the name of string variable from step 1.

4 Type a dot (.), and then call the **substr** method, passing the starting point and length of the string to extract.

5 Add an **alert()** to display the result variable.

6 Run the script in Photoshop or Illustrator.

■ The alert box shows the extracted portion of the string starting at the start point and including the specified number of characters.

CONVERT A STRING INTO AN ARRAY

onverting a string to an array using JavaScript is easy and useful for retrieving the individual words in a string. You can also format data using delimiters to separate values. When retrieving information from a spreadsheet or database, the data frequently has rows separated with a return, and columns separated with either a comma or a tab.

JavaScript has a built-in string method that allows you to convert this sort of data to an array. Arrays are often easier to work with than strings because you can more readily access individual values in an array. The `String.split()` method takes a string and returns an array by splitting it up using a specified delimiter. `Split` takes a single parameter, a string defining the delimiter. It returns the array with every instance of the delimiter removed.

For example, if you have a list of words in a string variable such as `names = 'bob mike jill';`, you can use the `split()` method to break this into an array of names by defining a space as the delimiter. `namesArray = names.split(' ');` namesArray now becomes an array containing the elements bob, mike, jill. The elements of the array appear in the same order they do in the string.

If you pass `split()` as an empty string, you can use it to convert a string into an array consisting of the characters of the string. To retrieve the individual letters from a string `str = 'abcdef';`, you can type **letters = str.split('');** **letters.** This becomes an array with one element for each character in the string.

The `split()` method removes the delimiter from the source string when creating the new array. The delimiter character does not appear in any of the elements of the resulting array.

CONVERT A STRING INTO AN ARRAY

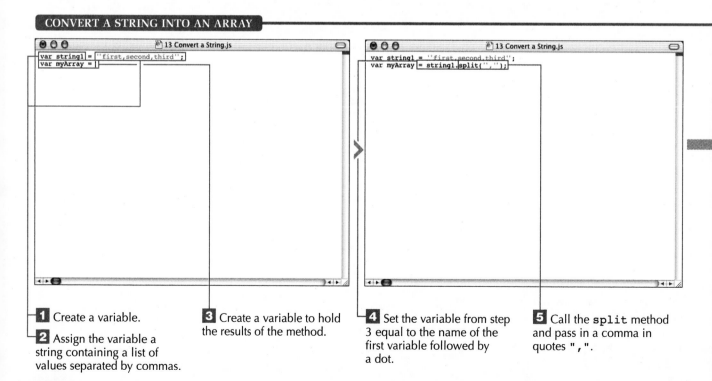

1 Create a variable.

2 Assign the variable a string containing a list of values separated by commas.

3 Create a variable to hold the results of the method.

4 Set the variable from step 3 equal to the name of the first variable followed by a dot.

5 Call the `split` method and pass in a comma in quotes **","**.

Apply It

The `Array` object also has a method called `join()`, which is the inverse of `split()`. `join()` returns a string consisting of the elements of the array with a delimiter character inserted between them. `Join` is useful for inserting a character between items without adding one to the end. If you have an array of names, you can loop through the array and append each name onto a string followed by a return, or you can use `join()` to insert a return for you. Not only does the loop require more coding, but you end up with an extra return on the end of the last name. You can rewrite this code and make it simpler using the `join()` method to achieve the same result.

TYPE THIS:

```
var names = ["michelle", "toby", "jon"];
var formatted = "";
for (var i=0; i<names.length; i++) {
  formatted += names[i] + "\r";
}
formatted = formatted.slice(0,-1);
```

OR TYPE THIS:

```
var names = ["michelle", "toby", "jon"];
var formatted = names.join("\r");
```

RESULT:

The `formatted` variable contains the values of the `names` array with a return between each, but not at the end.

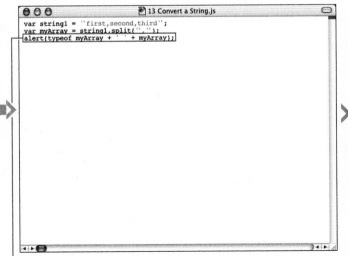

```
var string1 = "first,second,third";
var myArray = string1.split(",");
alert(typeof myArray + ' ' + myArray);
```

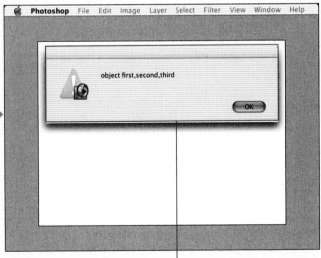

object first,second,third

6 Use the **typeof** operator and an **alert()** statement to display the type of the results variable and its values.

7 Execute the script in Photoshop or Illustrator.

■ An alert box shows that the variable is an array and lists its values.

COMMUNICATE WITH THE USER

You can communicate with a script user to retrieve information about what actions to take. JavaScript for Photoshop and Illustrator also allows you to display information to inform users of script actions. You can also use JavaScript to ask the user to respond to questions.

The section "Understanding JavaScript Syntax" illustrates one basic method of communication with the user — the alert() function, which takes a single parameter, the string to display to the user. JavaScript for Photoshop and Illustrator also supports the confirm() function to prompt a user to respond to a yes or no question.

When the alert() function is called, JavaScript displays a dialog box with a single OK button and waits for the user's response. You can use this function to debug scripts because it displays the value of variables and shows the results of conditionals. However, communication using

alert() is only one way; you can show the user a message, but the user has no way of responding to it other than accepting it.

You provide very basic two-way communication with confirm() because you prompt the user to respond to a yes or no question. Like alert(), confirm() takes a single parameter, the string to display to the user. But the alert box has two buttons, "No" and "Yes." Setting a variable to the return value of the function captures the response of the user. If the user clicks "Yes," JavaScript returns a value of true. If the user clicks "No," JavaScript returns a value of false.

Using confirm() with conditional statements creates scripts that communicate with the user and ask for input as to which operations to perform. You can also use confirm() to make sure a user understands the consequences of an action. For example, if your script changes every font in a document, you should verify that the user knows this and wants to continue.

COMMUNICATE WITH THE USER

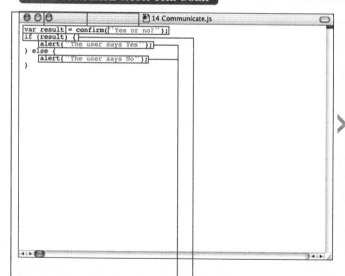

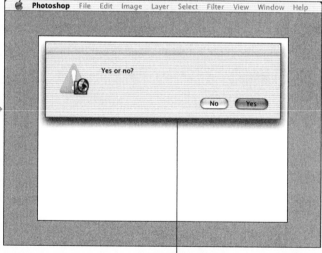

■1 Create a variable to store the result of the confirm() statement.

■2 Set the variable equal to confirm().

■3 Place a yes or no question in the parentheses.

■4 Add an if condition to test the result of the user's interaction.

■5 Add an alert() to display one message if the user replies "yes," and another if the user replies "no."

■6 Execute the script in Photoshop or Illustrator.

■ A different alert() box displays a different message depending on the user's choice.

ADD COMMENTS

Y ou can leave notes to yourself and others using *comments*. By describing your thought process in plain text, you make your scripts easier to read and modify, especially when you revisit them later. Because JavaScript does not execute any statements — including text and code — that appear within comments, you can use comments to debug code by temporarily disabling lines or blocks of code. You can also use them to locate important parts of long scripts and describe the behavior of functions. As you develop a library of functions, keep comments with the functions to remind you of their use.

You have two types of comments in JavaScript. *Single-line comments* begin with two forward slashes (//) and run until the end of the line. *Multi-line comments* begin with a forward slash and asterisk (/*) and end with a closing asterisk and forward slash (*/). When commenting out large blocks of code using multi-line comments, remember that you cannot nest them. Single-line comments can appear within multi-line comments.

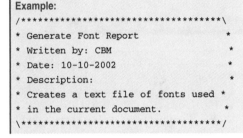

Extra

You must begin your scripts with an *explanatory header*, which may include the author, the creation date, a description of what it does, and any issues that the user may experience. If you distribute your scripts, include your e-mail address for feedback and suggestions. You can block off a header by boxing it inside of asterisks.

Example:
```
/***********************************\
* Generate Font Report             *
* Written by: CBM                  *
* Date: 10-10-2002                 *
* Description:                      *
* Creates a text file of fonts used *
* in the current document.         *
\***********************************/
```

ADD COMMENTS

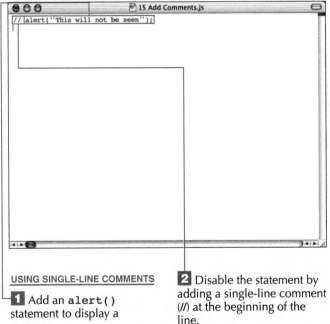

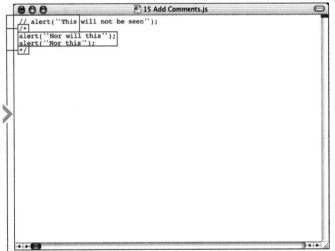

USING SINGLE-LINE COMMENTS

1 Add an `alert()` statement to display a message.

2 Disable the statement by adding a single-line comment (//) at the beginning of the line.

USING MULTI-LINE COMMENTS

3 Add two more `alert()` statements.

4 Add a multi-line comment to disable the alerts.

5 Execute the script in Photoshop or Illustrator.

■ No alerts display because of the comments.

UNDERSTANDING THE ADOBE SCRIPTING OBJECT MODEL

Scripting in Photoshop and Illustrator use an *Object-Oriented* approach to controlling the application. What this means is that the basic organizational unit is the object, and each object can have properties and methods. See Chapter 2 for more information. An object can also contain other objects, creating a hierarchy useful for organizing and expressing relationships between elements.

OBJECT-ORIENTED ORGANIZATION

You may find the Object-Oriented concepts somewhat difficult to grasp at first. For example, try to imagine a bookshelf. The bookshelf has properties like height, width, depth, and color. But it also has shelves, and each shelf is filled with books. The shelves and books can both be understood as objects inside the bookshelf object. To go further, each book has pages, and each page words. Each object along the way has its own set of properties; each book has a title, author, cover art, publication date, and so on. Considered in this way, the bookshelf all the way down to the words on the page of every book constitute a hierarchical object model. When you go searching for a quote from a book, you need to know what shelf the book is on, what book the quote is in, and what page the quote is on.

In JavaScript, you can navigate an object-oriented hierarchy using the dot (.) operator. First you specify the top-level object, and then step down to the data you need. For example, you can specify a word in the aforementioned example as: `bookshelf.shelf.book.page.word`.

In some cases, you may find it useful to organize elements into collections. A *collection* is a group of similar objects that share a common parent object. You can group the books on a shelf as an object and give each book an index to allow you to quickly reference it without knowing its name. Using a collection, you can loop through every book on a shelf and retrieve the author and title information.

OBJECTS IN PHOTOSHOP AND ILLUSTRATOR

Photoshop and Illustrator are organized very much like the bookshelf. At the top level, you have the `Application` object, which, because it is always present in JavaScript, you do not need to name explicitly. There are other objects in the hierarchy. For example, Photoshop includes the document, art layer, channel, history state, layer, and layer set. There is also a collection associated with each of these objects: documents, art layers, and so on.

The Adobe scripting model uses a simple method to add a new object to the hierarchy. Each collection has an `add()` method to create a new member of that collection. It is also easy to get the number of items in a collection using the `length` property. In this way, collection objects behave like arrays. For more information on using arrays, see Chapter 2.

Adobe scripting also makes wide use of constants. A *constant* is a built-in value that never changes over the course of a script. You use constants to refer to specific types of things; for example, you define the color space of a document in Illustrator using the `DocumentColorSpace` constant. For a complete list of all constants, see the quick references in Appendices A and B.

THE ILLUSTRATOR OBJECT HIERARCHY

The following diagram represents the Illustrator object hierarchy, and shows the relationships between the different objects you use for scripting Ilustrator.

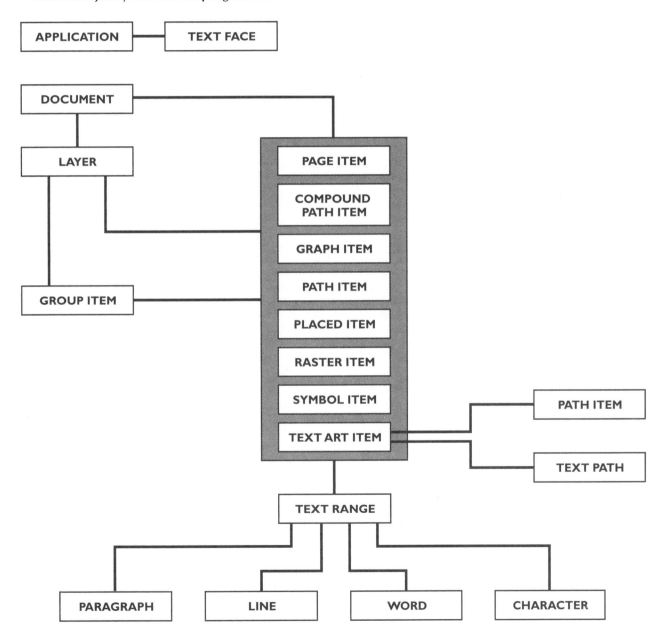

UNDERSTANDING COORDINATE SYSTEMS IN PHOTOSHOP AND ILLUSTRATOR

You can create documents and document elements in Photoshop and Illustrator if you understand the basic concepts of coordinate systems and units of measurement. Just like working with Photoshop and Illustrator by hand, scripting requires working with rulers and units to create documents of specific sizes and placing elements on a page.

THE COORDINATE SYSTEM

Photoshop and Illustrator use standard geometry to define the two-dimensional space of the page. You measure horizontal position on the x-axis, and vertical movement along the y-axis. The coordinate system also has an origin, or the *zero point*, where the two axes cross and measurement begins.

A pair of coordinates defines every point in a coordinate space. For example, the point at the origin is 0,0, while a point horizontally 10 units away is 10,0. In JavaScript, you define a point using an array, with the first value in the array specifying the x position, and the second element the y position. For example, to define a point with an x value of 100 and a y value of 50, your array is: `var myPoint = new Array(100, 50);`. You define more complex shapes as a set of points, or an array of point arrays. For example, you define a rectangle by the four points that make up its corners. A rectangle array is an array with four elements; each element in turn is a two-element array defining a point of the rectangle. The order of points in an array representing a shape moves counterclockwise. In the case of a rectangle, the order is upper-left, lower-left, lower-right, and upper-right.

Although both Photoshop and Illustrator use a coordinate system, there are some important differences. The origin in Photoshop always lies at the upper-left corner of the page. As you move from left to right along the x-axis, and top to bottom along the y-axis, numbers are positive and grow larger. In Illustrator, however, by default, the origin is in the lower-left corner of the page. As you move from left to right along the x-axis, and bottom to top along the y-axis, numbers are positive and grow larger. Notice that the y-axis in Illustrator is flipped with respect to the y-axis in Photoshop. Illustrator does, however, allow you to change the position of the origin with respect to the page. Using the `rulerOrigin` property of the `document` object, you can define a new origin point relative to the bottom-left corner of the page. See the section "Create a New Document in Illustrator" for more information on the `document` object.

UNITS AND RULERS

The coordinate systems in Photoshop and Illustrator rely on different units of measure to define the sizes of documents and objects. The most common unit for working with elements on the screen is the pixel; whereas, print work often requires working with real-world measurements like inches and centimeters.

There are some differences in the way Photoshop and Illustrator handle units of measure. Photoshop relies on two separate rulers when working with elements of a document. The *graphical ruler* defines the position and size of objects in the document, as well as the size of the document itself; the *text ruler* defines type elements such a leading, indentation, and font size. These units correspond to the setting in Units and Rulers in the Photoshop preferences. See the section "Set the Ruler Unit in Photoshop" for more information. Illustrator scripting has a more limited interaction with units. All units in Illustrator scripting are points. There are 72 points in an inch. To work in other units with Illustrator, you must convert the unit to points in your script to achieve the desired result. See Appendix A for conversions between points and other units.

SET THE RULER UNITS IN PHOTOSHOP

You can manipulate the way Photoshop understands units of measure using JavaScript. This lets you accurately write scripts that manipulate type and objects based on size. Photoshop uses two rulers to define the units when working with a document. The *graphics ruler* defines the size and position of graphics elements and the size of the document itself. The *type ruler* deals with textual elements, such as font size and paragraph indentations. These rulers correspond to the settings under Rulers and Units in the Photoshop preferences. For more on units and rulers, see the section "Understanding Coordinate Systems in Photoshop and Illustrator."

You can change a user's settings for rulers and units using JavaScript. You define the types of units using built-in constants, and you have different possible values when you use the graphics ruler instead of the type ruler. You define possible values for the graphics ruler in the `Units` constant,

and values for the type ruler as part of the `TypeUnits` constant. See Appendix B for a list of possible units for each constant.

The settings for ruler units are part of the `preferences` object, which allows you to access most of a user's Photoshop preference settings. When manipulating the values of a user's preferences, it is important to make a point of leaving things as you find them before your script finishes execution. You do not want to change a preference setting permanently and require the user to manually set things back to the way they were.

You define the settings for the graphical ruler in the `rulerUnit` property of the `preferences` object. You set the unit for the type ruler using the `typeUnit` property of the `preferences` object. You can save these values in a variable before you make any changes to make it easy to restore before the script ends. Possible values for `Units` and `typeUnits` are listed in Appendix B. Case is important, and you must place constant values in all caps.

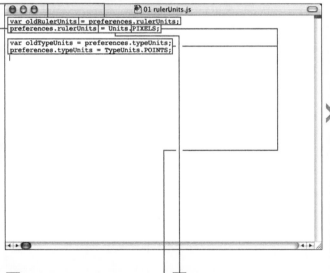

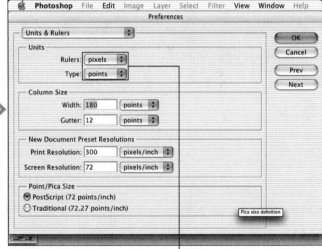

1 Create a variable to store the current settings for the graphical ruler.

2 Type an equal sign, and then **preferences.rulerUnits;**.

3 Change the ruler unit by typing **preferences.rulerUnits**.

4 Type an equal sign and then **Units**.

5 Type the name of the unit you want to use.

6 Repeat steps 1 to 5 with the **typeUnits** object in place of **rulerUnits**.

7 Execute the script in Photoshop.

■ The script changes the ruler and type units.

CREATE A NEW DOCUMENT IN PHOTOSHOP

Y ou can use JavaScript to create a new document in Photoshop. Photoshop stores all open documents in the documents object. Using the properties and methods of this object, you can create new documents and access currently open ones.

The basic Adobe scripting model employs an add() method to create a new instance of an object. In Photoshop, you create a new document by calling the add() method of the documents object. See Chapter 2 for more information.

The documents.add() method in Photoshop can take up to six optional parameters. The first two are width and height, which specify the size of the document. You set the unit for the width and height parameters to the current ruler unit. For more information, see the section "Understanding Coordinate Systems in Photoshop and Illustrator." You use the next parameter, resolution, to define the resolution of the new document in dpi. The

fourth parameter is the name of the document. Much like the manual File ⇨ New command, this parameter allows you to specify a name for the new document. The last two parameters are mode and initial fill. Using these parameters, you can define the mode of the document and the default fill type. The default fill type is equivalent to what appears in the Contents box in the New Document dialog box in Photoshop. Remember that function parameters are ordered. The order of the parameters for document.add() are width, height, resolution, title, mode, and initial fill.

The documents.add() method expects the mode and initial fill parameters to be predefined Photoshop constants. You should make the mode parameter a NewDocumentMode constant and the initial fill parameter a DocumentFill constant. You must pay close attention to the types of parameters that built-in methods expect. You can find the values for constants and determine the correct type for parameters in Appendix B.

CREATE A NEW DOCUMENT IN PHOTOSHOP

```
var oldRulerUnits = preferences.rulerUnits;
```

1 Create a variable and set it equal to **preferences.rulerUnits;**.

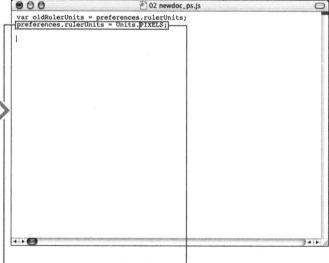

```
var oldRulerUnits = preferences.rulerUnits;
preferences.rulerUnits = Units.PIXELS;
```

2 Change the ruler unit by typing **preferences.rulerUnits = Units**.

3 Type the name of the unit you want to use.

Note: See Appendix B for possible values.

Extra

You can also close a document in Photoshop using the `document.close()` method. The `close()` method behaves very much like closing a document manually using File ⇨ Close. You receive different results depending on the status of the document you want to close. If the user has not applied any changes to the document, the `close()` method works without displaying any dialog boxes. This applies to new documents that users have not yet saved, but have not yet modified either, such as those created with the `documents.add()` method, or those users create in Photoshop using the File ⇨ New math path. If users have made changes to the document, the script presents them with an alert with three options. Users can either save the document, close it without saving it, or to cancel the close operation. The `close()` method can take an optional parameter specifying how the script should treat the document before closing it, essentially providing an answer to the Save Changes dialog box. You must make the parameter a `SaveOptions` constant value. The options are `DONOTSAVECHANGES`, `PROMPTTOSAVECHANGES`, or `SAVECHANGES`. It is good practice to specify save options explicitly to make sure you know how the method will behave in all situations.

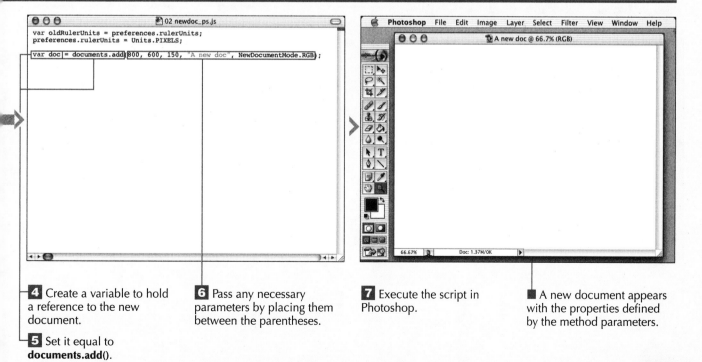

4 Create a variable to hold a reference to the new document.

5 Set it equal to **documents.add()**.

6 Pass any necessary parameters by placing them between the parentheses.

7 Execute the script in Photoshop.

■ A new document appears with the properties defined by the method parameters.

CREATE A NEW DOCUMENT IN ILLUSTRATOR

You can use JavaScript to create a new document in Illustrator. Creating new documents is useful for generating reports or simply making new art or patterns. As in Photoshop, Illustrator stores all open documents in the documents object. Using the properties and methods of this object, you can create new documents and access currently open ones.

Following the basic Adobe scripting model, you create a new document in Illustrator by calling the add() method of the documents object. To do this, you use the documents.add(), method — the same usage as in the section "Create a New Document in Photoshop." The documents.add() method returns a reference to the new document.

In Illustrator the documents.add() method takes up to three parameters, all of which are optional, with the following order: color space, width, height. As always, you can only define the later parameters by specifying earlier

ones. In the case of documents.add(), the first parameter is the color space of the new document. You have two possible values for a document's color space, which are constants that Adobe defines to represent possible values: DocumentColorSpace.RGB specifies the RGB color space, and DocumentColorSpace.CMYK specifies the CMYK color space. See Appendix A for a list of the values for constants.

The second and third parameters are width and height, respectively. Each of these parameters accepts a number specifying the size of the document. In Illustrator, the documents.add() method always interprets the width and height parameters in points. Illustrator does not offer the type of control over units available in Photoshop. You must specify the size of a new document in points. You can convert points to inches by multiplying the size in inches by 72. For example, to create an 8.5-inch by 11-inch document, you type **612 (8.5 * 72)** for the width and **792 (11 * 72)** for the height.

CREATE A NEW DOCUMENT IN ILLUSTRATOR

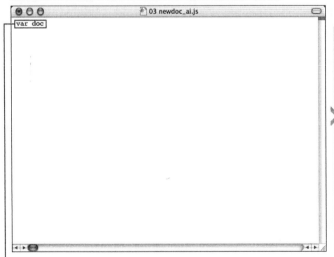

1 Create a variable to hold a reference to the new document.

2 Type an equal sign followed by **documents.add()**.

Apply It

Illustrator supports saving the current view state to make it easy to move between different areas of a large or complex document. Although you cannot create a new view using JavaScript, you can use the `document.views` collection to access the list of current views for this document. You create a new view manually in Illustrator with the View ⇨ New View menu path. After you create a new view, you save the center point of the window, zoom level, and screen mode of the document. You then access these views at the bottom of the View menu. With JavaScript, you can alter these properties for any view in a document.

TYPE THIS:

```
var myView =
activeDocument.views[0];

myView.centerPoint = [0,0];

myView.zoom = .8

myView.screenMode =
ScreenMode.FULLSCREEN;
```

RESULT:

First, the script creates the `myView` variable to reference the first view of the active document. Next, the view of the document changes so that the bottom left-hand corner of the document is in the center of the window. Then the zoom level of the document changes to 80%. The `zoom` parameter takes a numerical value with 1 being equal to 100%. Finally, the script sets the screen mode to full screen, which has the same effect as clicking the Full Screen Mode button on the bottom of the toolbar.

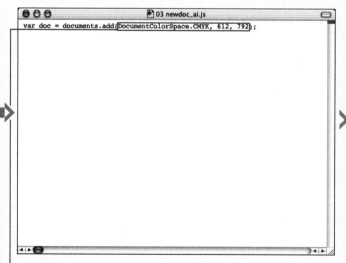

```
var doc = documents.add(DocumentColorSpace.CMYK, 612, 792);
```

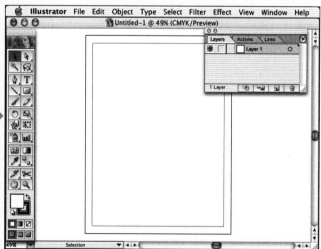

Untitled-1 @ 49% (CMYK/Preview)

3 Pass any necessary parameters to the method by placing them between the parentheses.

4 Execute the script in Illustrator.

■ A new document appears with the properties defined by the method parameters.

REFERENCE THE ACTIVE DOCUMENT IN PHOTOSHOP AND ILLUSTRATOR

You can reference the current document in Photoshop and Illustrator. Retrieving a reference to the currently active document allows you to manipulate the document and its contents. You use the *active document*, which refers to the currently selected document, in almost every script that works on a document.

Photoshop and Illustrator both have an implicit `Application` object when using JavaScript. Unlike other objects, the `Application` object has properties and methods that do not require you to name the object before making a method call or accessing a property. The properties and methods are globally accessible; this means you can simply type the name of the property or method without the `Application`.

One of the most useful properties is `activeDocument`. As long as you have a document open in Photoshop or Illustrator, there is a reference to the topmost document in the `activeDocument` property. Anytime you write a script that modifies the current selection or adds elements to a page, you need to make use of the `activeDocument` property.

Photoshop and Illustrator behave differently when your script accesses the `activeDocument` property, and you have no open documents. When you have no documents opened, Illustrator returns nothing for `activeDocument` — not `false`, not undefined. In fact, Illustrator does not even generate an error. Photoshop, on the other hand, does not allow JavaScript to access `activeDocument` if there is no current document. Instead of returning `false`, Photoshop displays an error and the script aborts.

To avoid receiving errors, you can make sure there are currently open documents. The `documents` object has a `length` property that contains the total number of currently open documents. If this number is greater than zero, your script can continue without errors.

REFERENCE THE ACTIVE DOCUMENT IN PHOTOSHOP AND ILLUSTRATOR

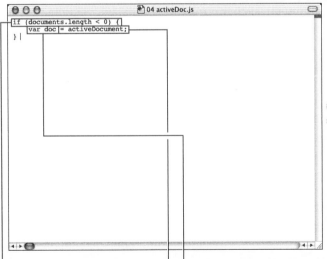

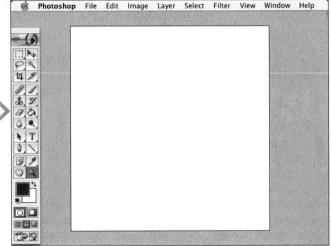

1 Create a condition to test for open documents by typing **if (documents.length > 0) {**.

2 If the condition is `true`, create a variable to hold a reference to the active document.

3 Set the variable equal to **activeDocument**.

4 Execute the script in Photoshop or Illustrator.

■ If a document is open, the script creates a reference.

SWITCH BETWEEN OPEN DOCUMENTS

Y ou can selectively move between currently open documents. The documents object contains a reference to every currently open document. You can reference each document using either an index or the name of the document.

The index of each document in the documents object is determined by the order in which you opened the documents. For example, if you open a few documents in Photoshop or Illustrator, you can see the document order by looking at the Windows menu in Illustrator, or the Windows ⇨ Documents menu in Photoshop. The top document is the *zeroith* document in the documents object. Remember that arrays in JavaScript are zero-index, meaning that the first item in the array is numbered 0.

You can also access each document in the documents object using the document name. The document name is the same as the file name, including the extension. For

example, you use documents['logo.ai'] to access the file named 'logo.ai'. However, using the document name ties your script to a particular situation, requiring a particular set of files. Depending on the application, you may find this acceptable behavior, but it is good practice to make your scripts as general as possible.

The activeDocument property references the currently active document, but you can also use it to set another document to active. By setting the value of activeDocument, you instruct Photoshop and Illustrator to bring that document into focus. Many common tasks, such as setting the visibility of a layer, require that you first set the document being modified as active. To avoid errors, you should always check that you have opened documents before attempting to switch the active document.

SWITCH BETWEEN OPEN DOCUMENTS

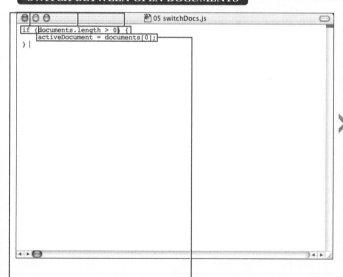

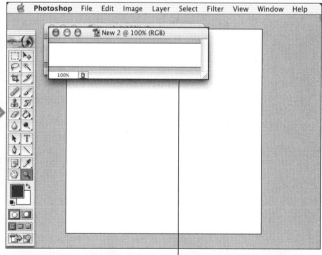

1 Create a condition to check for opened documents by typing **if() {**.

2 Type **documents.length > 0** in the parentheses to set the condition.

3 If the condition is met, switch to one of the documents by setting **activeDocument** equal to the **documents[i]**, replacing *i* with the index of the document to switch to.

4 Execute the script in Photoshop.

■ The script selects the specified document.

MANIPULATE A DOCUMENT IN PHOTOSHOP

You can manipulate a document in a number of ways using JavaScript. Photoshop provides powerful features that let you crop, trim, resize, and rotate. Many of these feature become very useful when batch processing a large number of images.

Photoshop makes a distinction between the image and the canvas. The *image* is defined as the entire document and its contents. The *canvas,* on the other hand, is the space in which the document sits. The modifications possible are the same as those available in the Edit and Image menus in Photoshop.

You access the main document manipulation functions through JavaScript as methods of the document object. A few require you to specify unit values. It is important to verify that your script is performing the correct

manipulation, so you should always set the ruler value before making any changes. Depending on the ruler setting, the same code can resize a document to 3 pixels or 3 inches. See the sections "Understanding Coordinate Systems in Photoshop and Illustrator" and "Set the Ruler Unit in Photoshop" for more information.

The available image manipulations are trim, crop, and resize. The canvas options are rotate, resize, and flip. Resizing the image stretches all of the art in the image, while resizing the canvas does not stretch the art but has the effect of adding more space around the current image area. Not all of the parameters for the manipulating methods are numbers. Some methods, such as trim, resize, and flip, use constant values for anchor position, trim type, and flip direction. See Appendix B for a list of constants and their values, and the required constant types for each operation.

MANIPULATE A DOCUMENT IN PHOTOSHOP

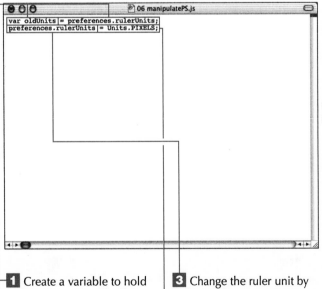

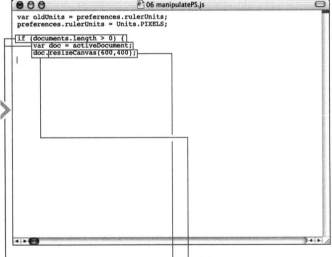

1 Create a variable to hold the current settings for the ruler unit.

2 Type an equal sign followed by **preferences.rulerUnits;**.

3 Change the ruler unit by typing **preferences.rulerUnits**.

4 Type an equal sign followed by **Units.** and the type of unit you want to use.

Note: See Appendix B for a list of possible values.

5 Check for open documents by typing **if (documents.length > 0) {,**.

6 If the condition is met, make a reference to the active document.

Note: See the section "Reference the Active Document" for more information.

7 Type the name of the document reference, followed by a dot.

8 Type **resizeCanvas();** placing the width and height of the resized image in the parentheses, separated by a comma.

Extra

The manual settings for resizing a canvas allow you to specify an anchor point for the resize operation. This permits you to add image area to only specific sides of a document. You can do this with scripting by passing an optional third argument to `document.resizeCanvas`. The third argument is an `AnchorPosition` constant. There are nine possible values, `BOTTOMCENTER`, `BOTTOMLEFT`, `BOTTOMRIGHT`, `MIDDLECENTER`, `MIDDLELEFT`, `MIDDLERIGHT`, `TOPCENTER`, `TOPLEFT`, and `TOPRIGHT`. Each of these values corresponds to one of the boxes in the Canvas Size dialog box. To keep the image in the upper-left corner of the newly resized canvas, you pass `AnchorPosition.TOPLEFT`.

You can also change the size of a document using the `document.crop()` method. Cropping is one of the most useful tools in Photoshop. You use the method by specifying what portion of the document you want to keep after Photoshop crops the document. The first parameter is an array of four numbers. The numbers define, in order, the left, top, right, and bottom coordinates of the cropped area. The second parameter is an optional parameter to specify a clockwise angle of rotation.

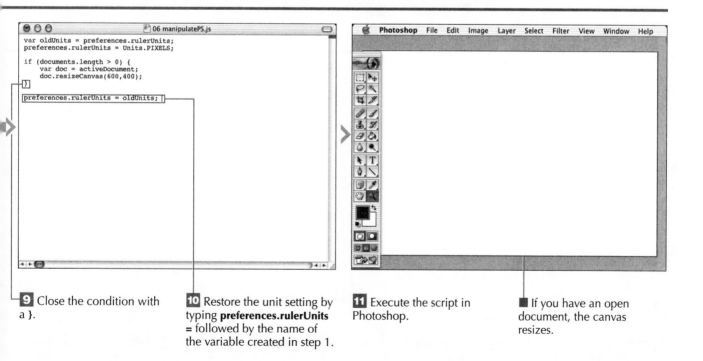

9 Close the condition with a }.

10 Restore the unit setting by typing **preferences.rulerUnits** = followed by the name of the variable created in step 1.

11 Execute the script in Photoshop.

■ If you have an open document, the canvas resizes.

USING THE DOCUMENT META-DATA IN PHOTOSHOP

You can access the document meta-data with JavaScript. All documents in Photoshop can have a set of meta-data containing information about the file such as author, title, copyright, and so on. You can view these settings in Photoshop by opening a new document via the File ⇨ File Info menu path.

When working in an environment where many different people work with the same file on a regular basis, document meta-data can help users keep track of important information about a file. Keeping relevant data about a file within the file itself makes it more difficult for a file to get separated from a project.

With scripting, you can make a document info template to stamp a document with common and important information such as your name, copyright, date, location, and so on. You may find a script like this useful for distributing in an organization to help keep track of assets.

The document meta-data is a docInfo object located in the info property of the document object. You must set the document to the activeDocument to make changes to the info object.

Almost all Adobe file types support document meta-data. In fact, Photoshop 7.0's built-in file browser displays this data for all Photoshop files. Document meta-data is also useful when using a workgroup server such as Adobe's Workflow Server. When using this workgroup file server, you can sort and search for files based on the document meta-data. Some other file viewers also support document meta-data such as Apple's QuickTime Player. In addition to Adobe's PSD and AI file formats, files that you save using Photoshop's File ⇨ Save As menu path also have meta-data information embedded in the document.

You can find a complete list of properties of the docInfo object in Appendix B.

USING THE DOCUMENT META-DATA IN PHOTOSHOP

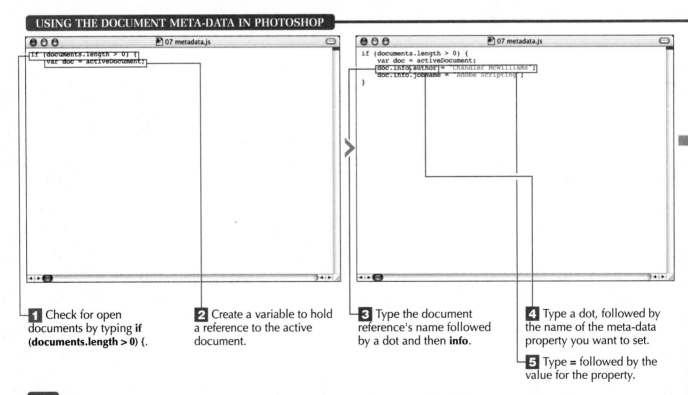

1 Check for open documents by typing **if (documents.length > 0) {**.

2 Create a variable to hold a reference to the active document.

3 Type the document reference's name followed by a dot and then **info**.

4 Type a dot, followed by the name of the meta-data property you want to set.

5 Type **=** followed by the value for the property.

Apply It

You can create a function to set all of the document meta-data properties for the active document. Creating a function makes it easy to set these properties for a large number of documents.

TYPE THIS:

```
function setMetaData() {
  if (documents.length > 0) {
    var doc = activeDocument;
    doc.info.author = 'Chandler McWilliams';
    doc.info.title = '';
    doc.info.ownerUrl = 'http://www.myurl.com';
    doc.info.category = 'VB';
    doc.info.credit = 'Chandler McWilliams';
    doc.info.jobName = 'Adobe Visual Blueprint'
    doc.info.keywords = ['photoshop' , 'scripting', 'visual blueprint'];
    doc.info.city = 'New York';
    doc.info.provinceState = 'NY';
    doc.info.country = 'USA';
  }
}
setMetaData();
```

RESULT:

When the `setMetaData ()` function is called, the File Info updates to show the values specified in the function.

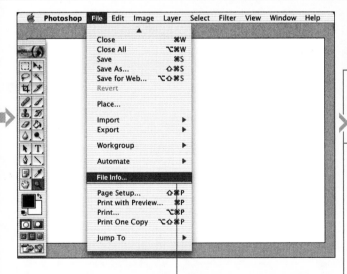

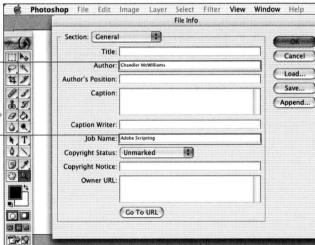

6 Open or create a document to modify.

7 Execute the script in Photoshop.

8 Click File ➪ File Info.

■ The File Info dialog box opens and shows that the specified document information has been set.

WORK WITH SELECTIONS IN PHOTOSHOP

Y ou can set and modify the current selection with JavaScript. One of the most common tools in Photoshop and Illustrator is the Marquee tool that you use to create selections. The selection is perhaps one of the most fundamental elements of working with these applications.

Both Photoshop and Illustrator have different ways of treating selections. Because Photoshop is a pixel-based application, you have no real objects to select. The selection is always a polygonal area defined by a set of points; each point in turn is defined as a set of x and y coordinates. See the section "Understanding Coordinate Systems in Photoshop and Illustrator" for more information on coordinates. When setting the selection in Photoshop, first you must describe the polygon that makes up the selection. In JavaScript, you do this by creating a multidimensional array. A *multidimensional array* is simply an array of arrays.

In the case of defining a polygon, each point is an array, with the x coordinate in the first position and the y coordinate in the second position. You collect these point arrays into a larger array to define the shape of the polygon. The order of the points in the array moves counter-clockwise.

Photoshop does not provide a way to test for a current selection. You receive an error if you attempt to access the selection object when you have no current selection. It is difficult to write a Photoshop script that operates on the user's selection without generating errors. One way to avoid errors is to use a Confirm dialog box to ask the user if there is a current selection. Although not ideal, it may prevent a possibly confusing error. You can also handle the errors using a `try...catch` statement. See Chapter 2 for more information about using confirm dialog boxes and Chapter 12 on handling errors.

WORK WITH SELECTIONS IN PHOTOSHOP

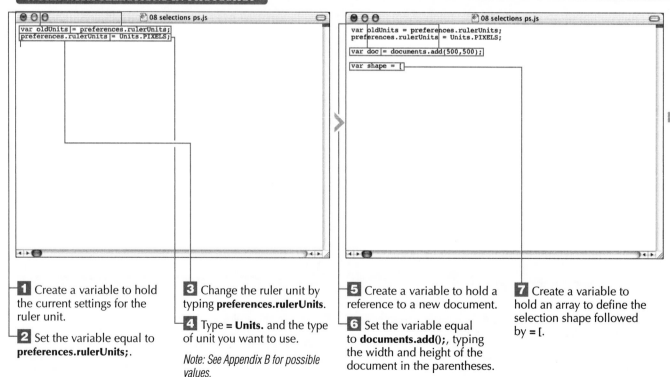

-◼1 Create a variable to hold the current settings for the ruler unit.

-◼2 Set the variable equal to **preferences.rulerUnits;**.

◼3 Change the ruler unit by typing **preferences.rulerUnits**.

-◼4 Type **= Units.** and the type of unit you want to use.

Note: See Appendix B for possible values.

-◼5 Create a variable to hold a reference to a new document.

-◼6 Set the variable equal to **documents.add();**, typing the width and height of the document in the parentheses.

◼7 Create a variable to hold an array to define the selection shape followed by **= [**.

Apply It

In Photoshop, you can modify the selection in a number of ways. You can rotate, expand, contract, feather, invert, stroke, and fill it. These methods correspond to the options in the Select menu, and the Fill and Stroke options in the Edit menu. Used together with the stroke and fill methods, selections are an easy way to create geometric shapes in Photoshop.

TYPE THIS:

```
if (documents.length > 0) {
  var doc = activeDocument;
  var shape = [
    [0,0],
    [0,100],
    [100, 100],
    [100,0]
  ];
  doc.selection.select(shape);
  var myColor = new SolidColor();
  myColor.rgb.red = 0;
  myColor.rgb.green = 0;
  myColor.rgb.blue = 0;
  doc.selection.stroke(solidColor, 1);
}
```

RESULT:

The script creates a selection in the active document and strokes the selection with the color created in the color object. See Chapter 6 for more information on changing the color a text item in Photoshop.

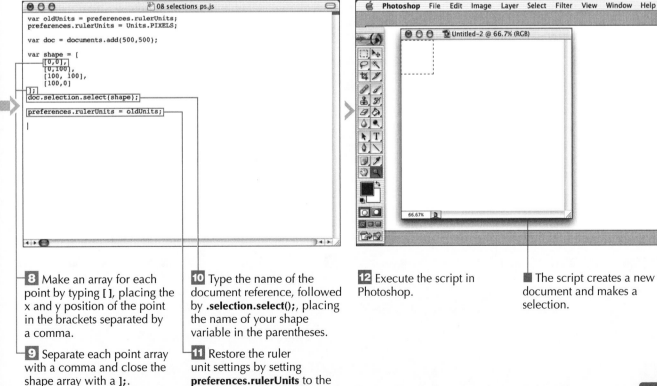

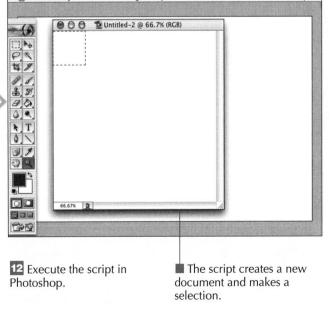

8 Make an array for each point by typing **[ ]**, placing the x and y position of the point in the brackets separated by a comma.

9 Separate each point array with a comma and close the shape array with a **];**.

10 Type the name of the document reference, followed by **.selection.select();**, placing the name of your shape variable in the parentheses.

11 Restore the ruler unit settings by setting **preferences.rulerUnits** to the variable created in step 1.

12 Execute the script in Photoshop.

■ The script creates a new document and makes a selection.

WORK WITH THE CLIPBOARD IN PHOTOSHOP

Using JavaScript, you can access Photoshop's clipboard, one of the most useful tools in Photoshop, and with it, the common copy, cut, and paste operations. JavaScript's clipboard methods are a powerful tool. For example, your script can take advantage of the clipboard to add a watermark to a number of documents.

In Photoshop, the clipboard interaction commands are all located in the Edit menu. The most common clipboard commands are copy, paste, and cut. The copy command makes a copy of the currently selected data in the clipboard; the cut command also adds the contents of the current selection to the clipboard, but it clears the current selection at the same time. Finally the paste command inserts the contents of the clipboard into the current document.

JavaScript can access these commands using methods of the `layer`, `document`, and `selection` objects. Both the `layer` and `selection` object have a `copy()` and `cut()`

method. Copy keeps the layer data intact, while cut removes everything from the layer. After the `copy()` method finishes, Photoshop selects the entire layer.

You can also use the `cut()` and `copy()` methods of the `selection` object to operate only on the current selection. Photoshop generates an error if you use these methods without an active selection. See Chapter 12 for more information on how to handle errors in JavaScript.

You add the contents of the clipboard to a document using the `document.paste()` method. Much like when using Photoshop by hand; the paste command inserts the clipboard contents in a new layer unless the currently selected layer is empty. If you create a new layer, it inserts itself on top of the currently selected layer. The `paste()` method returns a reference to the layer where you added the data. Like many other document manipulation methods, you can only use `paste()` on the active document.

WORK WITH THE CLIPBOARD IN PHOTOSHOP

COPY THE ACTIVE LAYER

1 Check for open documents by typing **if (documents.length > 0) {**.

2 Type **activeDocument. activeLayer.copy();**.

Note: See Chapter 4 for more information on the `activeLayer` *property.*

3 Execute the script in Photoshop with a document open.

■ The script selects the active layer and copies it.

Apply It

JavaScript also supports Photoshop's Copy Merged and Paste Into commands. The Copy Merged command copies the contents of all visible layers within the current selection. It is very useful for quickly moving art from document to document when preserving layers is not necessary. If you have no selection, an error generates.

TYPE THIS:
```
activeDocument.selection.copy(true);
```

RESULT:
The clipboard contains a copy of the artwork inside the selected area from all visible layers. If you have no selection, an error generates.

Photoshop's Paste Into command pastes the contents of the clipboard into the current selection. It adds a new layer containing the pasted information. Also, the selection border converts into a layer mask for the new layer. The clipboard contents are centered underneath the layer mask. See the Photoshop user's guide for more information on Layer Masks.

TYPE THIS:
```
var pasted = activeDocument.paste(true);
```

RESULT:
The script adds a new layer with the contents of the clipboard. The data centers itself under the current selection and the selection converts into a layer mask. An error occurs if you have no current selection.

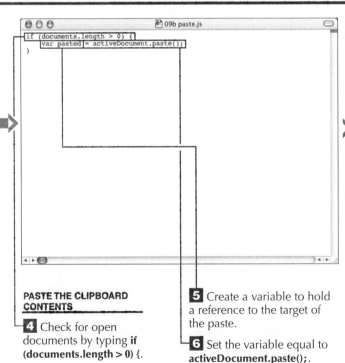

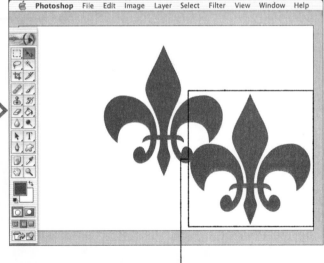

PASTE THE CLIPBOARD CONTENTS

4 Check for open documents by typing **if (documents.length > 0) {**.

5 Create a variable to hold a reference to the target of the paste.

6 Set the variable equal to **activeDocument.paste();**.

7 Execute the script in Photoshop with a document open.

■ The script adds the contents of the clipboard to the document.

CREATE A NEW ART LAYER IN PHOTOSHOP

You can use JavaScript to add a new layer, one of the most basic elements of a Photoshop document. You create layers to contain every visual element of a document, and because it is the first step in adding text, images, or other art to a document.

The main type of layer in Photoshop is the *art layer*, which contains all art, image, and text items. Photoshop also has a layer type called a *layer set*. A layer set is a group of art layers. See the section "Create a New Layer Set in Photoshop" for more information. Accessed from the document.layers collection, both art layers and layer sets share a few basic properties such as visibility and name. Unlike the documents collection, however, the layers collection does not have an add method.

You use the document.artLayers collection to access all current art layers in a document and to create new art layers using the add method. You must select or create a

document before attempting to add or manipulate a layer in the document. In this way, the layers and artLayers collections are properties of the document object. To understand more about the Adobe Scripting object model, see Chapter 3. Because the layers collection is a property of the document object, you should check for the existence of an open document before attempting to access any properties of the document.

The artLayers.add() method takes no parameters, so an extra step is involved to set any properties or to name the new layer. When the method is called, it returns a reference to the newly created layer. By capturing this reference, you can give a name to your layers. Naming layers helps keep your files easy to understand, but more importantly, it provides an easy way to reference the layer later in your script.

CREATE A NEW ART LAYER IN PHOTOSHOP

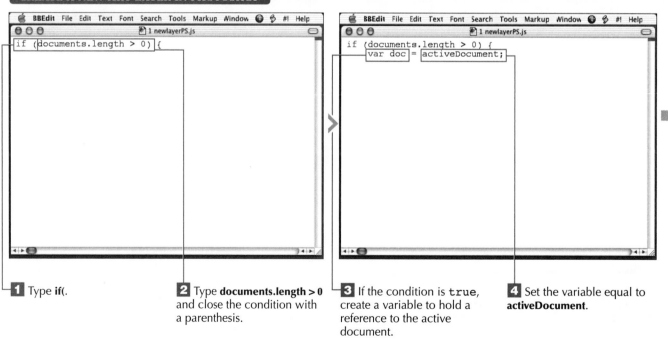

1 Type **if(**.

2 Type **documents.length > 0** and close the condition with a parenthesis.

3 If the condition is **true**, create a variable to hold a reference to the active document.

4 Set the variable equal to **activeDocument**.

Apply It

You can access all named layers as properties of the `artLayers` collection. For example, you can access a layer named TitleArt using `artLayers.TitleArt`. If your layer name contains spaces, you can use the `[]` operators to access the layer. Although it is easier to access a named layer if the name has no spaces, it is often easier to understand the file if the layers are given clearer names.

TYPE THIS:

```
if (documents.length > 0) {
    var doc = activeDocument;
    var theLayer = doc.artLayers.add();
    theLayer.name = "Title Art";
    var titleLayer = doc.artLayers["Title Art"];
}
```

RESULT:

The script creates a new layer in the active document. After the script creates the layer, it names it "Title Art". The `titleLayer` variable is then set to reference the new layer using the layer's name and the `document.artLayers` collection.

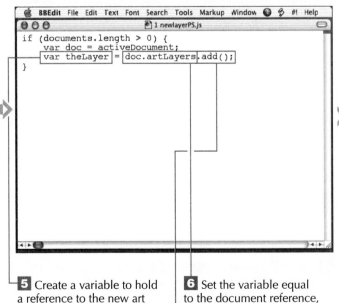

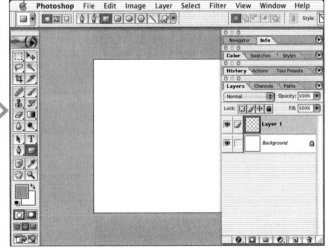

5 Create a variable to hold a reference to the new art layer.

6 Set the variable equal to the document reference, followed by a dot, and then **artLayers**.

7 Type a dot followed by **add();**.

8 Execute the script in Photoshop with a document open.

Note: See Chapter 1 for more information on running a sample script.

■ Photoshop creates a new layer.

57

CREATE A NEW LAYER SET IN PHOTOSHOP

*L*ayer sets are similar to folders that can hold other layers. You can create layer sets with scripting and control the contents and order of layers contained in the layer set. By using layer sets, you can organize changes and additions to a document made with scripting. When designing different sample compositions for a project, layer sets can help separate elements from the different versions. For example, you can write a script to export one layer set at a time as a JPEG or PDF file to show to a client.

You use the `layerSets` collection to access and manipulate the layer sets in a document. The `layerSets` collection is a property of the `document` object. Like the `artLayers`, the `layerSets` collection is one level deeper

than `documents` in the Photoshop object model hierarchy. Before manipulating a layer set, you must select a document in which to perform the modifications.

You create a new layer set by calling the `add` method of the `layerSets` collection. The method takes no parameters, so extra steps are required to add or modify properties of new layer sets. The `add` method returns a reference to the new layer set. You can add properties to the layer set by capturing the returned reference in a variable. It is always a good idea to name your layer sets. Naming helps keep your files organized and makes it easier to access layer sets later on in your scripts. See the section "Create a New Art Layer in Photoshop" in this chapter for more information on how to access named layers; the same methods also apply to accessing layer sets.

CREATE A NEW LAYER SET IN PHOTOSHOP

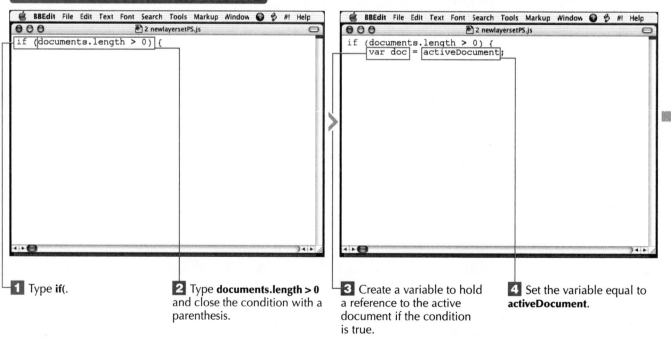

1 Type **if(**.

2 Type **documents.length > 0** and close the condition with a parenthesis.

3 Create a variable to hold a reference to the active document if the condition is true.

4 Set the variable equal to **activeDocument**.

Extra

You can access the layers in a layer set using the `layers` and `artLayers` properties of the `layerSet` object. Much like the `document` object has `layers` and `artLayers` properties, which allow you to access the layers in the document, each layer set also has these properties, which allow you to access the layers inside the layer set. You can add a new layer to a layer set in much the same way you add a new layer to a document. The `artLayers` property of a `layerSet` object works in the same way as the `artLayers` property of the `document` object.

Example:

```
if (documents.length > 0) {
    var doc = activeDocument;
    var mySet = doc.layerSets.add();
    mySet.name = "New Layer Set";
    var myLayer = mySet.artLayers.add();
    myLayer.name = "New Layer in Set";
}
```

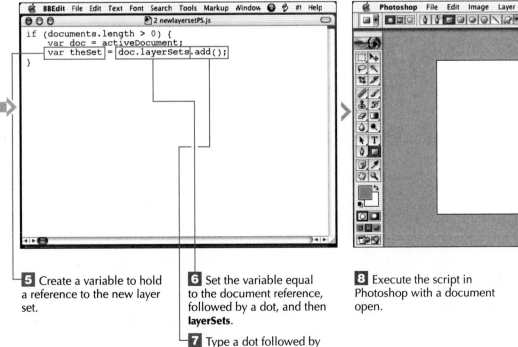

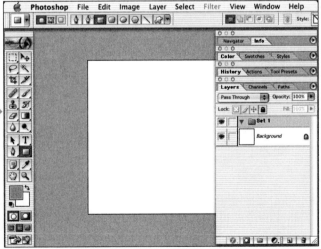

5 Create a variable to hold a reference to the new layer set.

6 Set the variable equal to the document reference, followed by a dot, and then **layerSets**.

7 Type a dot followed by **add();**.

8 Execute the script in Photoshop with a document open.

■ Photoshop creates a new layer set.

MANIPULATE LAYERS IN PHOTOSHOP

Y ou can use JavaScript to manipulate properties such as opacity, visibility, and blending modes of layers in Photoshop. Art layers and layer sets support settings and effects that are indispensable to most projects. You can also use JavaScript to rearrange the stacking order and link art layers and layer sets.

Art layers support many of the properties available in the Layers palette in Photoshop. You can lock pixels, transparency, and position, change the visibility, and set the blending mode. Many of the properties simply take a Boolean value to set them on or off. See Chapter 2 for more information about Boolean values.

`Layer` objects in Photoshop, which include both art layers and layer sets, have a set of methods to change the order of layers in a document. Using these methods, you can move layers to the top or bottom of the stacking order. You can also move a layer relative to other layers, moving it to a position before or after another layer.

You can also rotate, resize, and transform art layers and layer sets using scripting. When you transform a layer set, you change all of the layers contained in the set as well.

Layer sets have some properties in common with art layers, such as blending modes, visibility, and links. When you change a property of a layer set, the setting affects every layer within the set. Instead of setting the opacity of every layer in a set, you can change the set's opacity and affect every layer at once.

Before working on a layer or layer set, you must make the layer active. The built-in `activeLayer` property contains a reference to the currently selected art layer or layer set. You can also set this property to make a layer or layer set active. It is analogous to the `activeDocument` property discussed in Chapter 3.

MANIPULATE LAYERS IN PHOTOSHOP

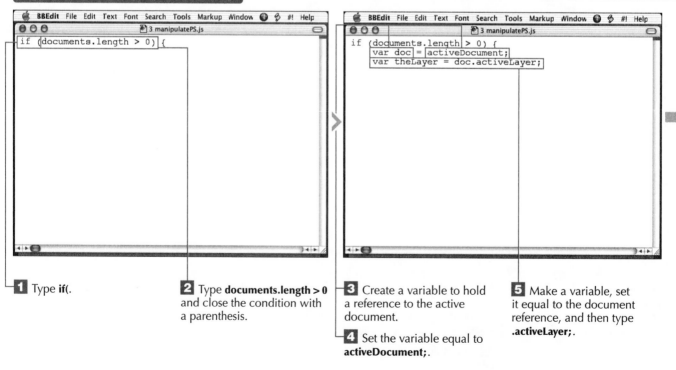

1 Type **if(**.

2 Type **documents.length > 0** and close the condition with a parenthesis.

3 Create a variable to hold a reference to the active document.

4 Set the variable equal to **activeDocument;**.

5 Make a variable, set it equal to the document reference, and then type **.activeLayer;**.

Apply It

You can add existing art layers to a layer set in Photoshop. You can use layer sets to organize changes made to a document, and are also a convenient way to apply changes to a large number of layers at once. The `moveToEnd` and `moveToBeginning` methods of the layer object allow you to move layers. Each method takes a single argument, which is the destination for the layer. The destination can reference a layer set or the document itself. Moving a layer to the end of a layer set or document moves it to the bottom of the stacking order. The "beginning" of a document or layer set is the top of the stacking order. When looking at the Layers palette in Photoshop, you can think of the "end" as the top and the "beginning" as the bottom.

TYPE THIS:

```
if (documents.length > 0) {
    var doc = activeDocument;
    var theLayer = doc.artLayers.add();
    var theSet = doc.layerSets.add();
    theLayer.moveToEnd(theSet);
}
```

RESULT:

The script creates a new art layer and layer set in the active document. After the script creates the layer set and art layer, it moves the layer to the top of the layer set.

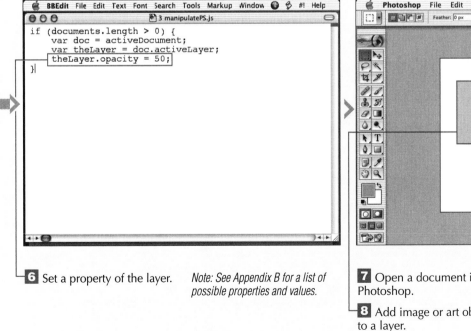

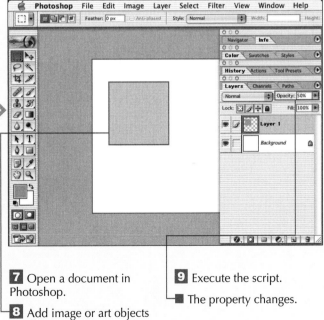

6 Set a property of the layer.

Note: See Appendix B for a list of possible properties and values.

7 Open a document in Photoshop.

8 Add image or art objects to a layer.

9 Execute the script.

■ The property changes.

DUPLICATE A LAYER IN PHOTOSHOP

You can use JavaScript to duplicate a layer in Photoshop — a good way to make a backup copy of a process before you begin. You can also repeatedly duplicate a layer and move it to a random position and scale to create background art.

You use the duplicate() method of the layer object to duplicate both art layers and layer sets. However, Photoshop 7 has a bug that causes an error when you use the duplicate() method with a layer set. Photoshop successfully duplicates the layer, but it gives an error and aborts the script. You can write your own script to duplicate a layer set by first creating a new layer set, duplicating each layer it the source set, and moving the layers into the newly created set. See the section "Manipulating Layers in Photoshop" for more information on moving layers into a layer set. You can also ignore the error by using a try-catch statement as illustrated in Chapter 12.

Extra

When using loops to create or duplicate objects, you may get stuck in an infinite loop. For example, you may need to write a script to duplicate every layer in a document, like the following example:

Example:
```
if (documents.length > 0) {
    var doc = activeDocument;
    for (var i=0; i<doc.layers.length; i++) {
        var theLayer = doc.layers[i];
        theLayer.duplicate();
    }
}
```

However, this code causes an infinite loop. Each time the condition is tested, doc.layers.length increases by one as a result of the duplicate operation, and so never meets the condition. If you get stuck in a script, you can always cancel it by pressing ⌘ + (Ctrl + in Windows).

DUPLICATE A LAYER IN PHOTOSHOP

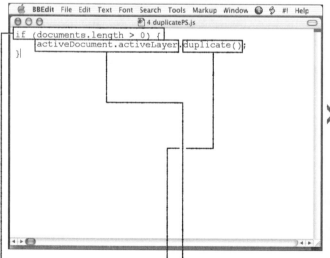

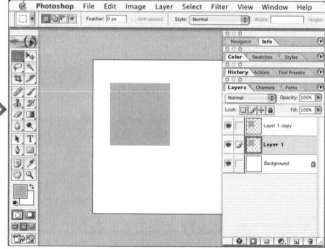

1 Type if(documents.length > 0) {.

2 Create a variable to hold a reference to the active layer of the active document.

3 Call the duplicate() method of the layer.

4 Execute the script in Photoshop with a document open.

■ The active layer duplicates.

APPLY A FILTER TO A LAYER IN PHOTOSHOP

You can apply filters to art layers in Photoshop to produce a wide variety of effects, including creating blurs, adding noise, and adding lens flares. You can access almost every standard filter using scripting. By applying these filters with scripting, you can combine commonly used effects into a single action. For example, you can write a script to create a large number of title images for a Web site all using a standard set of effects.

The available filters in JavaScript all exist as methods of the art layer object. All of the filter methods take the form `applyFilterName`, where `FilterName` is the name of the filter to apply. The parameters for each filter are different depending on the information required for the filter. For example, in the case of the `applyGaussianBlur` method, the method takes a single parameter that defines the radius of the blur operation.

You can only apply filters to art layers; an error occurs if a script attempts to apply a filter to a layer set. If an art layer contains text, Photoshop displays an alert telling the user that it will rasterize the text before applying the filter. See Chapter 6 for more information on working with text in Photoshop. You also cannot apply a filter to an empty layer. You can prevent errors from interrupting the script using a `try-catch` statement. See Chapter 12 for more information on `try-catch` statements.

Not all filters are available using JavaScript. You can find a complete listing of available filter methods and the required parameters in Appendix B. If you find that a filter is unavailable, you may be able to use it in conjunction with the Action Manager plug-in. See Chapter 11 for more information on using the Action Manager plug-in.

APPLY A FILTER TO A LAYER IN PHOTOSHOP

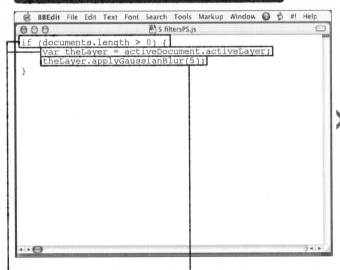

1 Type **if(documents.length > 0) {**.

2 Create a variable to hold a reference to the active layer of the active document.

3 Call a filter method of the layer.

Note: See Appendix B for a complete list of filters.

4 Execute the script in Photoshop with a document open.

■ Photoshop applies the filter to the active layer.

CREATE A NEW LAYER IN ILLUSTRATOR

Y ou can add new layers to an Illustrator document using JavaScript to help keep your documents organized and easy to edit. Using layers when scripting in Illustrator makes batch processing easier. For example, you can export layers to a Flash movie using three different options for treating layers; see Chapter 10 for more information on exporting a file to SWF from Illustrator.

Illustrator contains all document elements in a layer. Layers themselves contain other objects such as groups, page items, and path items. Although Illustrator allows you to add new groups and objects to one layer, it is good practice to use multiple layers to keep your documents organized.

You access all layers in Illustrator using the document.layers collection. Much like the documents collection discussed in Chapter 3, the layers collection contains a list of layers and includes methods to create and modify new layers. The layers collection is a property of

the document object. You must select an existing document or create a new one before you can access the layers collection.

You create new layers using the layers.add() method, which takes no parameters. This method generates a new layer at the top of the layer stacking order with default properties — the equivalent of clicking the Create a New Layer button in the Layers palette. You must add all properties, such as the name of a new layer, in additional steps. It is a good idea to name your layers for organization and for easy reference later in your scripts. You can apply the information on accessing named layers in the section "Create a New Art Layer in Photoshop" to Illustrator scripts as well.

Layers in Illustrator support *sub-layers*, which are layers contained in another layer. Every layer contains a layers collection that you can use to manipulate the sub-layers contained in that layer. The layers collection of a layer behaves in the same way as the document.layers collection.

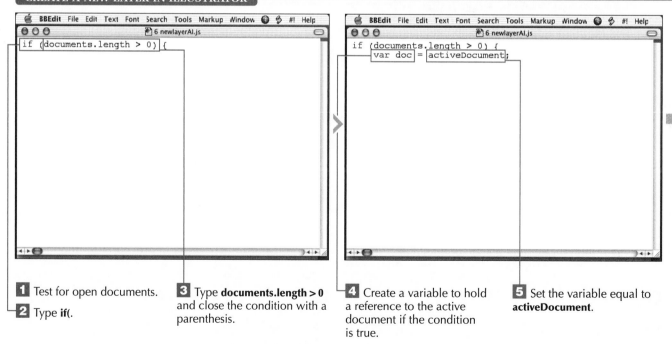

1 Test for open documents.

2 Type **if(**.

3 Type **documents.length > 0** and close the condition with a parenthesis.

4 Create a variable to hold a reference to the active document if the condition is true.

5 Set the variable equal to **activeDocument**.

Extra

When you create a new layer, Illustrator places it at the top of the layer stack, before all other layers. The `layer` object includes some methods to change the order of layers using scripting. You can move a layer relative to another layer, or move it to the absolute front or back of a document. JavaScript in Illustrator uses the language of before and after, beginning and end, to define the order of objects in a document. For example you can move a layer to the top of a document using the `moveToEnd()` method. When you look at the Layers palette in Illustrator, it makes more sense to talk about layer position in terms of top and bottom. You consider the top of the Layers palette as the beginning in JavaScript terms, and the bottom as the end.

The language of before and after extends to the methods that move layers to a new position relative to other layers or objects. You move an object "before" another object if you want it to appear on top of the object. You use the `moveBefore` and `moveAfter` methods to move a layer relative to another. See Appendix A for a complete list of methods for changing the order of layers.

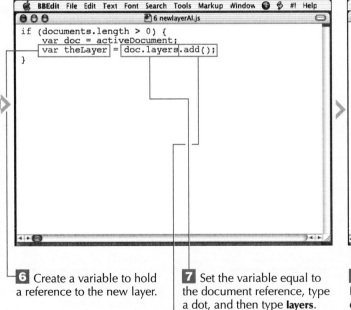

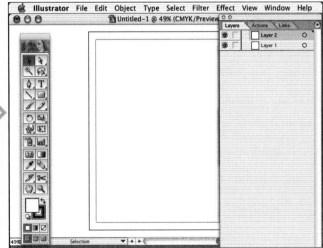

6 Create a variable to hold a reference to the new layer.

7 Set the variable equal to the document reference, type a dot, and then type **layers**.

8 Type a dot followed by **add();**.

9 Execute the script in Illustrator with a document open.

■ Illustrator creates a new layer.

RETRIEVE A LIST OF VISIBLE LAYERS IN PHOTOSHOP AND ILLUSTRATOR

You can create a report of visible layers in a document to help you remember the layout of a document at a given time. Using a simple loop, you can cycle through the layers of a document and execute an action when the layer is visible. Working with loops and layers is one of the most fundamental aspects of batch processing with Photoshop and Illustrator. When working with many different designs in a single document, it gets difficult to manage which layers are associated with which version. You can write a script to report which layers are visible at a given time as a reminder.

The `document.layers` collection has a `length` property that contains the number of layers in the collection. You can use this in the condition of a loop to access each layer in

the collection. See Chapter 2 for more information on using loops. However, this only allows you to access the top level of layer objects in a document.

To access sub-layers in Illustrator, and layers in layer sets in Photoshop, you need to use a recursive function. *Recursive functions* are functions that make a call to themselves during their operation. See p. 29 for an example of a recursive function. In the case of accessing layers, first you write a function to loop through all layers contained in a collection passed as a parameter. Then use a conditional to test each layer to see if it is a layer set in Photoshop, or if it has items in its `layers` property in Illustrator. If so, the script calls the original function and passes the `layers` property as the parameter. Because the function performs the same actions at each level, calling it makes your script better able to handle a wide variety of situations.

RETRIEVE A LIST OF VISIBLE LAYERS IN PHOTOSHOP AND ILLUSTRATOR

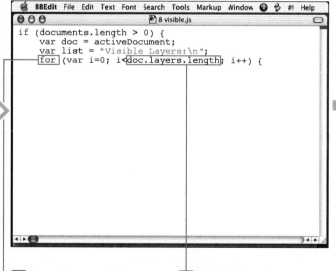

1 Type **if(documents.length > 0) {.**

2 Create a variable to hold a reference to the active layer of the active document.

3 Create a variable to hold the list of layers.

■ In this example, \n prints a return.

4 Create a **for** loop.

5 Retrieve the number of elements in the **layers** collection by typing your document reference, a dot, and then **layers.length**.

Extra

You can add a recursive function to access more than just the top level of layers. A script with a recursive function for Illustrator might look like:

Example:
```
function listVisible(theLayers) {
  var list = "";
  for (var i=0; i<theLayers.length; i++) {
    if (theLayers[i].visible) {
      list += theLayers[i].name + "\n";
      if (theLayers[i].typename == "Layer") {
        list += listVisible(theLayers[i].layers);
      }
    }
  }
  return list;
}


if (documents.length > 0) {
  var doc = activeDocument;
  var list = "Visible Layers:\n";
  list += listVisible(doc.layers);
  alert (list);
}
```

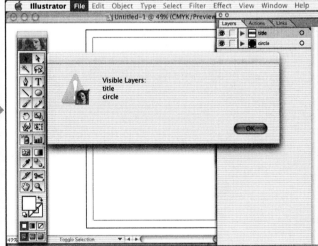

6 Test the visibility of each layer by typing the document reference, a dot, and then **layers[i].visible**.

7 Add the name of the layer and a '\n' to the list variable.

8 Display the list.

9 Execute the script in Illustrator.

■ A dialog box shows the visible layers.

CREATE PATH ITEMS

Almost all artwork created in Illustrator consists of paths, from the simplest squares and circles to very complex shapes and illustrations. You can manipulate and create new artwork using JavaScript and Illustrator. JavaScript gives you access to all elements of paths in Illustrator, allowing you to create art with scripting much as you can by hand.

A minimum of two points defines all path items. Every point is defined by three values: the anchor point and two control points. The *anchor point* is the position on the page of the point. The *control points*, or handles, control the curve of the point.

You access path items in a document using the `document.pathItems` collection. This collection is a list of references to every path item in the document, regardless of what layer or sub-layer contains the path item. Each layer also has its own `pathItems` collection, which

refers specifically to the path items contained in that layer. The `pathItems` collection has an `add()` method for creating new path items. Calling the `add()` method of the `documents.pathItems` collection adds a new path item to the top layer in the document. Using the `layer.pathItems` collection adds a path item to that particular layer.

After you create a path item, you can add points using the `pathItem.pathPoints.add()` method. The `pathPoints` collection of a `pathItem` contains a reference to every point in the path. The `anchor`, `leftDirection`, and `rightDirection` properties of the path point allow you to position the point and set its curve. Each of these properties is set to an array; the first element is the x position, and the second is the y.

Unless otherwise specified, the current setting of the drawing tools in Illustrator's Tools palette determines the way the path item is drawn.

CREATE PATH ITEMS

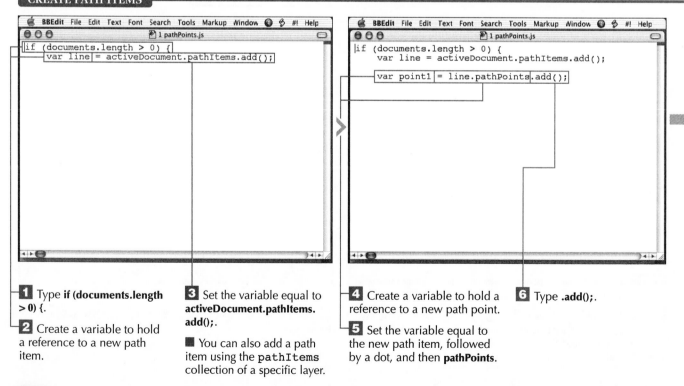

1 Type **if (documents.length > 0) {**.

2 Create a variable to hold a reference to a new path item.

3 Set the variable equal to **activeDocument.pathItems.add();**.

■ You can also add a path item using the **pathItems** collection of a specific layer.

4 Create a variable to hold a reference to a new path point.

5 Set the variable equal to the new path item, followed by a dot, and then **pathPoints**.

6 Type **.add();**.

Extra

You can define the points for an entire path at one time using the `pathItem.setEntirePath()` method. This method takes a single array as a parameter. The array should contain a list of points to add to the path item. Each point is an array of two numbers; the first is the x position, the second is the y position. See Chapter 2 for more information on arrays. The following code sets the position of all points for a `pathItem`.

One drawback of the `setEntirePath()` method is that you cannot set the `leftDirection` and `rightDirection` properties of each point at the same time that you set the position. One solution is to use `setEntirePath()` to set the positions of each point, and then use a loop to set the direction parameters for each point. See Chapter 2 for more information on using loops.

TYPE THIS:

```
if (documents.length > 0) {
  var line = activeDocument.pathItems.add();
  var points = [[0,700], [200,0], [300,300]];
  line.setEntirePath(points);
}
```

RESULT:

The path item is given three points, one for each point in the array.

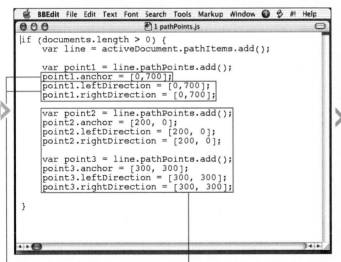

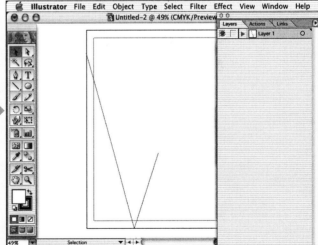

7 Set the **anchor** property of the new path point.

8 Set the **leftDirection** and **rightDirection** properties of the path point.

9 Repeat steps 4 to 8 to add other points to the path item.

10 Execute the script in Illustrator.

■ Illustrator creates a new path item with the defined points.

CREATE ELLIPSES

You can create an ellipse in Illustrator using JavaScript. The ability to create artwork is one of the most powerful features of Illustrator scripting. By using path items, you can access the drawing tools of Illustrator. You can write scripts to create many of the shapes you can draw by hand, and manipulate them further to create background patterns, repetitive shapes, or even animations.

In addition to the add() method, the pathItems collection has a method for drawing ellipses. The result is the same as using the Ellipse tool in Illustrator's Tools palette.

The ellipse() method takes up to six parameters. All parameters are optional. If you do not supply any, Illustrator draws the ellipse with an unpredictable shape and position. The first two parameters define the top and left of the new ellipse. Note that this is not the x and y position of the

center of the ellipse as might be expected, but rather the locations of the top and left sides. The next two parameters are the width and height. If you only supply the width, Illustrator draws the ellipse as a circle. You can position an ellipse according to its center point by accounting for the width and height when specifying the top and left. For example, to position a 100-point circle with x and y positions of 0 and 700, you can pass 750 for the top, because half of 100 is 50 plus the desired top position, and −50 for the left position.

By default, Illustrator draws all new path items using the current settings in the Tools palette. You can override this behavior using the filled and stroked properties of the pathItem object. Each of these parameters takes a single Boolean value to set whether it is active.

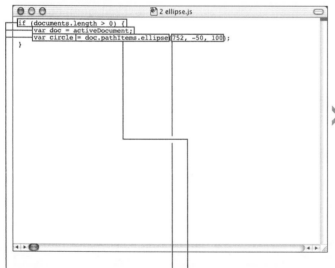

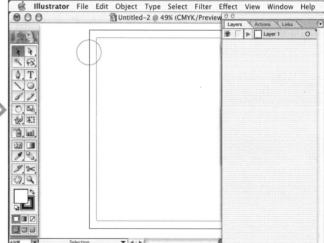

1 Type **if (documents.length > 0) {**.

2 Create a reference to the active document.

3 Create a variable to hold a reference to a new path item.

4 Set the variable equal to the document reference, and then type **.pathItems.ellipse();**.

5 Place the desired parameters in the parentheses.

6 Execute the script in Illustrator.

■ Illustrator creates an ellipse.

70

CREATE RECTANGLES

You can use JavaScript to create a rectangle in Illustrator. Scripting gives you access to many of the drawing tools that create artwork in Illustrator. Because artwork is composed of paths, you can generate a variety of shapes using the `pathItems` object and methods. You can write scripts to create complicated patterns and artwork that you may find too tedious to build by hand.

You use the `rectangle()` method of the `pathItems` collection to create rectangular and square shapes. This corresponds to the Rectangle tool in Illustrator's Tools palette.

The `rectangle()` method takes five parameters, all of which are optional. Together they control the shape of the rectangle. If you do not specify parameters, Illustrator creates rectangles with unpredictable locations and shapes. Like the `ellipse()` method, the first two parameters specify the `top` and `left` coordinates. The second two control the `width` and `height`. You use the fifth parameter to determine the direction of the path. All of the drawing methods of the `pathItems`

collection can optionally have the direction of their paths reversed. The path is not reversed unless you specify this parameter. The `width` and `height` parameters are measured in points. See Chapter 3 for more information on the coordinate systems in Photoshop and Illustrator.

Extra

You can also create a rounded rectangle with JavaScript using the `pathItems.roundedRectangle()` method. The first four parameters are the same as with the `rectangle()` method. The next two define the horizontal and vertical radius of the corners.

Example:
```
if (documents.length > 0) {
   activeDocument.pathItems.roundedRectangle
(500, 50, 300, 100, 15, 50);
}
```

CREATE RECTANGLES

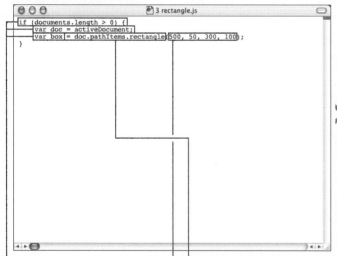

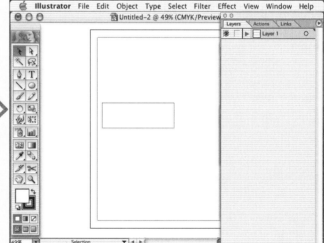

1 Type **if (documents.length > 0) {**.

2 Create a variable to reference the active document.

3 Create a variable to hold a reference to a new path item.

4 Type the document reference variable and then type **.pathItems.rectangle();**.

5 Place the desired parameters in the parentheses.

6 Execute the script in Illustrator.

■ Illustrator creates a rectangle.

CREATE STARS AND POLYGONS

Y ou can draw stars and polygons in Illustrator using JavaScript. Using the built-in methods of the `pathItems` object, you can draw complex shapes like stars and polygons. You can then use scripts to automate the creation of elaborate background patterns.

The `pathItems` object has a `star()` method that creates star shapes. The results of this method correspond to the Star tool in Illustrator's Tools palette. The `star()` method takes up to six optional parameters. If you do not specify parameters, Illustrator creates a star with an unpredictable shape and location. The first two parameters specify the center x and y position of the star. Unlike the `rectangle()` and `ellipse()` methods, you specify the *center point* of the new star. It is confusing at first to move between the ellipse and rectangle methods to the star method because of the order of the parameters. Make sure

the x position is first, and the y position second. The third parameter defines the outer radius of the star in points, and the fourth defines the inner radius, or the radius of the circle all of the inner points touch. You use the fifth parameter to specify the number of points on the star. A star cannot have less than two points. The sixth parameter determines the path direction.

The `pathItems.polygon()` method is used to create polygons and is very similar to the `star()` method. The first two parameters define the x and y positions of center of the polygon. The third parameter sets the `radius` of the shape in points, and the fourth specifies the number of sides the polygon should have. A polygon cannot have less than three sides. The fifth determines if the path is reversed. All five parameters are also optional.

CREATE STARS AND POLYGONS

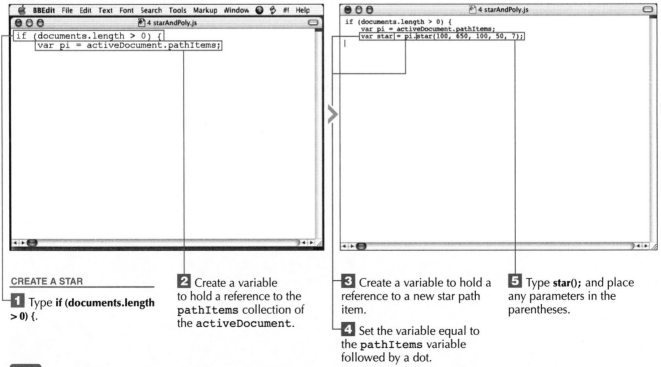

CREATE A STAR

1 Type **if (documents.length > 0) {**.

2 Create a variable to hold a reference to the `pathItems` collection of the `activeDocument`.

3 Create a variable to hold a reference to a new star path item.

4 Set the variable equal to the `pathItems` variable followed by a dot.

5 Type **star();** and place any parameters in the parentheses.

Apply It

You can use the JavaScript `Math` object to generate random numbers and create stars with random positions, sizes, and points. JavaScript has a built-in `Math` object with methods that give you access to a number of mathematical operations such as sine and cosine, absolute value, rounding, and random numbers. The `Math.random()` method returns a random number between 0 and 1. When this number is multiplied by a whole number, for example 5, the result is a number between 0 and 5. Using this in conjunction with `Math.round()`, which rounds numbers with decimal points to a whole number, you can generate a random whole number. Sometimes when working with random numbers, you want to set a lower limit to the number you get. You can accomplish this by adding the lower limit to the rounded random number.

TYPE THIS:

```
if (documents.length > 0) {
  var points = Math.round(Math.random() * 5) + 3;
  activeDocument.pathItems.star(300, 450, 200, 50, points);
}
```

RESULT:

This creates a star with an outer radius of 200, an inner radius of 50, and between 3 and 8 points.

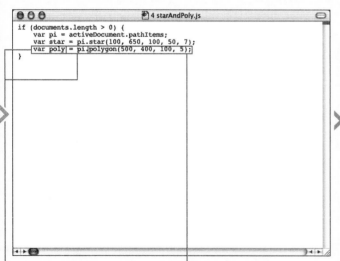

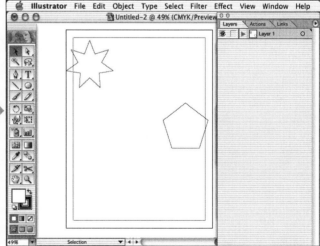

CREATE A POLYGON

■6 Create a variable to hold a reference to a new polygon path item.

■7 Set the variable equal to the **pathItems** variable followed by a dot.

■8 Type **polygon();** and place any parameters in the parentheses.

■9 Execute the script in Illustrator.

■ Illustrator creates a star and a polygon.

DEFINE AND APPLY COLOR VALUES

You can define color values to apply to swatches, gradients, and path items. You can create RGB colors, CMYK colors, and grayscale colors and apply them to objects in the document.

Illustrator only supports one color space for each document at a time. When you create a document, you must specify if it uses CMYK or RGB colors. When using colors in scripting, you must pay attention to the current color space of the document to ensure the correct results. If a script attempts to apply an RGB color to an object in a CMYK document, the color converts to a CMYK color, and a CMYK color is returned. This is not, however, a 100 percent accurate conversion, and some data loss occurs. You can use the documentColorSpace property of the document object to determine the color space. This property equals 2 for CMYK and 1 for RGB.

Creating a new color is a two-step process. You use the color object to change color values. When a new color object is created, you can access the properties for CMYK and RGB color as well as grayscale, pattern, gradient, and spot.

After you create the color object, you must create another object for the color type you want to use. There are objects for RGB, CMYK, grayscale, pattern, gradient, and spot. After a color type object is created, you can define the properties for that color. For example, a CMYK object has a property for black, cyan, magenta, and yellow. Each of these is set to a value between 0 and 100. An RGB object, on the other hand, has a property for red, green, and blue, and accepts a value between 0 and 255. See Appendix A for more information on the color type objects.

DEFINE AND APPLY COLOR VALUES

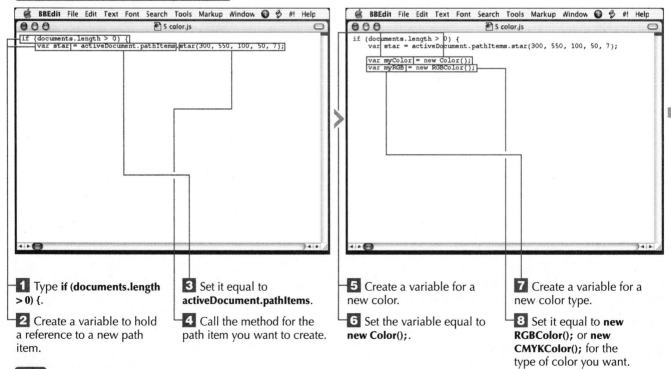

■1 Type **if (documents.length > 0) {**.

■2 Create a variable to hold a reference to a new path item.

■3 Set it equal to **activeDocument.pathItems**.

■4 Call the method for the path item you want to create.

■5 Create a variable for a new color.

■6 Set the variable equal to **new Color();**.

■7 Create a variable for a new color type.

■8 Set it equal to **new RGBColor();** or **new CMYKColor();** for the type of color you want.

Extra

Before setting the `fillColor` and `strokeColor` of a path item, it is good practice to set the corresponding `filled` or `stroked` property to `true` to ensure that the results of the color change appear. See the section "Working with Strokes" for more information.

The `fillColor` and `strokeColor` properties determine the colors of path items. These properties can also be read from an existing path item. You can compare the value of the `color` property of the color object retrieved from the `pathItem` a `ColorType` constant to determine the type of the color. For example, the following code sets the variable `myBlue` to the `blue` value of the first path item in the active document if the object's fill color type is RGB.

Example:
```
var pi = activeDocument.pathItems;
firstItem = pi[0];
firstItemFillColor = firstItem.fillColor;
if (firstItemFillColor.color == ColorType.RGB) {
  var myBlue = firstItemFillColor.rgb.blue;
}
```

See Appendix A for a complete list of possible values for the `ColorType` constant.

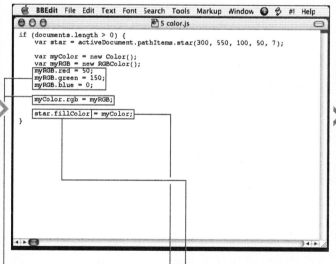

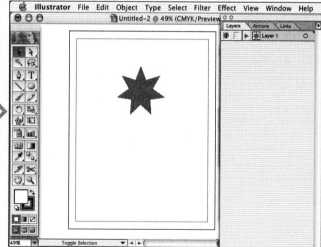

9 Set the properties for the color.

10 Set the `rgb` or `cymk` property for the color object to the color type object created in step 8.

11 Type the path item variable, a dot, and then **fillColor**.

12 Set the property equal to the color object.

13 Execute the script in Illustrator.

■ The script creates a new shape with the specified color.

MANIPULATE PATH ITEMS

You can use JavaScript to change properties of already existing path items. Path items have a variety of methods for altering the rotation, scale, and position. You can also duplicate a path item and change the stacking order. You can use these methods on path items that you create with scripting or with already existing path items.

With scripting you can access most of the options available under the Object ⇨ Transform and Object ⇨ Arrange menus. In addition to moving and resizing path items, you can also set properties such as name, polarity, and stroke-cap type. See Appendix A for more information about these properties.

All path items inhabit a particular location in the stacking order. This location determines which path items appear over and under others. This property is often referred to as the z-index. Whereas you define left and right along the x-axis, and top and bottom along the y-axis, you determine

the stacking order by what can be considered a third axis, called the z-axis. JavaScript provides a few different ways to modify the z-index of a path item. The moveBefore, moveAfter, moveToEnd, and moveToBeginning methods behave in the same way as the analogous methods for layer objects. See the section "Manipulate Layers in Photoshop" for more on these methods. The information there also applies to path items in Illustrator. In addition, you can arrange path items in Illustrator using the zOrder() method. This method takes a single ZOrderMethod parameter and performs the operations available under the Object ⇨ Arrange menu. See Appendix A for a complete list of values for the ZOrderMethod.

The movement and transformation methods of the pathItem object provide access to most of the commands under the Object ⇨ Transform menu. When working with rotation, keep in mind that positive angle values rotate the object counterclockwise, and negative values rotate the object clockwise.

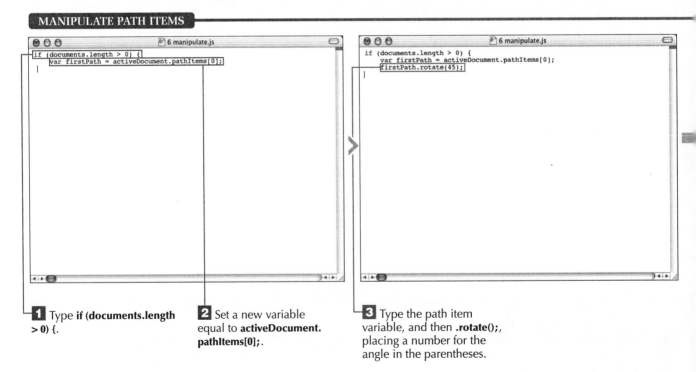

1 Type if (documents.length > 0) {.

2 Set a new variable equal to activeDocument.pathItems[0];.

3 Type the path item variable, and then .rotate();, placing a number for the angle in the parentheses.

Extra

You can manipulate the style of strokes using JavaScript. Illustrator provides a number of options that control the way strokes are drawn on an object. The most basic is the stroke width, which is set using the `strokeWidth` property. In addition, you can access many of the options that appear in Illustrator's Stroke palette. You may need to select Show Options from the palette's menu to see all options. The stroke cap and join styles control the way the ends and corners of path items are drawn. You can set these features using the `strokeCap` and `strokeJoin` properties. One of the most interesting features allows you to create a dashed stroke by specifying a pattern of how the dashes and spaces appear. You define the dash pattern using an array of numbers. The numbers in the array specify the length of the dash, and then the space for the pattern, in alternating order. Depending on the width of the stroke and the stroke cap type, the dash pattern may be difficult to see. Setting the cap type to Butt Cap increases the visibility of the dashes.

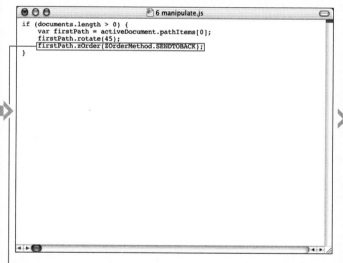

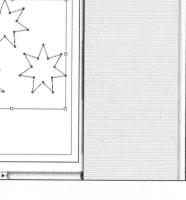

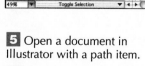

4 Type the path item variable, and then **.zOrder();**, placing a **ZOrderMethod** constant in the parentheses.

5 Open a document in Illustrator with a path item.

6 Execute the script.

■ The script rotates the path item and changes the stacking order.

WORK WITH SELECTIONS

You can set and modify a selection with JavaScript. Selections are one of the most important and powerful tools in Illustrator. You can write a script to operate on selected items, and make the script robust enough to understand when the correct type of object is selected.

Illustrator is a vector-based application and uses objects instead of pixels to define elements in a document. You access the selection in Illustrator using the `selection` property. This returns an array of items if there is a current selection. You can test for a current selection by testing if `selection.length` is greater than zero.

When working with selections, it is important to verify that the user has selected the correct type of object before attempting to perform an operation. Every item in

Illustrator scripting has a `typename` property that you can test to ensure the correct object type. For example, if a path item is selected, the value for `typename` is "PathItem."

You can also add an object to the current selection using the `selected` property of the object you want to select. Setting this selected property to `true` adds the object to the current selection. If you only need to select one item, you can set `selection` equal to a reference to the object you want to select. Likewise, you can unselect everything by setting the property to `false`.

If your script changes the user's selection, you might want to store the selection at the beginning of the script and restore it at the end. You can set a variable equal to `selection` to store it, and vice versa to restore it.

WORK WITH SELECTIONS

1 Type **if (documents.length > 0) {**.

2 Type **if (selection.length > 0) {**.

3 Create a variable and set it equal to **selection[0];**.

Extra

When you write a script that works with selections in Illustrator, you should make sure to check a few basic things about the selection. The first thing is to check that you have a object currently selected. After you know that a selection does exist, you should handle the possibility that the user has selected multiple, or in some cases not enough, objects for your script. It is hard to make a general rule about how to handle the number of items in a selection. If your script only requires you to select one object, you can use a `for` loop to loop through every item in the selection and perform the operation on each item. That way your script behaves as expected for both single and multiple selections. The last point to keep in mind when working with user selections is to verify that you select the expected type of object before performing any actions on it; you need to do this for each item in the selection if you are looping through the entire selection.

4 Create a condition to test the `typename` property of the reference variable.

5 If the item is the type you want, display an alert message.

6 Open a document with a selected path item in Illustrator.

7 Execute the script.

■ If the condition is `true`, Illustrator displays an alert.

CREATE GROUPS

You can use JavaScript to group items together in Illustrator. Groups are a great way to keep related items together, allowing you to scale, rotate, and move a number of items all at the same time. Also, groups are necessary for creating objects such as clipping masks and wrapping text around other page items. See Chapter 7 for more on working with wrapped text.

A group in Illustrator appears in the Layers palette as a special type of sub-layer. All groups belong to a particular layer; a reference to this layer is available in the group's `layer` property. A group can contain any other type of page item, even other groups. One great feature of using groups is that you can select the entire contents and move them together. This makes it easy to change the layout of documents while keeping related items together. When a group contains a `pathItem`, the `pathItem` still appears in the `document.pathItems` collection. However, the `pathItems` collection for the layer to which the group belongs does not contain a reference for any `pathItems` belonging to a group.

You can apply all of the movement and transformation methods discussed in the section "Manipulate a Path Item" to groups. You can also hide or show an entire group using the `hidden` property.

You create new groups using the `groupItems.add()` method. You can add a group to the top layer in a document using the document's `groupItems` collection, or to a specific layer using the collection in that layer. After you create a group, you use the `moveToEnd()`, `moveToBeginning()`, `move Before()`, and `moveAfter()` methods of the page item to add that items to the group. See the section "Manipulate Layers in Photoshop" for more on these methods. The information there also applies to path items in Illustrator, using the group name as the target.

CREATE GROUPS

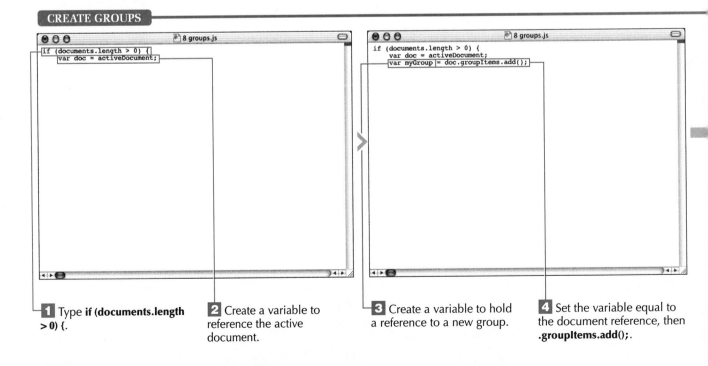

1 Type **if (documents.length > 0) {**.

2 Create a variable to reference the active document.

3 Create a variable to hold a reference to a new group.

4 Set the variable equal to the document reference, then **.groupItems.add();**.

Apply It

You can also create a new group using the `groupItems.createFromFile()` method. This method take a `File` object as a parameter and inserts the contents of the file as a group in the document. See Chapter 8 for more information on using and creating `File` objects. This method supports a number of different file types; you can even place the contents of text files. The following script opens a file specified by the `filepath` variable and inserts it as a group into the active document.

TYPE THIS:

```
var filepath = "//objects.pdf";
if (documents.length > 0) {
  var doc = activeDocument;
  var myFile = new File(filepath);
  var fileGroup = doc.groupItems.createFromFile(myFile);
}
```

▼

RESULT:

The script imports the objects.pdf file into the active document and places its contents in a new group item in the top-most layer of the document.

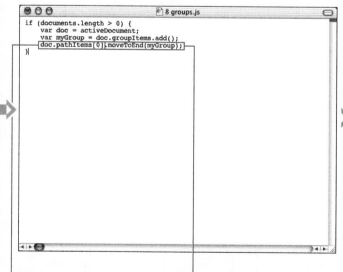

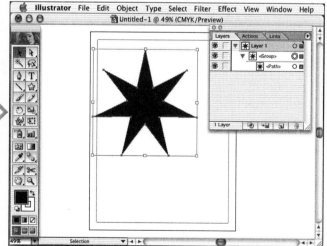

5 Type a reference to a path item in the document.

6 Type the method **moveToEnd()** or **moveToBeginning()**, placing the group reference in the parentheses.

7 Open a document in Illustrator containing a path item.

8 Execute the script.

■ Illustrator creates a new group and adds the referenced path item to it.

CREATE AND PLACE SYMBOLS

You can create new Illustrator symbols using JavaScript. As of version 10, Illustrator supports a symbol library that lets you reuse art elements in a document. Using symbols can greatly reduce the size of your file because you do not need to duplicate the information for the artwork. Symbols also allow you to quickly and easily edit a large number of items in a document. When exporting artwork from Illustrator to Macromedia Flash's SWF format, the symbol associations remain intact, letting you take advantage of symbol-based design in Flash.

You can create symbols out of a number of different types of page items including paths, text, compound paths, groups, placed items, and placed raster artwork. JavaScript has a couple of different collections and objects necessary for creating symbols in a document. The `document.symbols` collection is a list of all `symbol` objects currently contained in the document. You can see

the symbols in a document by using the Symbols palette. When you create a new document, Illustrator adds a few default symbol items. You create new symbols items using the `add()` method of this collection.

The `document.symbolItems` collection refers to every `symbolItem` object contained in the document. A `symbolItem` is an instance of a symbol that you have placed in the document. You can place symbols either by hand or by using the `document.symbolItems.add()` method.

You can think of the `symbol` object as a prototype, or master, version of the symbol artwork. When you place a symbol in a document, the script creates an instance of this master version. Every instance is a `symbolItem` and each `symbolItem` links to a particular symbol. The `symbol` property of a `symbolItem` is a reference to the `symbol` object of which it is an instance.

CREATE AND PLACE SYMBOLS

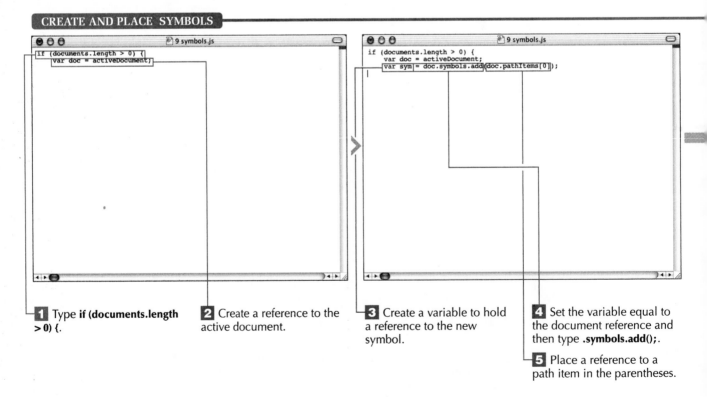

1 Type **if (documents.length > 0) {**.

2 Create a reference to the active document.

3 Create a variable to hold a reference to the new symbol.

4 Set the variable equal to the document reference and then type **.symbols.add();**.

5 Place a reference to a path item in the parentheses.

Extra

Symbol-based design is a strong element of creating animations using Macromedia's Flash. As in Illustrator, symbols in Flash keep the file size small and make documents easier to edit. When you export an Illustrator document using symbols into Flash's SWF format, Illustrator symbols are preserved and used in the Flash animation. This allows you to make very small Flash animations using artwork created in Illustrator.

As of Illustrator 10, the PDF file format that stores Illustrator documents does not provide native support for symbols. If you use symbols in your document and do not need to have Adobe Acrobat read the file, you may want to disable PDF support for the file using the Save Options dialog box. This makes your document much easier to edit, and enhances the performance of Illustrator. To disable PDF support on an existing document, click File ⇨ Save As, and deselect the Create PDF Compatible File option (☑ changes to ☐). You can also use the `pdfCompatibility` property of and `IllustratorSaveOption` object when saving a document with JavaScript. See Chapter 8 for more information on saving a file with JavaScript.

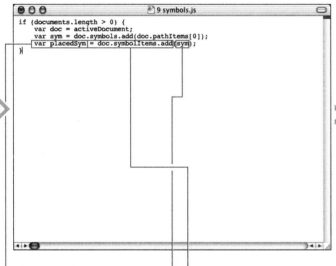

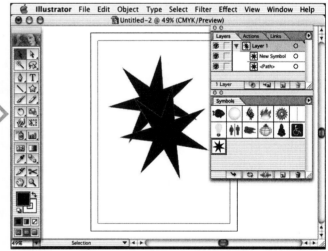

6 Create a variable to hold a reference to a new symbol instance.

7 Set the variable to the document reference and then type **.symbolItems.add();**.

8 Place the reference to the symbol in the parentheses.

9 Open a document containing a path item in Illustrator.

10 Execute the script.

■ Illustrator creates a new symbol from the specified path item and an instance of the symbol is created in the document.

CREATE GRADIENTS

Y ou can create and apply gradient fills using JavaScript. Gradients are a fundamental element to most artwork you create in Illustrator. JavaScript allows you to create new gradient types and edit existing gradients. You can use scripting to edit and apply a gradient to a number of objects in a document.

You use the gradient object to define a gradient in Illustrator. All gradients in a document are represented in the document.gradients collection; the add() method of this collection creates a new gradient. When you create a new gradient, it appears in Illustrator's Swatches palette. New gradients, by default, move from black to white. You can also edit an exiting gradient using the document.gradients collection.

Gradients fall into two categories depending on the way the gradient fills an area. *Linear* gradients move from color to color along a single line. Linear gradients often look

something like a series of color bars placed one after another. The other type of gradient is radial. *Radial* gradients start from a center point and cycle through colors moving out from the center. They can appear as a number of color concentric circles places one inside the next. You can set the type of gradient in JavaScript using the type property. This property is set to a GradientType constant value.

You apply a gradient to a new object by creating a GradientColor object. After the object's creation, you set the gradient property of this object to a gradient object. Next, create a new Color object and set its gradient property to the GradientColor object. Finally, you are ready to apply the gradient to a pathItem using the fillColor property. See the section "Define and Apply Color Values" for more information about the Color object and the fillColor property.

CREATE GRADIENTS

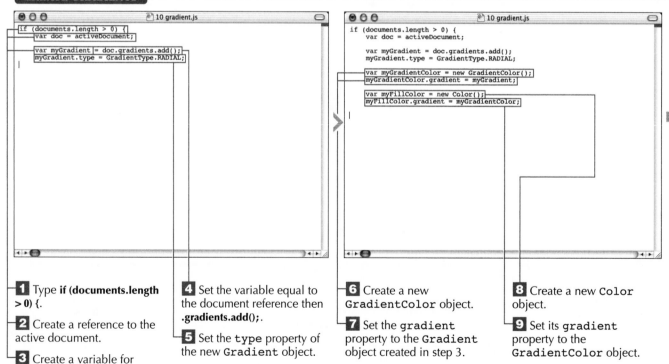

1 Type **if (documents.length > 0) {**.

2 Create a reference to the active document.

3 Create a variable for a reference to a new Gradient object.

4 Set the variable equal to the document reference then **.gradients.add();**.

5 Set the **type** property of the new Gradient object.

6 Create a new GradientColor object.

7 Set the gradient property to the Gradient object created in step 3.

8 Create a new Color object.

9 Set its gradient property to the GradientColor object.

Apply It

Gradients can also have an origin point that defines where in the path item the gradient should start. Linear gradients can also have an angle associated with them to specify the angle of the line the gradient moves along. You can create a wide range of effects by changing the origin and angle of gradients. For example, this script creates a new linear gradient beginning in the center of the first path item in the document, with an angle of 45 degrees.

TYPE THIS:

```
if (documents.length > 0) {
  var doc = activeDocument;
  var myGradient = doc.gradients.add();
  myGradient.type = GradientType.LINEAR;
  var myGradientColor = new GradientColor();
  myGradientColor.gradient = myGradient;
  myGradientColor.origin = [0, 100];
  myGradientColor.angle = 45;
  var myFillColor = new Color();
  myFillColor.gradient = myGradientColor;
  var pi = doc.pathItems[0];
  pi.filled = true;
  pi.fillColor = myFillColor;
}
```

RESULT:

The first path item in the document has a gradient with a fill angle of 45 degrees and an origin at 0,100.

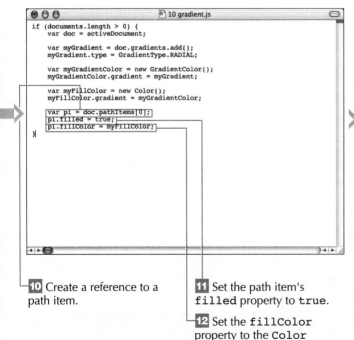

```
if (documents.length > 0) {
  var doc = activeDocument;

  var myGradient = doc.gradients.add();
  myGradient.type = GradientType.RADIAL;

  var myGradientColor = new GradientColor();
  myGradientColor.gradient = myGradient;

  var myFillColor = new Color();
  myFillColor.gradient = myGradientColor;

  var pi = doc.pathItems[0];
  pi.filled = true;
  pi.fillColor = myFillColor;
}
```

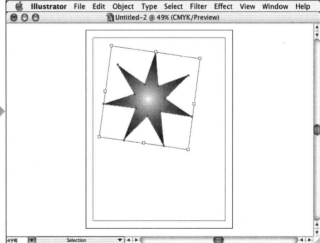

■10 Create a reference to a path item.

■11 Set the path item's `filled` property to `true`.

■12 Set the `fillColor` property to the `Color` object from step 8.

■13 Open a document with a path item in Illustrator.

■14 Execute the script.

■ Illustrator applies the gradient to the path item.

EDIT A GRADIENT'S STOP POINTS

You can modify a gradient's stop points to create more interesting gradients. *Stops* are the parts of gradients that define the colors the gradient cycles through. You also use stops to define where in the gradient the different points of pure color appear, and how the colors of the gradient blend together.

Every gradient also requires at least two stops. You can access all stops in a gradient using the `gradient.gradientStops` collection. You use the `add()` method to create a new stop on the gradient. When you create a gradient, it is automatically given two stops, so make sure to account for them when editing a gradient.

A `gradientStop` object defines each stop for the gradient. A stop must have a color value set using a `Color` object. See the section "Define and Apply Color Values" for more

information on creating a `Color` object. Stop points also have a position in the gradient. You define the position by setting the `rampPoint` property to a percentage value where 0 is the beginning of the gradient, and 100 is the end.

The colors on a gradient can blend into each other at different rates. Between any two stops on a gradient, there is a point where the colors of the stops are present in equal amounts. You can set the position of this point using the `midpoint` property, assigning it a percentage value between 0 and 100, much like the position of the stop points. Because you define gradient stops in order, the `midpoint` property for a stop sets the midpoint between it and the next stop in the gradient. The closer a `midpoint` is to a stop, the more quickly that color dissipates in the gradient.

EDIT A GRADIENT'S STOP POINTS

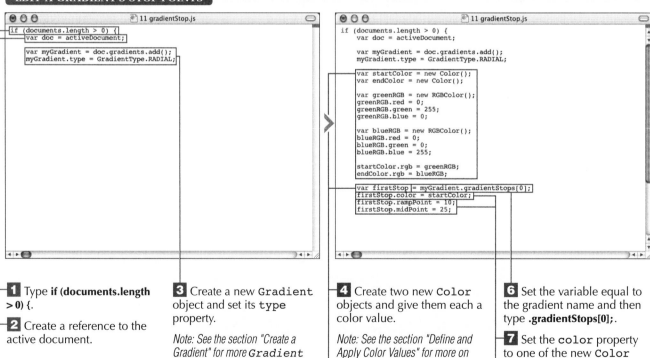

1 Type **if (documents.length > 0) {**.

2 Create a reference to the active document.

3 Create a new `Gradient` object and set its `type` property.

Note: See the section "Create a Gradient" for more `Gradient` objects.

4 Create two new `Color` objects and give them each a color value.

Note: See the section "Define and Apply Color Values" for more on `Color` objects.

5 Create a variable for a reference to the first stop on the gradient.

6 Set the variable equal to the gradient name and then type **.gradientStops[0];**.

7 Set the `color` property to one of the new `Color` objects.

8 Set the `rampPoint` and `midpoint` properties of the stop.

Apply It

Gradients in Illustrator have a few features in common with symbols. Every gradient, as it appears in the Swatches palette, acts as a prototype for that gradient style. This includes the position and color of stops as well as the type of gradient. When you apply a gradient to an object in a document, the size of object determines the size of the gradient. This is why you specify the position of stops in terms of percentages. You can set the length of the instance of a gradient using the `length` property of the `GradientColor` object. For example, this script creates and applies a gradient and sets its length.

TYPE THIS:

```
if (documents.length > 0) {
  var doc = activeDocument;
  var pi = doc.pathItems[0];
  var myGradient = doc.gradients.add();
  myGradient.type = GradientType.LINEAR;
  var myGradientColor = new GradientColor();
  myGradientColor.gradient = myGradient;
  myGradientColor.length = 50;
  var myFillColor = new Color();
  myFillColor.gradient = myGradientColor;
  pi.filled = true;
  pi.fillColor = myFillColor;
}
```

RESULT:

The script applies a new gradient to the first path item and gives the gradient a length of 50.

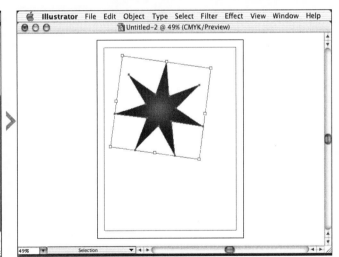

9 Repeat steps 7-10 for the second stop in the gradient.

10 Create a `GradientColor` object and fill a path item with the gradient.

Note: See the section "Create a Gradient" for more information.

11 Open a document with a path item in Illustrator.

12 Execute the script.

■ Illustrator applies the gradient to the path item.

WORKING WITH COMPOUND PATHS

You can create and edit compound paths in Illustrator using JavaScript. Compound paths are powerful tools for creating complex shapes in Illustrator. With JavaScript, you can create new compound paths or edit an existing one. You can also edit or remove paths from a compound path.

A *compound path* is a special type of object that consists of many separate path items. Illustrator uses the fill color of the bottom-most item in the compound path to fill the shapes of items in the compound path. Which parts of the shapes are filled with which color depends on how the elements in a compound path overlap. In addition to filled areas, compound paths also create transparent areas inside of other shapes. The shapes in a compound path act like windows or holes that you can move around inside of the other objects in the compound path to create interesting shapes. In effect, one item in a compound path punches a hole in another, letting you see through to the artwork underneath.

The path items that comprise a compound path cannot have separate settings for fills and strokes. In this respect, all elements of the compound path are treated as a single path item. This behavior differs from that of groups because the individual paths in a group still retain a certain degree of independence from the other items with which it is grouped.

Designing letters for typefaces is a common use of compound paths. Whenever you convert a text item to outlines using the Type ⇨ Create Outlines menu or by calling the `textArtItem.createOutline()` method, JavaScript creates a compound path for each letter in the text item. Another source of compound paths that Illustrator automatically creates occur when you apply some of the tools in the Pathfinder palette.

WORKING WITH COMPOUND PATHS

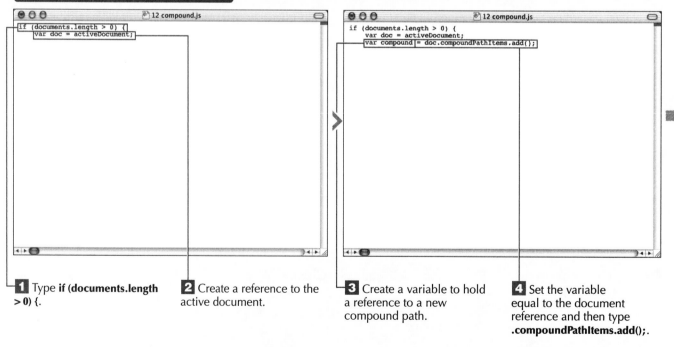

1 Type if (documents.length > 0) {.

2 Create a reference to the active document.

3 Create a variable to hold a reference to a new compound path.

4 Set the variable equal to the document reference and then type **.compoundPathItems.add();**.

Extra

Illustrator uses a few different factors to determine what parts of a shape it should fill. The main way is by using a fill rule. Every path and text item has a fill rule set that determines how Illustrator should treat it in a compound path. There are two options, even-odd or non-zero winding. The even-odd rule counts the overlapping space on objects and fills every other overlapping space. The non-zero winding rule determines the transparent space using path direction. Overlapping objects with paths flowing in opposite directions have transparent space drawn where they overlap. You can set the fill rule for a path item using the `evenodd` property. You use the even-odd rule when this property is `true` and the non-zero winding rule when it is `false`. Setting this property for a single path item in a compound path sets it for the entire compound path. You cannot change the direction of a path using JavaScript. You can, however, create new path items by setting the `reversed` parameter to `true`. See Appendix A for a list of parameters for methods of the `pathItems` collection.

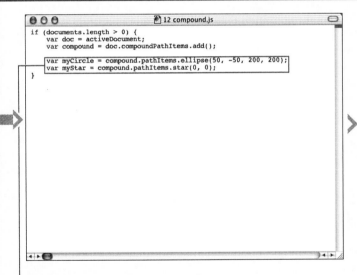

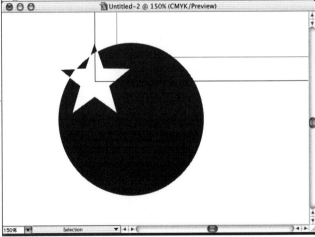

5 Create two path items using the **pathItems** collection of the **CompoundPathItem** you just created.

6 Open a document in Illustrator.

7 Execute the script.

■ Illustrator creates a compound path item.

CREATE CLIPPING MASKS

Y ou can create clipping masks with JavaScript. Illustrator lets you mask objects to create complex shapes. Clipping masks provide yet another way to create interesting artwork using Illustrator. Creating clipping masks with JavaScript can help you automate repetitive tasks and save time.

A *clipping mask* is a shape that limits the visible area of the shapes it masks. In a way, clipping masks are the opposite of compound paths. Compound paths are often thought of as floating holes that punch through an object to show the background. Clipping masks, on the other hand, are like windows that show only a small area of an object. Only shapes that intersect the clipping mask are visible.

You create a clipping mask by grouping objects together. The top-most object in the group serves as the mask for all elements of the group. You can only use one object as a

mask, meaning that you cannot use a group as a mask. This makes it very difficult to make a mask out of outlined text. The mask applies to as many items as are present in the group. You can make a mask out of almost any page item, including compound paths, path items, and text items.

After you collect the items that you want to include in the mask into a group, you can set the `clipped` property of the group to `true` to convert it into a clipping mask group. Because you must collect the mask and the items it masks together in a group, you may find it difficult to organize documents when you use clipping masks. Clipping masks can also cause printing problems when they become too complex.

When you create a clipping mask, you set the stroke and fill of the object that you use for the mask to transparent. There is no way to set these properties beforehand to avoid this behavior.

```
if (documents.length > 0) {
    var doc = activeDocument;
```

```
if (documents.length > 0) {
    var doc = activeDocument;
    var group = doc.groupItems.add();
```

1 Type **if (documents.length > 0) {**.

2 Create a reference to the active document.

3 Create a variable to hold a reference to a new group.

4 Set the variable equal to the document reference and then type **groupItems.add();**.

Apply It

After you create the clipping mask, you can reapply a stroke and fill to the object. When you apply a stroke to a mask, it appears normally, outlining the entire shape of the mask. When a fill applies, only the sections of the mask that do not overlap with underlying art fill in. This can create some very interesting effects.

TYPE THIS:

```
if (documents.length > 0) {
  var doc = activeDocument;
  var group = doc.groupItems.add();

  var circle = group.pathItems.ellipse(140, 50, 100, 100);
  var star = group.pathItems.star(100, 90, 100, 20, 7);
  group.clipped = true;

  var bColor = new Color();
  var black= new RGBColor();
  black.red = 0;
  black.green = 0;
  black.blue = 0;
  bColor.rgb = black;

  var rColor = new Color();
  var red = new RGBColor();
  red.red = 255;
  red.green = 0;
  red.blue = 0;
  rColor.rgb = red;

  circle.fillColor = bColor;
  star.fillColor = rColor;
}
```

RESULT:

The script masks a black circle with a red-filled star.

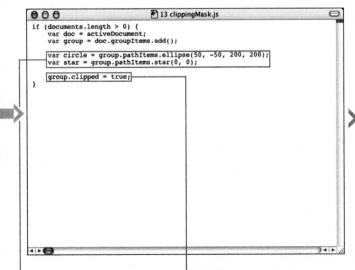

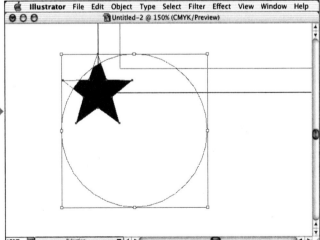

5 Add two or more path items to the group using the **pathItems** collection of the group.

■ You must overlap the path items to make the mask visible.

6 Set the **clipped** property of the group to **true**.

7 Open a document in Illustrator.

8 Execute the script.

■ Illustrator creates a clipping mask.

CREATE A TEXT LAYER

You can add text to a document in Photoshop using JavaScript. Using scripting to manipulate text in a document is a powerful way to automate repetitive tasks. You can generate font reports, remove text, change text, change character and paragraph formatting, and even add effects.

Before you can add text to a document, you must create a new art layer. The art layer cannot have any contents before you add text. Similar to using Photoshop by hand, only a single text item can exist on a text layer. Also, you cannot have any other objects on the layer. If you try to add text to a layer that contains other art or objects, Photoshop generates an error. See Chapter 12 for more information on handling errors.

After you create a new art layer, you can convert it into a text layer by modifying its `kind` property. The `kind` property takes a `LayerKind` constant value. Setting its

value to `LayerKind.TEXT` allows you to add text to the layer. You can also check if a layer is a text layer by comparing its `kind` property to the `LayerKind.TEXT` value.

After you make a layer into a text layer, you can access the layer's `textItem` property. You use the `textItem` property to make modifications to the text on the layer. You can use the `contents` property of `textItem` to access the text on the layer. The `textItem` property also provides access to the justification, font, scale, leading, and so on.

To convert a text layer into an art layer, or rasterize the text, you can set the `layer.kind` property to `LayerKind.NORMAL`. This has the same effect as selecting Rasterize from the Layers menu.

CREATE A TEXT LAYER

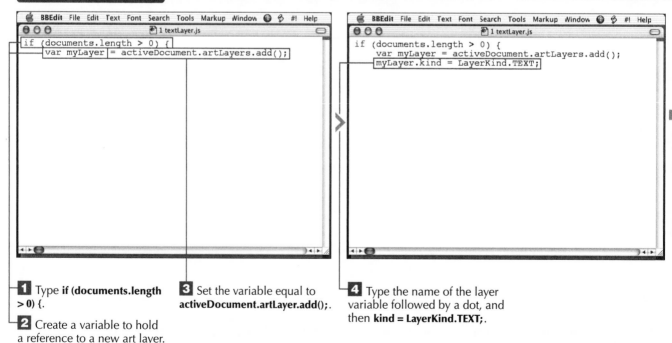

1 Type **if (documents.length > 0) {**.

2 Create a variable to hold a reference to a new art layer.

3 Set the variable equal to **activeDocument.artLayer.add();**.

4 Type the name of the layer variable followed by a dot, and then **kind = LayerKind.TEXT;**.

Extra

Every `textItem` object has a `kind` property that determines if the text object is paragraph text or point text. *Point text* is the equivalent of selecting the Text tool and clicking once. The content of the text box continues on a single line until the text ends. The content of the text item and the size of the font you use determines the size of a point text item. You cannot set size properties like width and height on a point text item. However, you can change the size of the text item using the `verticalScale` and `horizontalScale` properties of the text item. Point text is the default type for all `textItem`s that you create with scripting.

The other type of text item is *paragraph text*. Paragraph text is the type of text area you create by clicking and dragging the Type tool in Photoshop. Paragraph text has a height and width, and the content wraps to these dimensions. Setting the `kind` property of the `textItem` to `TextType.PARAGRAPHTEXT` changes the `textItem` to paragraph text.

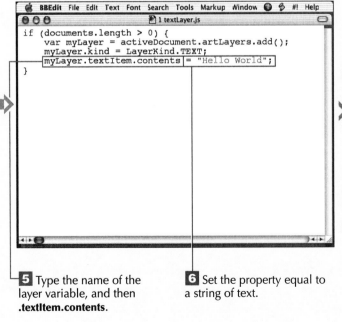

5 Type the name of the layer variable, and then **.textItem.contents**.

6 Set the property equal to a string of text.

7 Execute the script in Photoshop with a document open.

■ Photoshop creates a new text layer containing the string.

RETRIEVE THE NAME OF A FONT

You can retrieve the font name of a text item in Photoshop using JavaScript. When you create new text items with JavaScript, the font of the newly created text item is set to the default font. Using fonts is an important aspect of all design. Accessing and setting fonts with scripting is a powerful way to save time because you can automate common tasks such as changing or updating the fonts in a document.

Working with fonts in Photoshop is somewhat difficult. To change a font, you set the font property of a textItem object to the PostScript name of the font. However, the PostScript name of the font is not the name that appears in Photoshop's Character palette.

The best way to find the PostScript name of a font is to use scripting. By creating a text object and setting the desired font by hand, you can use an alert() to display the name

of the text item. This additional step is not too bothersome when creating a script for an environment where the installed fonts are previously known, such as a workplace. It becomes more difficult when you try to write scripts for distribution to a wider audience.

Whenever you explicitly set a font in a script, it is good practice to define the font near the top of the document and draw attention to it using comments. This makes it easier for users of your scripts to change and tweak the font name as needed. You might also want to use comments to describe the process for determining a font's name. This makes it easier for others to follow your steps in the future. Whenever your scripts require steps outside of simply running the script, you should make comments for the user. See Chapter 2 for more information on how to add and use comments.

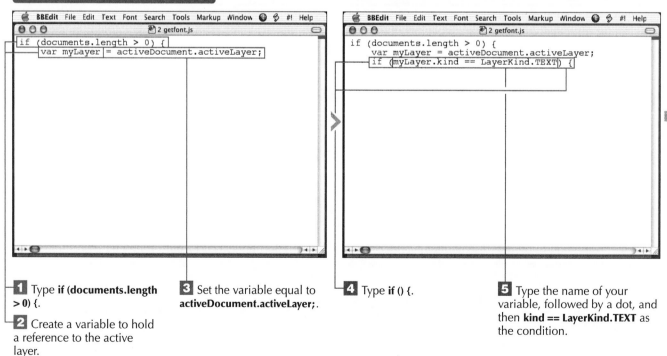

1 Type **if (documents.length > 0) {**.

2 Create a variable to hold a reference to the active layer.

3 Set the variable equal to **activeDocument.activeLayer;**.

4 Type **if () {**.

5 Type the name of your variable, followed by a dot, and then **kind == LayerKind.TEXT** as the condition.

Extra

Keeping a file with the PostScript names of commonly used fonts is a great way to save time. Saving the names is quicker and less hassle than looking up a font name every time you need it.

Some font management applications like Font Reserve show the PostScript name of a font in the font's info palette listing. Using a font manager is a great way to retrieve a quick list of available fonts and font names.

When testing the name of a text item, you should always make sure that you are testing against the PostScript name of the font. You can also use the `String.indexOf()` method to test if one string appears in another. The method takes a single parameter for the string to locate. The index of the first instance of the string to locate is returned. If the test string is not found, the method returns a value of –1, because strings are zero-indexed. A value of 0 means that the test string has been found at the very beginning of the target string. For example, you can use this method to test if a text item is using any font with the word "Arial" in the title.

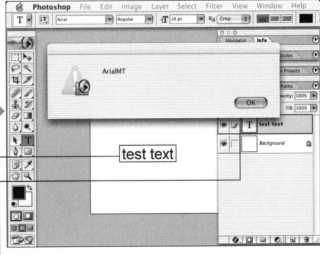

6 Type **alert();**.

7 Type the name of your variable, followed by a dot, and then **textItem.font** in the parentheses.

8 Type text in the desired font to a document in Photoshop.

9 Select the layer.

10 Execute the script.

■ An alert displays the name of the font.

Note: Make sure you do not have text selected when you run the script. See Chapter 1 for more information.

SET THE FONT OF A TEXT ITEM

With JavaScript, you can set the font of a text item in Photoshop. All created text items in Photoshop are set to the default font and default size. You can change the font of a text item to create more interesting compositions. Using custom fonts and sizes can give your design more interesting and distinctive characteristics.

After you determine the PostScript name for the desired font, you can change the font property of the textItem object. See the section "Retrieve the Name of a Font" for more information. The names that appear in the Character palette do not always work for setting the font of a text item.

If your script attempts to change the font of a text item to an unrecognizable font, Photoshop displays an alert telling the user that the current font is unavailable, and that font substitution will occur. If you see this dialog box when you run a script that manipulates fonts, you may not have entered the font name correctly, or the font you are using is not currently available to Photoshop. Make sure that you enter the font name exactly as it appears at the end of the section "Retrieve the Name of a Font," including case and punctuation.

Extra

You can change the weight and style of a font using the `fauxBold` and `fauxItalic` properties of the `textItem` object. These properties correspond to the buttons in the Character palette. If your font does not have a bold or italic weight available, these properties, when set to `true`, approximate bold or italic for you. To set the text on the selected layer to faux bold:

Example:
```
if (documents.length > 0) {
    var myLayer = activeDocument.activeLayer;
    myLayer.textItem.fauxBold = true;
}
```

SET THE FONT OF A TEXT ITEM

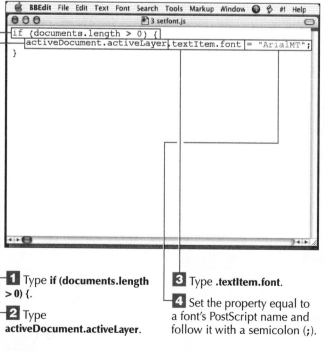

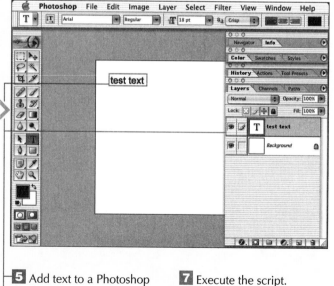

1 Type **if (documents.length > 0) {**.

2 Type **activeDocument.activeLayer**.

3 Type **.textItem.font**.

4 Set the property equal to a font's PostScript name and follow it with a semicolon (**;**).

5 Add text to a Photoshop document.

6 Select the layer.

7 Execute the script.

■ The font changes.

CHANGE THE COLOR OF A TEXT ITEM

You can change the color of newly created or existing text in Photoshop with JavaScript. Color adds a new element to the range of possibilities available with scripting. You can write a script to change the color of every piece of text in a document. This saves you time when you make updates and design changes.

As explained in more detail in Chapter 5, color in Photoshop is similar in many ways to color in Illustrator. Before you can set the color of a text item in Photoshop, you must create a color object to hold the values for the new color. The SolidColor object supports five different color specifications: CMYK, gray, HSB, lab, and RGB. Photoshop converts between color spaces if you create a SolidColor object and specify values for a color space different from the current color space of the document. However, this is not a perfect conversion and the resulting color does not perfectly match the original color. You can always test the color space of the document using the document.mode property.

The SolidColor object also has some useful properties for working with Web safe colors. After you create a SolidColor object and the properties for a color set, you can use the nearestWebColor property to retrieve an RGBColor object with red, green, and blue values for the nearest Web safe color that corresponds to the created color.

Unlike Illustrator, you do not need to create a separate color object for each color space type. The SolidColor object's color type properties are pre-defined objects for the color type they support. For example, the cmyk property of a SolidColor object has pre-existing cyan, magenta, yellow, and black properties that you can set directly to the desired values.

CHANGE THE COLOR OF A TEXT ITEM

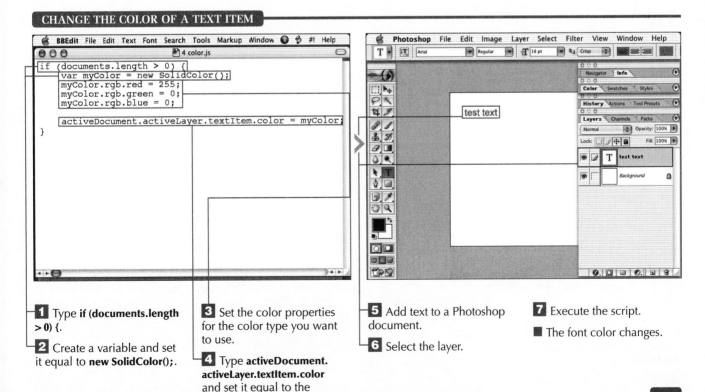

■1 Type **if (documents.length > 0) {**.

■2 Create a variable and set it equal to **new SolidColor();**.

■3 Set the color properties for the color type you want to use.

■4 Type **activeDocument. activeLayer.textItem.color** and set it equal to the color variable.

■5 Add text to a Photoshop document.

■6 Select the layer.

■7 Execute the script.

■ The font color changes.

CREATE A DROP SHADOW EFFECT

You can create a drop shadow-like effect using JavaScript. One way to create a crisp drop shadow is to duplicate a text layer, set its color to black, and offset it underneath the original text layer. Using JavaScript, you can easily automate this process. With scripting, you can quickly add new text that uses this effect.

Understanding the steps necessary to achieve a drop shadow effect helps you better plan the script. The first step is to duplicate the layer containing the text item, and then to move the new layer under the original. You can use the moveAfter() method of the layer object to change the order of the layers in the layers palette. See Chapter 4 for more information on duplicating and manipulating layers.

After you position the layer underneath the original, you offset the layer down and to the right. The position property of the textItem object is an array with two

values: the first is the x position and the second is the y position. By adding a small number to each value and then setting the position property with the new values, you can offset the layer by any amount. You must set the position property equal to an array. You cannot set the individual values one at a time. You must store the x and y values, plus the offset amount, and then set the position property to an array of the two values.

The final step is to change the color of the text so that it stands out against the original text and the background. See the section "Change the Color of a Text Item" for more on changing the color of your text. By changing the relationships between the color of the source text, the shadow, and the background, you can create a wide range of effects.

CREATE A DROP SHADOW EFFECT

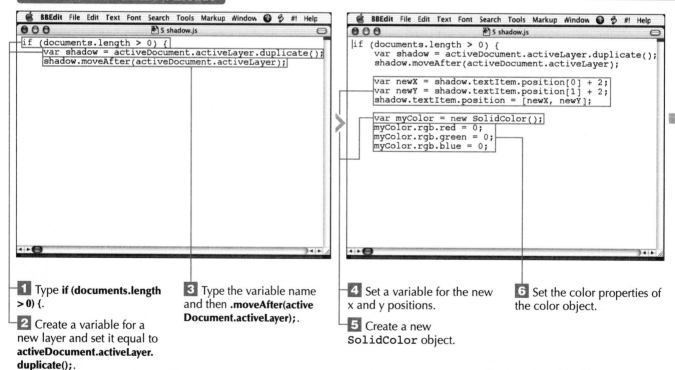

1 Type if (documents.length > 0) {.

2 Create a variable for a new layer and set it equal to **activeDocument.activeLayer.duplicate();**.

3 Type the variable name and then **.moveAfter(activeDocument.activeLayer);**.

4 Set a variable for the new x and y positions.

5 Create a new SolidColor object.

6 Set the color properties of the color object.

Apply It

You can use JavaScript to add a text-warp effect to text items. The `warpStyle` property of the `textItem` object lets you set the warp to one of Photoshop's built in warp styles. This is the equivalent of using the Create Warped Text button in the Text tool's Options palette. The values are a `WarpStyle` constant. You can find a complete list of available warp styles in Appendix B.

TYPE THIS:

```
if (documents.length > 0) {
  var myLayer = activeDocument.artLayers.add();
  myLayer.kind = LayerKind.TEXT;
  myLayer.textItem.contents = "Hello World";
  myLayer.textItem.warpStyle = WarpStyle.FLAG;
}
```

RESULT:

If you have any documents open, this script first creates a new art layer. Once the script creates the art layer, the script makes it into a text layer, and then adds the text "Hello World" to the text layer. See the section "Create a Text Layer" in this chapter for more information on creating a text item. After the script creates the text item and adds the text, it sets the `warpStyle` for the text item to the Flag warp style. See the Photoshop User Guide for more information about text effects.

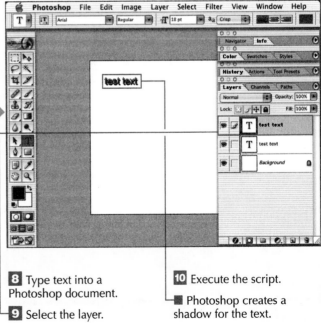

7 Set the `textItem.color` property of the layer to the color object.

8 Type text into a Photoshop document.

9 Select the layer.

10 Execute the script.

■ Photoshop creates a shadow for the text.

ADD TEXT TO A DOCUMENT

You can add text to a document in Illustrator using JavaScript and open up a wide range of possibilities. You can automate repetitive text changes easily. You can pull text from external sources, such as an easy-to-edit text file or script, and dynamically add it to a new or existing document. For example, you can create a system for generating pages of mailing labels automatically and then save the results as a PDF.

Unlike text in Photoshop, Illustrator does not require the creation of a special layer type to add text. The document, group, and layer objects in Illustrator contain a textArtItems collection that lists all of the text items contained within each container. Using the textArtItems.add() method adds a new text item to an existing layer or document. You create the new text item in a different location in the layer stack depending on which textArtItems collection you use. If you need to add text

to a specific layer or group, use the textArtItems collection for that object. Using the textArtItems collection of the document object adds the text item to the top-most layer of the document.

There are three kinds of text items in Illustrator: point text, path text, and area text. *Point text* is the default type of text. It is the same type of text that you create using the Type tool in Illustrator. For more about path text and area text, see the section "Create Path and Area Text."

All text items are associated with at least one textPath object. The textPath is not the same as a normal pathItem. The textPath object defines the position and orientation of its text item. Every text item has a textPaths collection; the first member of this collection is the default textPath associated with the text item.

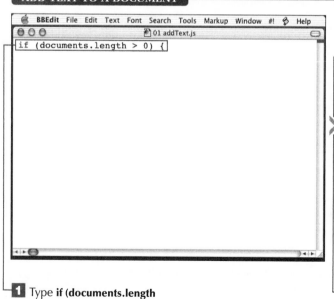

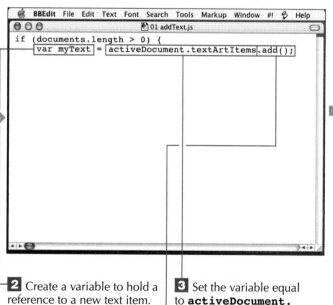

1 Type **if (documents.length > 0) {**.

2 Create a variable to hold a reference to a new text item.

Note: See Chapter 2 for more information.

3 Set the variable equal to **activeDocument. textArtItems**.

4 Type a dot, then **add();**.

You can change the orientation of a text item with JavaScript. The first `textPath` object in the `textPaths` collection of a text item controls some of the basic properties of the text item. To change the orientation, set the `orientation` property to a `TextOrientation` constant. See Appendix A for possible values of the `TextOrientation` constant.

After you add the text item, and set the contents of the text item equal to `"Hello world."`, consider adding text to a text item before manipulating any of its other properties. The final line of code changes the orientation of the text item to vertical, so the text reads from top to bottom.

TYPE THIS:

```
var doc = activeDocument;
var myText = doc.textArtItems.add();
myText.contents = "Hello world.";
myText.textPaths[0].orientation = TextOrientation.VERTICAL;
```

RESULT:

This script first adds a new text item to the active document.

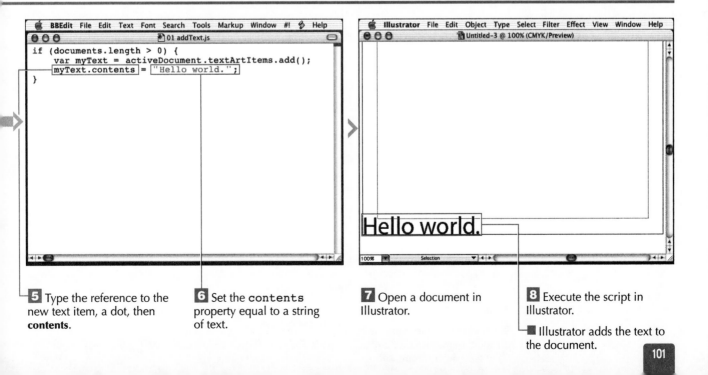

5 Type the reference to the new text item, a dot, then **contents**.

6 Set the **contents** property equal to a string of text.

7 Open a document in Illustrator.

8 Execute the script in Illustrator.

■ Illustrator adds the text to the document.

CREATE PATH AND AREA TEXT

You can create path and area text using JavaScript. Path and area text are essential tools for many common tasks and layouts. Using scripting to create and modify these text types is a great way to automate common repetitive tasks, or swap out text for newer or different versions.

There are three types of text items in Illustrator. The first is *point text*, discussed in the section "Add Text to a Document." The second type is *area text*, which you create by either clicking and dragging the Type tool, or drawing a shape and clicking it using the Area Type tool. The third type is *path text*, which you create by drawing a path and using the Path Type tool.

The area text and path text items are each associated with a pathItem object as well as their textPath object. The key difference between these text types is the relationship

they hold to their path items. The pathItem of area text is a shape that constricts the shape of the text. For example, an area text item with a square path fills the inside of the square shape and wraps at the edges of the square. Path text, on the other hand, follows along the path and uses it as the baseline of the text. Path text with a square path follows the edge of the square. See Chapter 4 for more information on creating paths in Illustrator.

You can set the kind property of a textArtItem to a TextType constant in order to create area or path text. The possible values for this constant are: POINTTEXT, PATHTEXT, and AREATEXT. You can access the pathItem object of area and path text using the textPathObject property of the first item in the textPaths collection of a textArt object.

CREATE PATH AND AREA TEXT

```
BBEdit  File  Edit  Text  Font  Search  Tools  Markup  Window  #!  Help
02 addPathText.js
if (documents.length > 0) {
    var doc = activeDocument;
    var myText = doc.textArtItems.add();
```

```
BBEdit  File  Edit  Text  Font  Search  Tools  Markup  Window  #!  Help
02 addPathText.js
if (documents.length > 0) {
    var doc = activeDocument;
    var myText = doc.textArtItems.add();
    myText.contents = "Hello world.";
    myText.kind = TextType.AREATEXT;
```

1 Type **if (documents.length > 0) {**.

2 Create a variable to reference the active document.

3 Create a variable to hold a reference to a new text item.

Note: See Chapter 2 for more information.

4 Set the variable equal to the document variable, and then type **.textArtItems.add();**.

5 Set the **contents** property of the new text item equal to a string of text.

6 Set the **kind** property of the new text item equal to **TextType**.

7 Type a dot, and then the value for the type of text to create.

Extra

You may find it easy to create area and path text by drawing a path with the drawing tools and attaching text to the new path to achieve the desired effect. Unfortunately, this is a little more difficult, but not impossible, in JavaScript. You must copy over each path point in a `for` loop.

Example:
```javascript
var doc = activeDocument;
var myText = doc.textArtItems.add();
myText.kind = TextType.AREATEXT;
myText.contents = " lots of text to wrap...";
ar circle = doc.pathItems.ellipse(500, 200, 200, 200);
var textPoints = myText.textPaths[0].textPathObject.pathPoints;
var circlePathPoints = circle.pathPoints;
for (var i=0; i<circlePathPoints.length; i++) {
  if (i >= textPoints.length) {
    var myPoint = textPoints.add();
  } else {
    var myPoint = textPoints[i];
  }
  myPoint.anchor = circlePathPoints[i].anchor;
  myPoint.leftDirection = circlePathPoints[i].leftDirection;
  myPoint.rightDirection = circlePathPoints[i].rightDirection;
}
circle.remove();
```

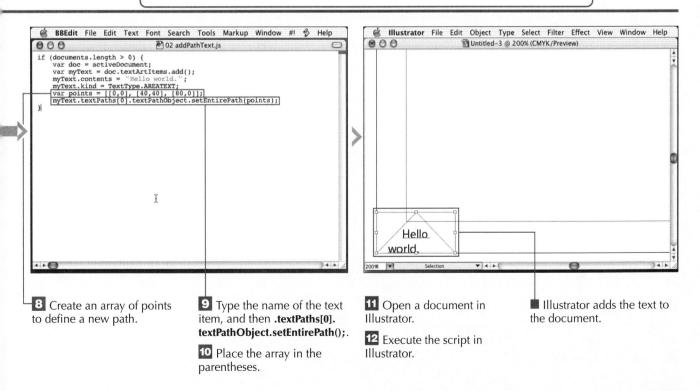

8 Create an array of points to define a new path.

9 Type the name of the text item, and then **.textPaths[0].textPathObject.setEntirePath();**.

10 Place the array in the parentheses.

11 Open a document in Illustrator.

12 Execute the script in Illustrator.

■ Illustrator adds the text to the document.

MANIPULATE PART OF A TEXT ITEM

You can use Illustrator's powerful text scripting features to manipulate parts of a text item. Unlike Photoshop, Illustrator lets you access and manipulate parts of a piece of text. For example, you can change the font of every occurrence of a certain word in a document, or increase the size of the first line of every paragraph.

Illustrator scripting allows you to access specific portions of a text item. This means you can set properties of only a part of a larger text item. You can break down each text item into characters, words, paragraphs, lines, and even arbitrary ranges of characters.

You use the `textArtItem.textRange()` method to extract a reference to a particular range of characters. The behavior of this method is similar to the `String.slice()` method described in Chapter 2. The method returns a `textRange` object with many of the properties and methods of the `textArtItem` object. For example, setting

the `contents` property of a `textRange` object replaces the text referenced when the `textRange()` method was initially called.

Every `textRange` object has a collection for the characters, words, and paragraphs it contains. These collections provide access to specific parts of the text. For example, `textArtItem.words[0]` refers to the first word of a text item. Each of these collections also has `add()` and `addBefore()` methods to make it easier to tack on additional text. For example, you can add a number to the beginning of every paragraph in a text item.

The `textRange` object also has a collection of the lines of text it contains called `textLines`. A *line* of text is defined as all text up until a line break. Unlike the collections for words, paragraphs, and characters, the `lines` method does not have an `add` method. You can add lines to a piece of text by using the return character, `\r`.

MANIPULATE PART OF A TEXT ITEM

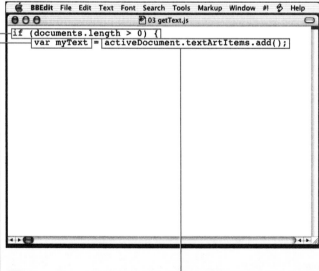

1 Type **if (documents.length > 0) {**.

2 Create a variable to reference a new text item.

3 Set the variable equal to **activeDocument.textArtItems.add();**.

4 Set the **contents** property of the new text item.

Apply It

Using the collections of the `textRange` object makes it easy to save text effects as easy-to-use functions. For example, a function can change the size of every character in a `textRange` object to slope from one size to another, starting big and getting smaller.

The first parameter defines the range of characters to use, the second sets the font size with which you start, and the third sets the font size with which you end. The function works by first determining how much smaller each character must be, which is the `step` variable, and then looping through each character and setting the font size. You find the size for each character by subtracting the step multiplied by the index of the current character from the maximum font size.

TYPE THIS:

```
function slopeText(range, startsize, endsize) {
  var step = (startsize - endsize)/range.characters.length;
  for (var i=0; i< range.characters.length; i++) {
    range.characters[i].size = startsize - (step*i);
  }
}
```

⌄

RESULT:

This script creates a function that slopes the characters in a text range.

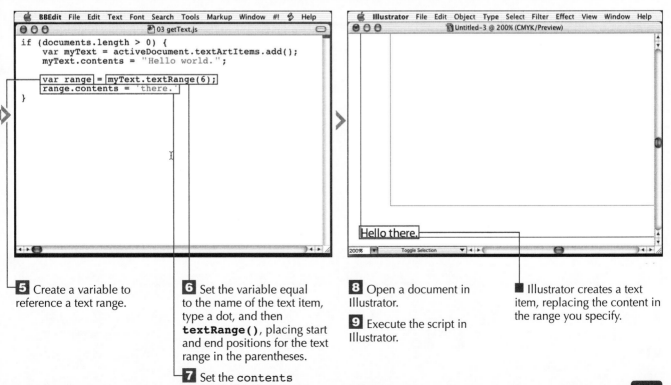

5 Create a variable to reference a text range.

6 Set the variable equal to the name of the text item, type a dot, and then **textRange()**, placing start and end positions for the text range in the parentheses.

7 Set the **contents** property of the range.

8 Open a document in Illustrator.

9 Execute the script in Illustrator.

■ Illustrator creates a text item, replacing the content in the range you specify.

RETRIEVE A LIST OF AVAILABLE FONTS

With JavaScript, you can access the entire Illustrator font list and retrieve a list of every font available to Illustrator. This allows you to write script that can work in a wider variety of situations because you can determine the availability of a desired font before you start a project. For example, you can create a script and define an ordered list of fonts that you can use. You can then arrange your script so it uses the second font on the list if your first choice is not available.

Accessing a list of preferred fonts allows you to create advanced user interactions by prompting the user to confirm the use of a font in a specific situation. For example, you can write a function that searches the list of available fonts for one with a name *close* to but not exactly the font defined. This makes it easy to distribute your scripts and allows users to specify the common name, instead of the PostScript name, for a font.

The textFaces collection makes it much easier to work with type in Illustrator as opposed to Photoshop. The textFaces collection contains a list of every font available to Illustrator. This collection is not a property of a specific document, but much like the activeDocument property, it belongs to the implicit application object. Each item in the textFaces collection is a textFace object. The name property of a textFace object is a string containing the full PostScript name of the font.

Currently, only the name of every font is available with scripting. You can, however, change other font related properties such as baseline shift, leading, and tracking for characters, words, paragraphs, and textRanges. See Appendix A for a complete list of available type manipulation properties.

RETRIEVE A LIST OF AVAILABLE FONTS

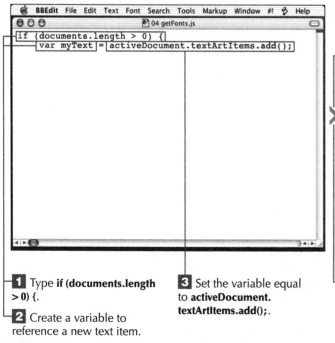

1 Type **if (documents.length > 0) {**.

2 Create a variable to reference a new text item.

3 Set the variable equal to **activeDocument.textArtItems.add();**.

4 Create a variable to hold the text range of the entire text item.

5 Create a loop, using **i<textFaces.length** as the condition.

Extra

You can search for the availability of a font by looping through the `textFaces` collection and testing each value to see if it equals the name of the font for which you are searching. When a function encounters the `return` statement, the value after the statement is returned and the function stops executing. This function takes advantage of this fact by looping through the available fonts and returning a `true` value if it finds the font. If the loop completes and the function does not find the font, it returns the value `false`. The function does not execute the `return false` if it finds the font because the earlier `return` statement stops the execution of the function. See p. 28–29 for more information.

Example:
```
function checkForFont(myfont) {
  for (var i=0; i<textFaces.length; i++) {
    if (textFaces[i].name == myfont) {
      return true;
    }
  }
  return false;
}
```

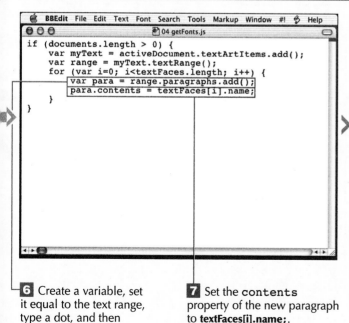

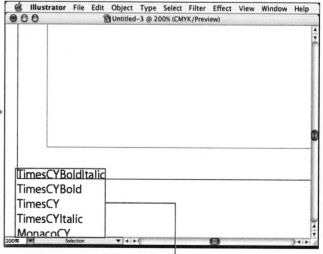

6 Create a variable, set it equal to the text range, type a dot, and then **paragraphs.add();**.

7 Set the **contents** property of the new paragraph to **textFaces[i].name;**.

8 Execute the script in Illustrator with a document open.

■ Illustrator creates a text item with the name of every font.

■ The list appears in the lower-left corner, the default position.

SET THE FONT OF A TEXT ITEM

You can change the font of an entire text item, paragraph, word, character, or text range with JavaScript. You can create powerful, time-saving scripts and keep documents up-to-date. For example, you can write a script to apply style guidelines to the text in a document, setting the font and size of specific parts of the text.

You use the `font` property of the `textRange`, `paragraph`, `word`, `character`, and `textLine` to set and retrieve the font of a piece of text. The property is simply the PostScript name of the font as a string. Setting this property to a new PostScript font name changes the font for that object.

It is confusing at first that `textArtItems` does not have a `font` property, and that you must set the font for a `textRange`. To set the font for an entire `textArtItem`,

you must first retrieve a `textRange` object that refers to the entire contents of the `textArtItem`. See the section "Manipulate Part of a Text Item" in this chapter for more information.

Remember, you must use the PostScript name for a font for the operation to be successful. If a script tries to set the `font` property to an unrecognizable font name, it generates an error. One way to avoid this is to create a list of installed fonts and copy the font name from the list.

Another way to retrieve the name of a font is to create a text item with the desired font by hand, and then use scripting to retrieve the name of the font. Unfortunately, this places a lot of pressure on users who work with your scripts because they must step through this process to make sure the font name is correct.

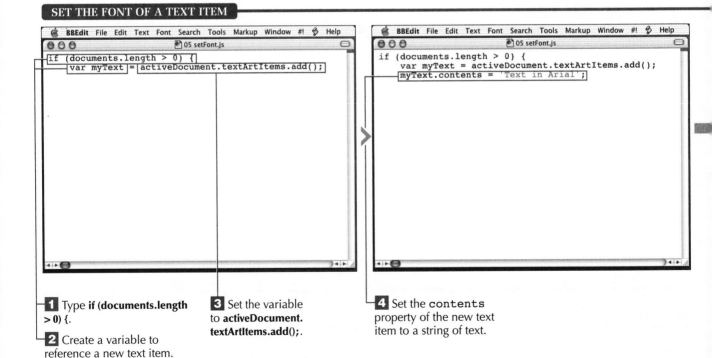

SET THE FONT OF A TEXT ITEM

1 Type **if (documents.length > 0) {**.

2 Create a variable to reference a new text item.

3 Set the variable to **activeDocument. textArtItems.add();**.

4 Set the **contents** property of the new text item to a string of text.

Extra

You can improve the font list script in the section "Retrieve a List of Available Fonts" by setting the font of each item to the font it represents. After creating the paragraph item, you can set the font for just that item. The body of the loop may look like the following example:

TYPE THIS:

```
if (documents.length > 0) {
  var myText = activeDocument.textArtItems.add();
  var range = myText.textRange();
  for (var i=0; i<textFaces.length; i++) {
    var para = range.paragraphs.add();
    para.contents = textFaces[i].name;
    para.font = textFaces[i].name;
  }
}
```

RESULT:

This script creates a list of available fonts much like you find in the section "Retrieve a List of Available Fonts," but it also changes the font of the name to reflect the font.

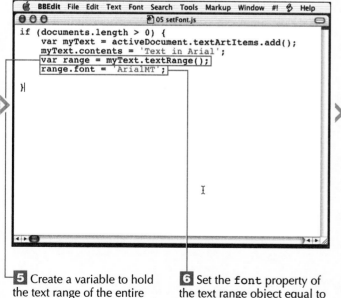

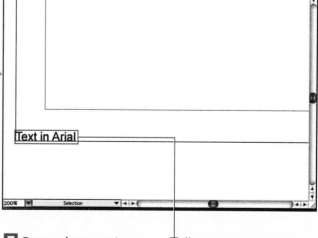

5 Create a variable to hold the text range of the entire text item.

6 Set the **font** property of the text range object equal to the PostScript name of a font.

7 Open a document in Illustrator.

8 Execute the script in Illustrator.

■ Illustrator creates a text item with the set font.

FLOW TEXT BETWEEN PATHS

You can flow text between multiple path items using JavaScript. Flowing text through different path items gives you powerful control over the layout of your document. You can quickly create columns for a newspaper feel, or even have text flow through different items on the page, each with different shapes.

In Illustrator, you can flow text between different area text items by selecting the text items and using the menu path Type ➪ Blocks ➪ Link. The logic when using Illustrator by hand is that you create two area text items, and then link them together to create flowing text. Although the result of creating flowed text with scripting is the same, the logic and the steps necessary are a bit different.

To create flowed text using JavaScript, you must add new `textPath` objects to the `textPaths` collection of the area text item you want to flow. After you create and shape the

initial area text item, you must add new paths to create the text flow. See the section "Create Path and Area Text" in this chapter for more information on creating area text. The `textPaths.add()` method of the `textArtItem` object adds new `textPaths` to the text item, which you can, in turn, modify using the `textPathObject.setEntirePath()` method.

You can make each path through which the text flows a different shape and size. However, you may find it difficult to achieve the path shapes that you want, particularly when you are dealing with elliptical and rounded shapes. One limitation of the `setEntirePath()` method is that you can only specify the anchor points of the path item. To achieve a rounded path, you must set the `leftDirection` and `rightDirection` properties of each path point using a loop. See Chapter 5 for more information.

FLOW TEXT BETWEEN PATHS

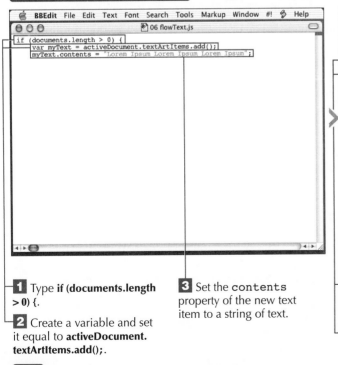

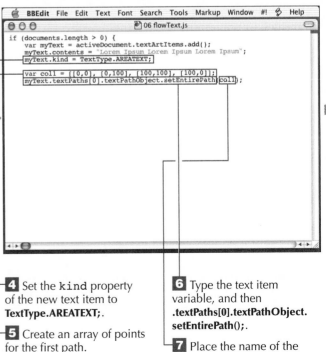

1 Type if **(documents.length > 0) {**.

2 Create a variable and set it equal to **activeDocument.textArtItems.add();**.

3 Set the **contents** property of the new text item to a string of text.

4 Set the **kind** property of the new text item to **TextType.AREATEXT;**.

5 Create an array of points for the first path.

6 Type the text item variable, and then **.textPaths[0].textPathObject.setEntirePath();**.

7 Place the name of the array in the parentheses.

Extra Every flowed area text item can contain multiple path items; you may find it helpful to determine which range of text belongs to which paths. Every `textRange` object contains a reference to the `textPath` that contains it. The `textPath` property of a `textRange` object is a reference to the `textPath` on which the contents of the `textRange` currently lie. By default, Illustrator wraps the contents of an area text item on a word-to-word basis. By obtaining a reference to the entire `textRange` of a text item, you can loop through the words in the range and find the path. For example, to find the first word that is a member of the second `textPath` of the first text item in the current document is, you use the following code:

Example:
```
var doc = activeDocument;
var myText = doc.textArtItems[0];
var fullRange = myText.textRange();
for (var i=0; i<fullRange.words.length; i++) {
  var testWord = fullRange.words[i];
  if (testWord.textPath == myText.textPaths[1]) {
    alert("The first word of the 2nd path item is: " +
fullRange.words[i].contents);
    break;
  }
}
```

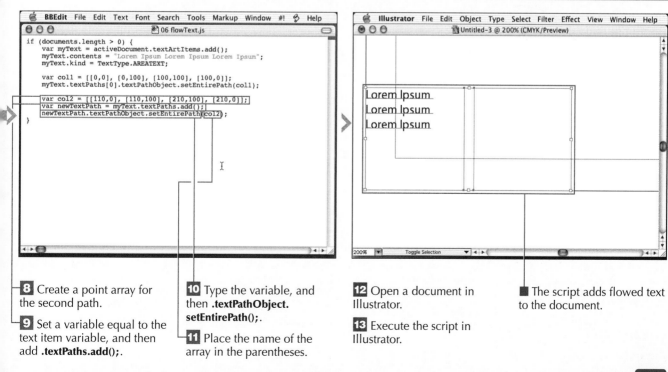

8 Create a point array for the second path.

9 Set a variable equal to the text item variable, and then add **.textPaths.add();**.

10 Type the variable, and then **.textPathObject. setEntirePath();**.

11 Place the name of the array in the parentheses.

12 Open a document in Illustrator.

13 Execute the script in Illustrator.

■ The script adds flowed text to the document.

WRAP TEXT AROUND OTHER OBJECTS

You can wrap text around other objects using JavaScript. You can do this to easily to create interesting page layouts with text, images, and art objects. You can also create integrated designs using drawings, images, and text. Creating wrapped text using scripting has the same effect as selecting an art object and a text item and then using the Type ⇨ Wrap ⇨ Make menu path from Illustrator.

You can set all `textArtObjects` to wrap around other objects with which they are grouped. Before you can set any text item to wrap around another page element, you must group them together. See Chapter 5 for more information on creating groups in Illustrator. Grouping the items together lets Illustrator know what objects the text should wrap around. You can create multiple instances of wrapped text by creating multiple groups of page items and text art items.

After you group a text item with another page element, you can enable wrapping by setting the `wrapped` property of the `textArtItem` object to `true`. When you enable wrapping with JavaScript, the view of the document in Illustrator occasionally does not refresh automatically. If you create wrapping text and it does not appear to work, you may want to first save and then reopen the document. Alternatively, you can drag the group containing the art item, and then use the Undo command to restore the positioning; this forces Illustrator to redraw the window. Yet another option is to set the position of the group containing the text item to its current position. Although no change occurs, doing this forces Illustrator to redraw the screen.

If the text item and the page item it should wrap around do not overlap, you cannot view the results of the wrapping operation.

WRAP TEXT AROUND OTHER OBJECTS

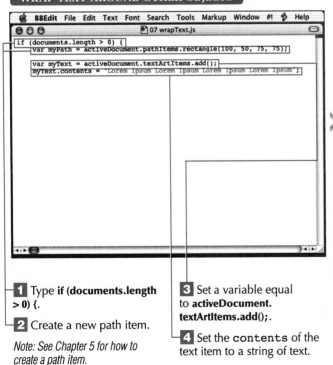

■1 Type **if (documents.length > 0) {**.

■2 Create a new path item.

Note: See Chapter 5 for how to create a path item.

■3 Set a variable equal to **activeDocument. textArtItems.add();**.

■4 Set the **contents** of the text item to a string of text.

■5 Set the **kind** property of the text item to **TextType.AREATEXT;**.

■6 Create a point list to shape the path of the text item.

■7 Type a text item variable, and then **.textPaths[0]. textPathObject.setEntirePath();** placing the point list variable in the parentheses.

Extra You can wrap a `textArtItem` around almost any other type of page item in a document. The main exception is that you cannot wrap text around a group. If you must wrap text around a group, you can copy the text item into the group and set the `wrapped` property to `true`. One disadvantage of this is that the text wraps around each item in the group, rather than the bounding box of the group itself. You can resolve this situation by retrieving the dimensions and position of the group and drawing a path item of the same size in the same place, with `stroked` and `filled` properties both set to `false`. Next, group the text item with this path to make it appear as though the text wraps around the group. You can use either the `top`, `left`, `height`, and `width` properties of the `groupItem` object, or you can retrieve the entire bounds of the object as an array using the `geometricBounds` property. Make sure to clearly label the "dummy" box so that its purpose is clear to someone looking at the Illustrator document.

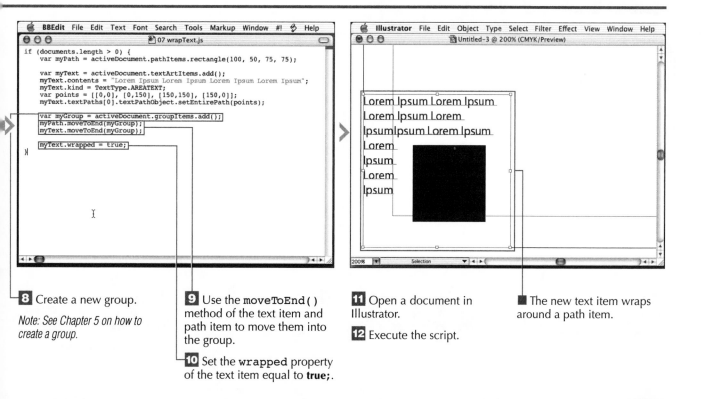

8 Create a new group.

Note: See Chapter 5 on how to create a group.

9 Use the `moveToEnd( )` method of the text item and path item to move them into the group.

10 Set the `wrapped` property of the text item equal to **true;**.

11 Open a document in Illustrator.

12 Execute the script.

■ The new text item wraps around a path item.

SET PARAGRAPH OPTIONS

You can add complex paragraph formatting to your text items using JavaScript. Illustrator supports a wide variety of text formatting options such as indents, word spacing, and hyphenation. You can save common formatting styles as easy-to-use functions so you can quickly apply them to a large number of text items or documents.

The `paragraph` object supports many formatting features not available to other text range items such as `character`, `word`, and `textRange`. Most of the options that you can apply to paragraphs using the Paragraphs palette in Illustrator are also available with JavaScript. Each `textRange` object has a `paragraphs` collection that provides access to the paragraphs it contains. You create a paragraph when you enter a hard return in the text area. You can also add a new paragraph to a text range using the `paragraphs.add()` method. See the section "Retrieve a

List of Available Fonts" in this chapter for an example of using the `paragraphs.add()` method to add text to a text art item.

Some of the most useful options for paragraph formatting are indention, hyphenation, and alignment. These features are only available for the `paragraph` object. You cannot quickly change the paragraph formatting options for an entire text art item. You can loop through the `paragraph` objects in the `paragraphs` collection of a `given` `textRange` object and set the formatting for each paragraph. Some paragraph formatting options require you to set other options before you can see their effects. For example, the minimum and maximum word spacing options are only valid for paragraphs with justification set to `ALLLINES` or `FULLLINES`. Also, many of the paragraph formatting options are only visible for area text items. The amount of text determines the size of point text items, so spacing and alignment features do not apply.

SET PARAGRAPH OPTIONS

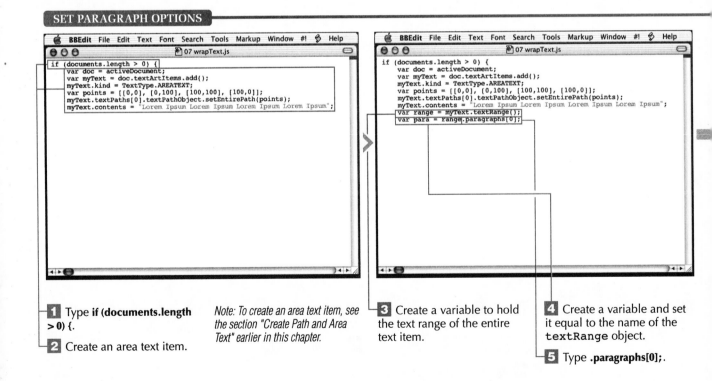

1 Type **if (documents.length > 0) {**.

2 Create an area text item.

Note: To create an area text item, see the section "Create Path and Area Text" earlier in this chapter.

3 Create a variable to hold the text range of the entire text item.

4 Create a variable and set it equal to the name of the **textRange** object.

5 Type **.paragraphs[0];**.

Apply It

You can apply paragraph and text formatting to the currently selected text in Illustrator. Unlike Photoshop, Illustrator allows you to run a script when a section of text in a text art item is selected. If you run a script while text is selected, the `document.selection` object returns a `textRange` object that refers to the selected text. If you do write scripts to operate on the user's selection, you should check that the user has selected the correct type of data before continuing the script to avoid errors.

TYPE THIS:

```
if (documents.length > 0) {
  var doc = activeDocument;
  if (doc.selection instanceof TextRange) {
    var para = doc.selection.paragraphs[0];
    para.size = 50;
    para.firstLineIndent = 15;
    para.justification = Justification.ALLLINES;
  }
}
```

RESULT:

The above code changes the font, justification, and indention for the selected paragraph. If the user does not select an entire paragraph, the properties change for the entire selection.

```
if (documents.length > 0) {
  var doc = activeDocument;
  var myText = doc.textArtItems.add();
  myText.kind = TextType.AREATEXT;
  var points = [[0,0], [0,100], [100,100], [100,0]];
  myText.textPaths[0].textPathObject.setEntirePath(points);
  myText.contents = "Lorem Ipsum Lorem Ipsum Lorem Ipsum Lorem Ipsum";
  var range = myText.textRange();
  var para = range.paragraphs[0];
  para.firstLineIndent = 15;
  para.justification = Justification.ALLLINES;
}
```

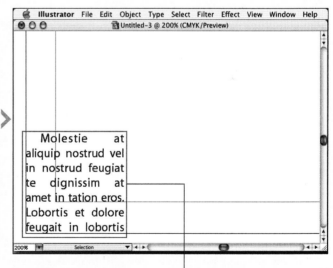

6 Set the `firstLineIndent` property of the paragraph object to a number.

7 Set the `justification` property of the paragraph object to a `Justification` constant value.

Note: See Appendix A for a list of possible values.

8 Open a document in Illustrator.

9 Execute the script in Illustrator.

■ Illustrator adds the text to the document.

UNDERSTANDING THE FILE SYSTEM

The *file system* is the basic structure and layout of files on a computer. The dominant model of a file system is the hierarchical system with which most users of both MS Windows and Macintosh computers are familiar. Drives are organized into *directories*, or *folders*, and folders in turn contain *files* or other folders. The file system is hierarchical in that each folder or file has a position relative to the "top" of the file system, with the top folder holding all other files and folders.

PLATFORM DIFFERENCE

One major difference between the way the file system is implemented in MS Windows, Macintosh, and UNIX platforms is the notation for specifying a file in the file system. The complete description of a file's location in the file system is called a *path*. The following table outlines the notation for all three platforms.

PLATFORM	PATH
Windows	C:\Documents\Important Papers
Macintosh	Macintosh HD:Documents: Important Papers
UNIX	/Documents/Important Papers

Neither Photoshop nor Illustrator are available for any UNIX or Linux platform, the closest being Mac OS X, but Mac OS X recognizes the traditional Macintosh path names. However, the UNIX style path notation might look familiar because it is the standard notation for Internet addresses.

Each of these operating systems uses a different delimiter to indicate a folder in the file system. In MS Windows, you separate each folder and file using a \ while you use the : on Macintosh systems. This can make it difficult to specify a file path in a script because you can never be completely sure on which file system your script will run. Things are further complicated by the fact that although most MS Windows systems use the C: drive as the primary drive, this is not always the case. Similarly, in the Macintosh environment, users can give the main hard drive almost any name they want.

ADOBE'S SOLUTION TO PLATFORM DIFFERENCES

Luckily, Adobe has included a few shortcuts to make working with the file system easier. Both Photoshop and Illustrator support working with the file system using JavaScript. The Folder and File objects provide access to a wide range of file system features. The Folder object has a few properties that are useful for locating commonly needed items in the file system.

PROPERTY	DESCRIPTION
Folder.startup	The location of the current application, for example, Photoshop or Illustrator.
Folder.system	The location of the operation system.
Folder.temp	Default location of temporary files.
Folder.trash	Location of the Trash (Mac) or Recycle Bin (Windows).

The file system objects in JavaScript also support the use of UNIX style URI syntax. This is the syntax familiar from Internet addresses. Each item in the path is delimited by a /. This syntax is then translated to work with whichever file system the script is running on. To get around the issue of hard drive names and locations, you can begin your paths with // to indicate the primary hard drive of the computer on which the script is running. However, it is possible that JavaScript will interpret the same path in URI notation with unexpected results on different platforms. For example, in a Windows system with a default drive of C: and a Macintosh with a default drive named Macintosh HD, the same URI can be interpreted differently.

URI	WINDOWS	MACINTOSH
/c/myDocs/file.txt	C:\myDocs\file.txt	Macintosh HD:c:myDocs:file.txt
//myDocs/file.txt	C:\myDocs\file.txt	Macintosh HD:myDocs:file.txt
/Macintosh HD/ myDocs/file.txt	C:\Macintosh HD\ myDocs\file.txt	Macintosh HD:myDocs:file.txt

You must be careful when specifying pathnames that you take into consideration problems that may arise if your script is run on a platform other than the one you intended. You can make your scripts more cross platform accessible by detecting the user's operating system and behaving accordingly. The Folder.fs property returns a string containing the name of the operating system in use. For example, the Folder.fs property on a computer running Mac OS X is "Macintosh".

LINE ENDINGS

Different operating systems also use different default line endings, or line *feeds*, for files. Sometimes, when you open a file from a different operating system, the file appears on a single line, with odd characters interspersed — this is an effect of the differences between system line endings. The File and Folder objects in JavaScript for Photoshop and Illustrator attempt to detect what line endings are in use when opening a file. This way files from different systems can be read without a problem. The File.lineFeed property is a string set to macintosh, windows, or

unix, depending on the file system currently in use. The writeLn method of the File object will write the correct type of line ending for the operating system running the script. See the section "Write Data to a File" in this chapter for more information on using the writeLn method.

Some text editing applications allow you to view and change the line endings for a file. For example, BB Edit lets you change all line endings in a file to unix, macintosh, or windows.

OPEN OR CREATE A FILE AND FOLDER

You can create new files and folders using JavaScript in both Photoshop and Illustrator. Creating new folders lets you organize the output of your scripts when you export. You can use new files to save textual information about the result of a script or information about documents. Accessing and creating already existing files and folders lets you organize your documents for use with your scripts.

You use the File and Folder objects to access and create new items in the file system. Both objects have constructors much like the Array object. When you create a new Folder or File object, you can pass a path to specify where in the file system the object is located. If the path refers to an already existing item, the constructor returns a

reference to the item; otherwise, it creates a new object. If no path is passed, the constructor creates the object in a temporary location.

When you create a new File object, a new file does not necessarily appear in the file system. Likewise, the creation of a new Folder object does not automatically create a new folder in the file system. The File object does not create an actual file until your script uses the open() method of the file. The open method of the File object can accept up to three parameters. The first is the open mode, the second is the Macintosh type code, and the third is the Macintosh creator code. You create a folder using the create() method of the Folder object.

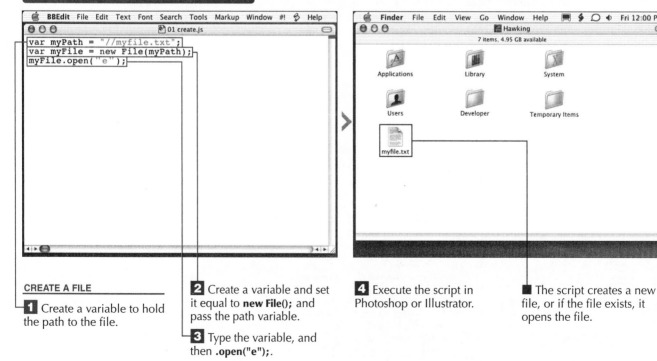

OPEN OR CREATE A FILE AND FOLDER

CREATE A FILE

1 Create a variable to hold the path to the file.

2 Create a variable and set it equal to **new File();** and pass the path variable.

3 Type the variable, and then **.open("e");**.

4 Execute the script in Photoshop or Illustrator.

■ The script creates a new file, or if the file exists, it opens the file.

Extra

Windows users do not have much need for the type or creator codes for the `open` method of the `File` object, but you can use them to determine what application opens the files you create on a Macintosh. All Macintosh files have a type code that specifies the file type. For example, a text file you create with BB Edit has a type code of "TEXT". The creator code determines which application opens the file. For example, a file with a creator code of "R*ch" opens in BB Edit. To create a new file that opens in the BB Edit by default, you type:

Example:
```
var myPath = "//myfile.txt";
var myFile = new File(myPath, "TEXT", "R*ch");
myFile.open('e');
```

JavaScript ignores the type and creator parameters if the script is run on Windows, and does not generate an error.

The available modes for the first parameter of the `open()` method are as follows:

PARAMETER	DESCRIPTION
r	Opens a file for reading only. The method call fails if the file does not exist.
w	Opens a file for writing. If the file exists, the method destroys the contents; otherwise it creates a new file.
e	Opens a file for both reading and writing. If the file does not exist, the method creates a new one.

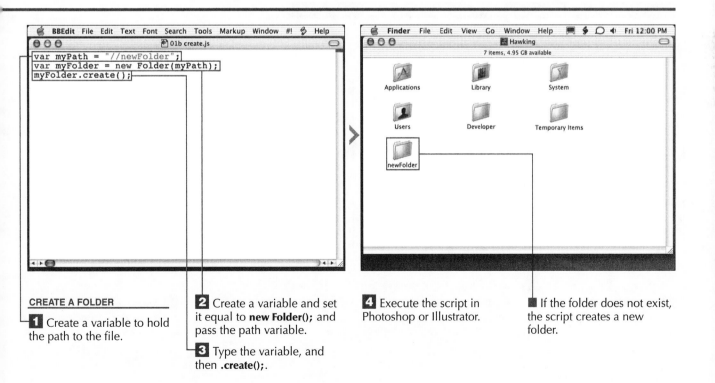

CREATE A FOLDER

1 Create a variable to hold the path to the file.

2 Create a variable and set it equal to **new Folder();** and pass the path variable.

3 Type the variable, and then **.create();**.

4 Execute the script in Photoshop or Illustrator.

■ If the folder does not exist, the script creates a new folder.

SAVE THE ACTIVE DOCUMENT IN PHOTOSHOP AND ILLUSTRATOR

You can use JavaScript to save documents in Photoshop and Illustrator. Using the `File` object allows you to specify the name and location to save documents from Photoshop and Illustrator. For example, you can make changes to every open file and save a copy of each newly modified file in another location. The `File` object is required for many common functions in both Photoshop and Illustrator. Opening, saving, exporting, and importing all require the use of a `File` object to specify the source or destination of these operations.

Photoshop and Illustrator each have `document.save()` and `document.saveAs()` methods that allow you to save the active document. Much like when working with either of the applications by hand, Photoshop and Illustrator do not make the Save command available until you save the document to a specific location. If you try to use the

`save()` method on a previously unsaved file, an error occurs. Every document has a `true` or `false` `saved` property, which checks for modifications to the file since the last save. Be aware that the `saved` property for a new document is `true` until you save and modify the file. This behavior is a bit counter-intuitive in the case of a new file that you have not yet saved.

The `saveAs()` method requires one parameter, a `File` object that defines where in the file system you want to save the file. Other than the first `File` object parameter, the implementation of the `saveAs()` method differs only slightly between Illustrator and Photoshop. The method can accept different parameters in each application. See Appendix A and Appendix B for more information on the optional parameters for the `saveAs()` method in Illustrator and Photoshop.

SAVE THE ACTIVE DOCUMENT IN PHOTOSHOP AND ILLUSTRATOR

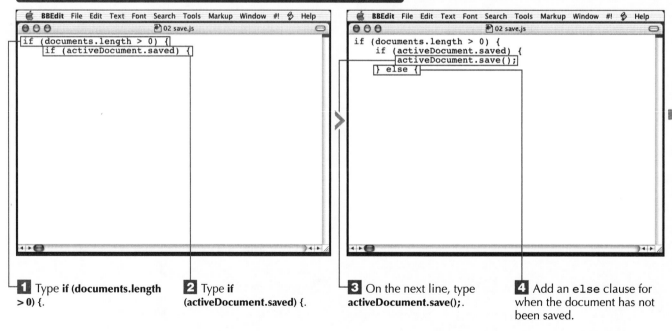

1 Type **if (documents.length > 0) {**.

2 Type **if (activeDocument.saved) {**.

3 On the next line, type **activeDocument.save();**.

4 Add an **else** clause for when the document has not been saved.

Apply It

You can prompt the user to save the current file using the `confirm()` method. See Chapter 2 for more information of the `confirm()` method. Asking the user to confirm before a `save` operation helps ensure that you do not lose data.

TYPE THIS:

```
if (documents.length > 0) {
  var myPath = "//newFile";
  var results = confirm("Would you like to save the current document as " + myPath + "?");
  if (results) {
    var myFile = new File(myPath);
    activeDocument.saveAs(myFile);
  }
}
```

RESULT:

If a document is open, the user sees a confirm dialog box with this text: "Would you like to save the current document as //newFile?" If the user replies "yes," the script saves the file to the new location.

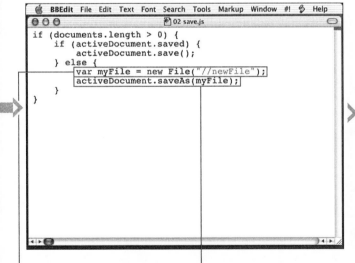

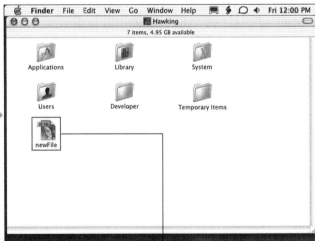

5 Create a variable and set it to **new File();**, placing the path to the file that you want to save in the parentheses.

6 Type **activeDocument. saveAs();** with the name of the `File` object in the parentheses.

7 Execute the script in Illustrator or Photoshop with a document open.

Note: Make sure that you have made changes to the document before running the script.

■ The script saves a file.

RETRIEVE A LISTING OF FILES IN A FOLDER

Because JavaScript in Photoshop and Illustrator can access and read the contents of files and folders, you can retrieve a list of all files in a given folder. Organizing files into folders for use with scripts is a good way to prepare files for batch processing. It is much easier to specify a folder and have a script operate on the contents of the folder than it is to manually list all files with which a script needs to work. For example, you can create source and destination folders and write a script that performs some action on every file in the source folder and save the result in the destination folder. See Chapter 11 for more information on batch processing.

The `Folder` object has a `getFiles()` method that it uses to return an array of all files and folders in a folder. The array that returns consists of `File` and `Folder` objects, one for each file or folder.

The `getFiles()` method takes an optional parameter to specify a mask for listing files. The *mask* is a string that can contain characters and the asterisk (*) as a wild card. For example, if you have a directory with many different files and only want to work with files having an `.ai` extension, you can pass `*.ai` as the mask to restrict the contents of the array of returned files.

You can also pass the name of a function in place of a mask string. The script calls the function, which passes a `File` or `Folder` object for every file or folder in the directory. If the function returns a value of `true`, the script adds the file to the array. See Chapter 2 for more on creating functions and returning values from a function.

RETRIEVE A LISTING OF FILES IN A FOLDER

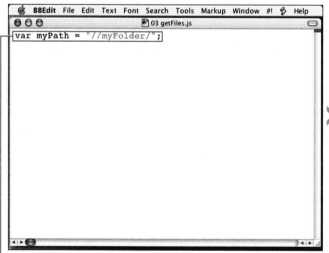

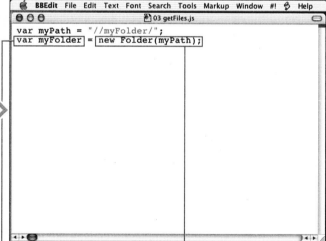

1 Create a variable to hold the path to the file.

2 Create a variable to hold a reference to a new **Folder** object.

3 Set the variable equal to **new Folder();** and pass the path variable.

Apply It

You can differentiate between a `File` and `Folder` object using the `instanceof` operator. The `instanceof` operator compares two values. The first is a specific instance of an object, for example a `File` object, and the second is the name of the object as it appears in the constructor, such as `File`. The operator returns `true` if the item is the same type as the object. You can test each returned item as the result of a `getFiles()` call and display an alert if the item is a folder.

```
var myFolder = new Folder("//myFolder");
var files = myFolder.getFiles();
for (var i=0; i<files.length; i++) {
  if (files[i] instanceof Folder) {
    alert(files[i].name + " is a folder");
  }
}
```

RESULT:

The `files` variable contains an array of all folders and files in the //myFolder directory. As the loop moves through the array, the script tests each item to see if it is a folder. If it is, an alert displays with the name of the folder and a message.

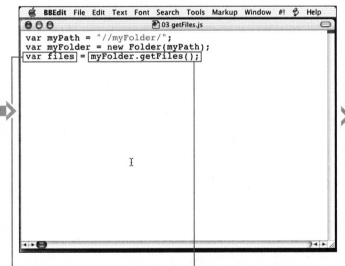

```
var myPath = "//myFolder/";
var myFolder = new Folder(myPath);
var files = myFolder.getFiles();
```

4 Create a variable to hold an array of the contents of the folder.

5 Set the variable equal to the name of the `Folder` object, and then type **.getFiles();**.

6 Execute the script in Illustrator or Photoshop.

■ The script creates an array representing the files in the specified folder.

READ A FILE

You can use JavaScript to read the contents of a specific file. Reading the contents of a file is a vital part of creating dynamic documents in Photoshop and Illustrator. One of the advantages of scripting is that you can use a text file to specify the content of a document. See Chapter 11 for more on retrieving content from external files.

You use the open() method of the File object to open a file and gain access to its contents. See the section "Open or Create a File and Folder" for more information on the open() method. The result of the open method is a true or false value, and you can use these values to verify the successful opening of the file. If the file opens successfully, the script can continue to read and manipulate the file. Verifying that the file is open helps to prevent further errors down the line and helps isolate problems with the script.

Every open file has an internal pointer to a specific position in the file, much like the needle on a record player sitting at a specific location on the record. You can move the pointer using the seek method. It is a good idea to get in the habit of setting the pointer position before any attempt to read the contents of a file. To rewind the file, use the seek method, passing two arguments, 0 and 0.

The read method reads from the current point in the file for a certain number of characters or to the end of the file. After the method reads the data from the file, it is important to close the file using the close method. You must do this as soon as the reading operation stops so that the file is available to other applications and processes.

READ A FILE

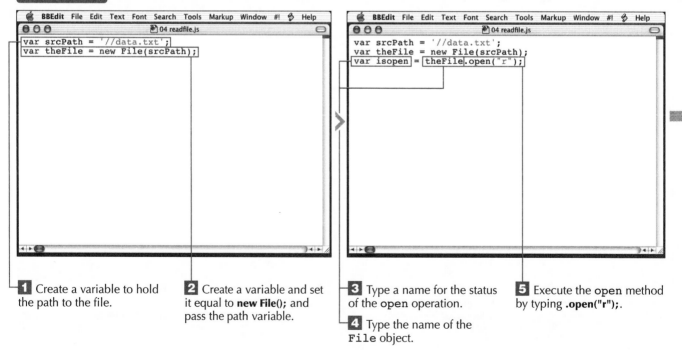

1 Create a variable to hold the path to the file.

2 Create a variable and set it equal to **new File();** and pass the path variable.

3 Type a name for the status of the **open** operation.

4 Type the name of the **File** object.

5 Execute the **open** method by typing **.open("r");**.

Apply It

Using any of the `read` methods automatically forwards the file pointer to the end position of the section of text that was read. The `read` method sets the pointer to the end of the file, the `readch` method forwards the pointer one character, and the `readln` method forwards the pointer to the beginning of the next line. You can use the `tell` method of the `File` object to retrieve the current position of the file pointer. When you want to append data to the end of a file, verify that the file pointer is at the end of the file so that you do not lose data.

TYPE THIS:

```
var theFile = new File("//data.txt");
var success = theFile.open("r");
if (success) {
 theFile.seek(0,0);
 var startPos = theFile.tell();
 theFile.readch();
 var endPos = theFile.tell();
 alert("The start position was: " + startPos);
 alert("The end position was: " + endPos);
}
```

RESULTS:

The first alert indicates that the pointer was initially at 0, and after the `readch` operation, the position moves to 1.

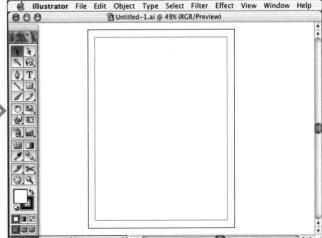

6 Type **if() {** with the status variable as the condition.

7 Create a variable and set it equal to the name of the file variable, and then type **.read()**.

8 Type the name of the file variable, and then **close();**.

9 Execute the script in Photoshop or Illustrator.

■ The script stores the contents of the file in a variable.

WRITE DATA TO A FILE

Y ou can create a new file or add text to an existing one with JavaScript. The `File` object provides powerful tools for writing to and reading from text files. You can create text files to store information about documents or the results of a script. See Chapter 11 for more information on creating document reports with JavaScript.

After you open a file for writing using the `open()` method, with the mode set to either `"w"` or `"e"`, you can add to or overwrite the contents of a file. There are a few methods for adding text to a file. The `write()` method takes the string you want to add to the file as an argument and writes it to the file starting with the current location of the file pointer. The `writeln()` method also takes a string as a parameter and writes the string to the file beginning at the current position of the file pointer, but after the method writes the string, it inserts a line break.

If you need to add text to the end of a file, make sure to open the file in edit mode using the `"e"` parameter of the `open()` method. After the file opens, you should move the file pointer to the end of the file to make sure that you do not overwrite data. You can move a file pointer to the end of a file using the `seek(0,2)` method.

Be very careful when opening files in write mode. Even if you do not perform other operations on the file, after you open it in write mode, you will lose the entire contents of the file. Unless you are sure you need to replace all of the data in the file, it is often safer to open files in edit mode to make sure not to accidentally lose any data.

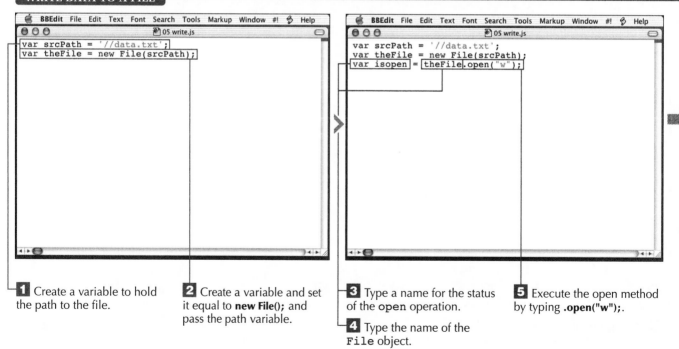

1 Create a variable to hold the path to the file.

2 Create a variable and set it equal to **new File();** and pass the path variable.

3 Type a name for the status of the **open** operation.

4 Type the name of the **File** object.

5 Execute the open method by typing **.open("w");**.

Apply It

When working with files, be careful that you do not have the same file open in two different objects. If you write data to a file with one object, and then write data with another, you run the risk of overwriting the results of the first operation. Each `File` object has its own file pointer, making it difficult to keep two copies of the same file synchronized.

Both the `write()` and `writeln()` methods accept multiple string parameters. All parameters are then concatenated into a single string and written to the file.

TYPE THIS:

```
var srcPath = '//data.txt';
var theFile = new File(srcPath);
var isopen = theFile.open("w");
if (isopen) {
  theFile.write("This is a new file named ", theFile.name);
  theFile.close();
}
```

RESULTS:

The file now contains the string and the name of the file, for example, "This is a new file named data.txt".

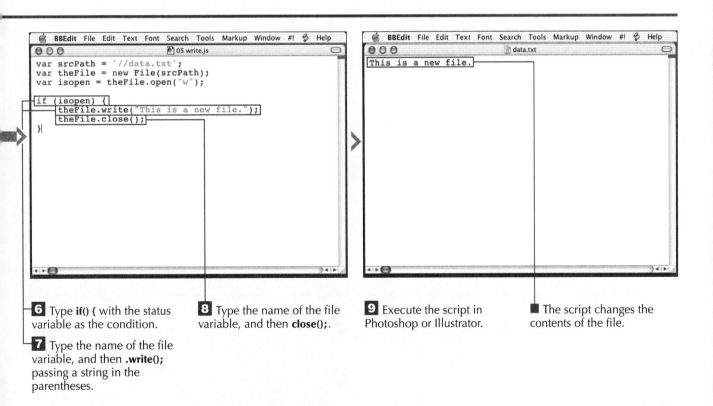

6 Type **if() {** with the status variable as the condition.

7 Type the name of the file variable, and then **.write();** passing a string in the parentheses.

8 Type the name of the file variable, and then **close();**.

9 Execute the script in Photoshop or Illustrator.

■ The script changes the contents of the file.

PLACE A FILE IN ILLUSTRATOR

You can add placed images to an Illustrator document with JavaScript. *Placed files* are art and image files that appear in the file, but remain independent from the Illustrator document. An advantage of using placed files for artwork is that you can easily change the artwork without opening Illustrator and placing the image all over again. Placed files are useful when creating dynamic, data-driven pages. Illustrator can bind a variable to the contents of a placed file and change the current file with each dataset. See Chapter 9 for more information about using variables and datasets in Illustrator.

There are two main types of placed files, raster files and vector files. *Raster files* are bitmap files such as JPEGs, BMPs, GIFs, and TIFFs. Most file formats that you generate with Photoshop are raster files. You create *vector files* in a vector art application like Illustrator and generate files such as AI and EPS.

The document object contains a separate collection for each of the two possible placed art item types. All vector items are available with the placedItems collection, while the raster files are in the rasterItems collection. Each of these collections has an add() method that adds a new element to the document. After the method adds the item, you can specify which file it links to using the file property of the newly created object.

When the file property of a rasterItem or placedItem is set to a File object, Illustrator attempts to replace the object with the specified file. If you try to load the wrong type of file, for example, a raster item into a placedItem, an error occurs.

Although the example in this section places a raster file, you can use the steps to place other file formats in Illustrator.

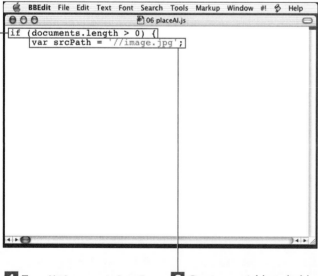

1 Type **if (documents.length > 0) {**.

2 Create a variable to hold a path to the raster file or placed item you want to place.

3 Create a variable and set it equal to **new File();**, passing the path variable.

4 Create a variable and set it equal to **activeDocument. rasterItems.add();**.

■ You can place a vector item by replacing *rasterItem* with *placedItem*.

Extra

You can ascertain the color space of a raster item with JavaScript. Each `rasterItem` object has an `imageColorSpace` property that contains a reference to an `ImageColorSpace` constant value. By comparing the property to the possible values for the constant, you can establish the color space. It is a good idea to match the color space of your documents and the images you place. Images in the RGB color space are optimized for display on the screen, and some colors might not look quite right when printed. You can alert the user when placing a raster item with a color space different from that of the document.

Example:
```
if (documents.length > 0 &&
activeDocument.rasterItems.length > 0) {
  var mySpace = activeDocument.rasterItems[0];
  if (mySpace == ImageColorSpace.CMYK) {
    alert("First raster item has a CMYK color space");
  } else if (mySpace == ImageColorSpace.RGB) {
    alert("First raster item has a RGB color space");
  } else if (mySpace == ImageColorSpace.GRAYSCALE) {
    alert("First raster item has a Grayscale color space");
  }
}
```

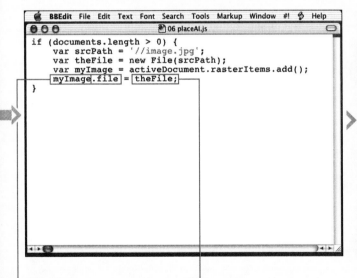

5 Type the name of the variable created in step 4, and then **.file**.

6 Set the property to the file variable.

7 Open a document in Illustrator.

8 Execute the script.

■ The script places the raster or placed item in the document.

UNDERSTANDING VARIABLES AND DATASETS IN ILLUSTRATOR

Y ou can create dynamic content using variables and datasets in Illustrator. Illustrator variables allow you to connect the contents of text items, the visibility of objects, the data of graphs, and the file linked to a placed item. When you use them in conjunction with datasets, you can create multiple versions of the same design in one

document. For example, you can create a document for many different languages, and you can store the text for each language in a dataset. This makes it easy to add new languages and apply changes to the design in one location, without repeating your work.

VARIABLES

Illustrator 10 introduced variables and the Variables palette, which make it easy to create dynamic content. You should not confuse Illustrator variables with the variables you use in scripting. You only use scripting variables to create and manipulate documents with JavaScript, AppleScript, or Visual Basic. Illustrator variables do not require the use of scripting; you can create them by hand in Illustrator with the Variables

palette. To open the Variables palette, you select Variables from the Windows menu. Illustrator variables make content dynamic and separate the form of a document from its content. The content of a document can be the images shown or the text that appears in text items. The form of the document is the design of the document. Elements like font, color, and layout are all elements of the design of the document.

DATASETS

Variables work in conjunction with datasets. A *dataset* represents the values for all variables in a document. Capturing the current values of all variables creates a dataset. After you create a dataset, you can change the contents and the states of the variables to create new datasets. You can then switch between datasets to change the content and configuration of the document. Capturing a dataset is sort of like taking a picture of the document, or at least of the items that are bound to variables. After you capture a dataset, you can change the values for all items on the page; the

name of the dataset appears in italics if it is not current with the data in the document. If you make changes to a document, you can either update the data in the dataset or capture a new one.

You can also manipulate Illustrator variables and datasets with JavaScript. This not only allows you to create dynamic content, but also allows you to automate of the presentation and export of content. See p. 164 for more information on batch processing with datasets.

USING DATASETS AND VARIABLES

The basic process for using variables and datasets in Illustrator, either by hand or using JavaScript, is simple. First, you create a number of variables in the document. You then must *bind* them to an item on the page; this essentially establishes a relationship between the variable

and the page item. After you associate the variables with page items, you create, or *capture*, a dataset. This saves the current value of all variables in the document. After that, you can change values and add new datasets to create multiple versions of your document.

A VIEW OF THE VARIABLES PALETTE

Before you begin working with variables, you may want to familiarize yourself with the Variable palette. The Variable palette offers a place to easily switch datasets, view a list of created datasets, create new variables, and name variables and datasets. See the Illustrator user guide for more on the Variable palette.

CYCLE THROUGH DATASETS

You can use this feature to view the previous or the next dataset in the Datasets menu.

CAPTURE DATASET

Allows you to create a new dataset for the current state of all the variables in a document.

DATASETS MENU

This button allows you to access many other features of datasets. You can export and import variable libraries, select bound objects, rename datasets, or update the values for an existing dataset.

VARIABLE TYPE

Indicates the type of the variable. Double-clicking the variable name allows you to edit the variable type.

VARIABLE VALUE

Shows the value for the variable in the current dataset.

VARIABLE NAME

Displays the name of the variable. You can edit the name by double-clicking it.

CREATE NEW VARIABLE

Allows you to create a new variable. The variable will not have a type set for it.

CREATE A TEXT STRING VARIABLE

You can link a text item to a text string variable with JavaScript. With Illustrator variables, you can give a single text item multiple values for its contents. This makes it easy to create multiple versions of the same layout using different text. Keeping different copies of the same file, or separate copies of the same layer, each with different content, makes it difficult to make even minor changes to the design. Illustrator variables make it easy because you keep the content separate from the design.

You access all of the variables in a document using the `document.variables` collection. Much like other collections in Illustrator and Photoshop, you use the `add()` method to create a new variable. When you create a new variable, Illustrator gives it the default `unknown` type. All possible values for variable types are part of the `VariableKind` constant. Before you can bind a variable to an object, you must explicitly set its type; your scripts are

easier to understand if you do this. When you bind a variable to an object, Illustrator automatically sets the variable to the appropriate type. However, it is not always possible for Illustrator to determine what type of variable you intend for every situation.

Every text item, whether it is point text, area text, or path text, has a `contentVariable` property that refers to the text string variable associated with it. If there is no variable associated with the text item, this property is `null`. For more on text items, see Chapter 7.

You use the `name` property of a `variable` object to give the variable a meaningful name. The name is a string and must follow the same conventions as variable names in JavaScript: no spaces, special characters, and so on. See Chapter 2 for detailed information on variable name requirements.

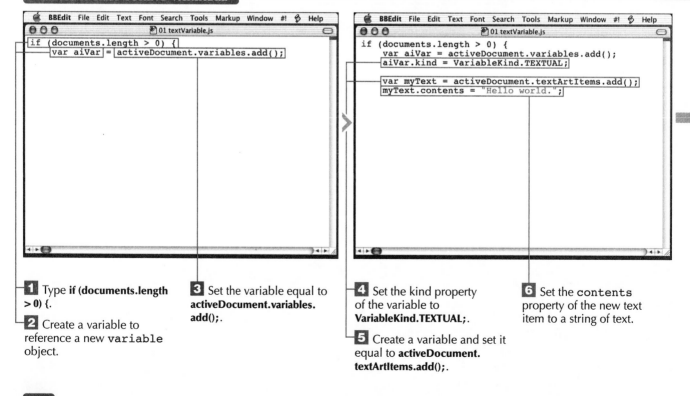

1 Type **if (documents.length > 0) {**.

2 Create a variable to reference a new `variable` object.

3 Set the variable equal to **activeDocument.variables.add();**.

4 Set the kind property of the variable to **VariableKind.TEXTUAL;**.

5 Create a variable and set it equal to **activeDocument.textArtItems.add();**.

6 Set the `contents` property of the new text item to a string of text.

Apply It

Every variable that you bind to an object contains a reference to the object with which it is associated. The `pageItems` property of the `variable` object is a collection of all page items with which the current variable is associated. You can associate a variable with more than one object and affect both objects simultaneously. You can retrieve a list of all `pageItems` currently bound to variables in a document. This script creates an array of all page items that have a variable bound to them.

TYPE THIS:

```
if (documents.length > 0) {
  var doc = activeDocument;
  var boundItems = new Array();
  for (var i=0; i<doc.variables.length; i++) {
    var myPI = doc.variables[i].pageItems;
    for (var j=0; j<myPI.length; j++) {
      boundItems.push(myPI[j]);
    }
  }
}
```

RESULT:

The script creates an array of items associated with variables.

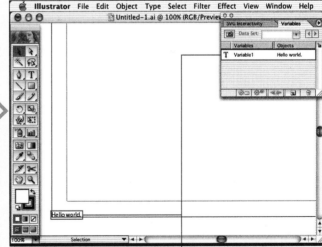

7 Set the `contentVariable` property of the new text item equal to the variable object.

8 Open a document in Illustrator.

9 Execute the script in Illustrator.

■ The script creates a variable and text item, binding the variable to the text item.

CREATE VISIBILITY AND LINKED FILE VARIABLES

Y ou can create data driven documents using variables and JavaScript. *Visibility variables* control what objects, layers, and groups are visible in a given dataset. They make it easy to create documents that change to fit a variety of situations while maintaining the same basic design. *Linked file variables* allow you to change the currently displayed external art file. Linked files can include raster files, such as JPEG, or vector files, such as EPS. Using linked files for the art in an Illustrator document makes it easy to change the art in Illustrator. For example, you can have a file with a different icon and photo for each person in a company, and using variables and datasets, dynamically create a biography of each person, display the correct images for each person, and export each dataset to a PDF.

You can control almost all objects in an Illustrator document with a visibility variable. You use the `visibilityVariable` property of an object to bind an

object's visibility to an Illustrator variable. When working with visibility in Illustrator, you can set the current visibility of an object using the Visibility toggle icon in the Layers palette. In JavaScript, each object has a `hidden` property. You must set this property to a `true` or `false` value to determine if the object appears in the current document. In the case of variables and datasets, you use the `hidden` variable to toggle the visibility of an object in the current dataset.

You can bind linked file variables to either a `rasterItem` or a `placedItem`. It is important to know what type of placed file you are dealing with so that you can locate the item in the appropriate collection. Each of these items has a `contentVariable` that binds a linked file variable to the object.

CREATE VISIBILITY AND LINKED FILE VARIABLES

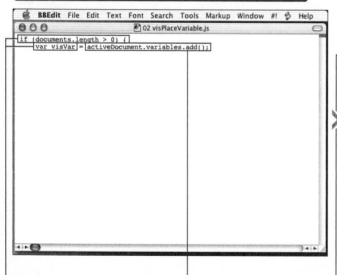

1 Type **if (documents.length > 0) {**.

2 Create a variable to reference a new `variable` object.

3 Set the variable equal to **activeDocument.variables. add();**.

4 Set the `kind` property of the variable to **VariableKind.VISIBLITY;**.

5 Repeat steps 2 to 4, but set the `kind` property of the second variable to **VariableKind.IMAGE**.

Apply It

When placing a file with JavaScript, you can use the reference to the object that the `placedItems.add()` method creates when it places the file, no matter what the file type, to access the `contentVariable` of the object. See Chapter 8 for more information on placing files using JavaScript.

If you are uncertain about the type of placed image with which you need to work, you can create a new array containing a reference to both `rasterItems` and `placedItems`. After creating the single array, you may find it easier to locate the object using its `name` property. The following code loops through the `placedItems` and `rasterItems` collections and adds the members of both to a new array.

TYPE THIS:

```
if (documents.length > 0) {
  var linkedArt = new Array();
  for (var i=0; i<activeDocument.placedItems; i++) {
    linkedArt.push(activeDocument.placedItems[i]);
  }
  for (var i=0; i<activeDocument.rasterItems; i++) {((te)
    linkedArt.push(activeDocument.rasterItems[i]);
  }
}
```

RESULT:

Illustrator creates an array containing all `rasterItems` and `placedItems`.

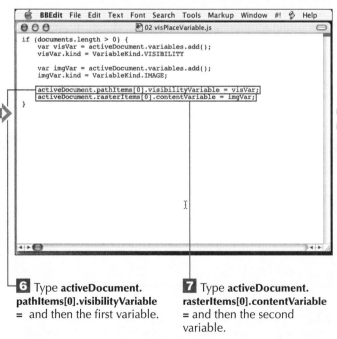

6 Type **activeDocument.pathItems[0].visibilityVariable** = and then the first variable.

7 Type **activeDocument.rasterItems[0].contentVariable** = and then the second variable.

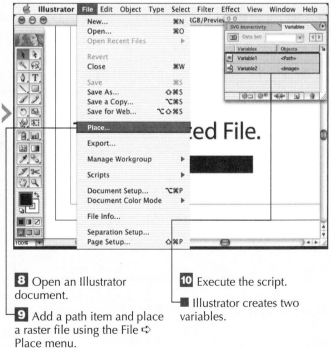

8 Open an Illustrator document.

9 Add a path item and place a raster file using the File ➪ Place menu.

10 Execute the script.

■ Illustrator creates two variables.

CREATE A NEW DATASET

You can use the power of variables by creating datasets to store the state of bound objects. A dataset is like a snapshot of the current state of all variables in a document. Without datasets, Illustrator variables are useless because you have no way to alter the contents of the variable data. You can use datasets to create different versions of a document, or even save the current configuration of layer and object visibility to organize multiple comps into a single document.

When working with variables in Illustrator, a window in the Variables palette shows the name of the currently active dataset, if one exists. After you capture a dataset using the Capture Dataset button in the Variables palette, the default name of the new dataset appears. The disclosure triangle in the upper-right corner of the window lets you access an

Options menu. One of the options in the menu allows you to give a meaningful name to the dataset. If the name of the dataset appears in italics, the contents or state of one or more variables have changed since you first captured the dataset. The Update Dataset option in the menu makes sure the dataset contains the current values for all variables.

Datasets only become useful when you have more than one present in a document. Each dataset contains a snapshot of the values of all variables when you created or last updated the set. When working with datasets in a script, you may find it useful to add a dataset as a point in a timeline running top to bottom. If you set values for a variable, create a dataset, and then change the values, the dataset contains the values of the variables at the time you created it.

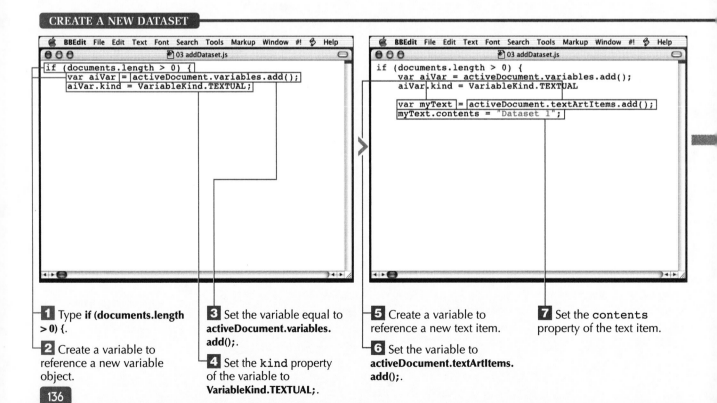

1 Type if (documents.length > 0) {.

2 Create a variable to reference a new variable object.

3 Set the variable equal to activeDocument.variables.add();.

4 Set the kind property of the variable to VariableKind.TEXTUAL;.

5 Create a variable to reference a new text item.

6 Set the variable to activeDocument.textArtItems.add();.

7 Set the contents property of the text item.

Extra

You can change the currently displayed dataset using the `display()` method. Displaying the dataset makes the document appear with the content of the variables associated with that dataset. The contents of text items and images all change to show the current values for the displayed dataset.

Illustrator stores all datasets in the `datasets` collection of the `document` object. If you name your datasets using the `name` property, it is much easier to reference them later on in your scripts, or in the future when you revisit a document.

You retrieve a reference to the currently visible dataset using the `document.activeDataset` property. This property is useful when looping through the `datasets` collection to test if the current item in the collection is the same as the currently displayed dataset.

Looping through the `datasets` collection, you can display and manipulate every dataset in a document. The following code loops through every dataset in the active document and displays it. You can add code where the comment is to execute some action while each dataset is visible. For example, you may want to save the document as a JPEG.

Example:
```
for (var i=0; i<activeDocument.datasets; i++) {
  activeDocument.datasets[i].display();
  // manipulate dataset
}
```

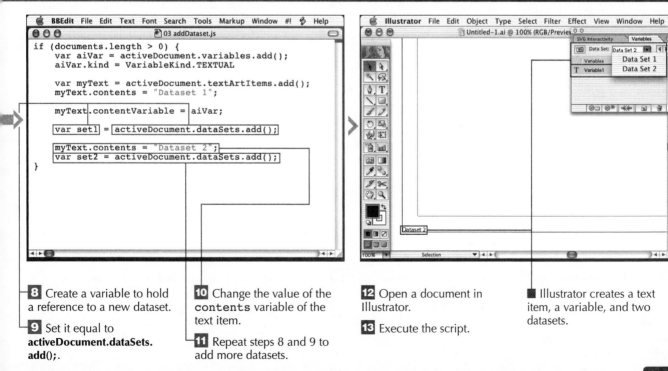

```
if (documents.length > 0) {
    var aiVar = activeDocument.variables.add();
    aiVar.kind = VariableKind.TEXTUAL

    var myText = activeDocument.textArtItems.add();
    myText.contents = "Dataset 1";

    myText.contentVariable = aiVar;
    var set1 = activeDocument.dataSets.add();

    myText.contents = "Dataset 2";
    var set2 = activeDocument.dataSets.add();
}
```

8 Create a variable to hold a reference to a new dataset.

9 Set it equal to **activeDocument.dataSets. add();**.

10 Change the value of the **contents** variable of the text item.

11 Repeat steps 8 and 9 to add more datasets.

12 Open a document in Illustrator.

13 Execute the script.

■ Illustrator creates a text item, a variable, and two datasets.

EXPORT AND IMPORT VARIABLE LIBRARIES

You can save the current value of all variables in all datasets into an external XML file using JavaScript. Saving the datasets lets you create variable libraries that you can edit by hand or generate with another application. You can import external variable files into an existing document. Using variables, datasets, and external variable libraries make it easy to integrate Illustrator documents with data from external sources such as spreadsheets and databases. For example, you can create a variable library file containing personnel information, including the locations of pictures. Then, by importing the variable library into different Illustrator documents, you can easily create a wide variety of different designs without reentering the information.

When you export a variable library, Illustrator creates an XML document that describes the variables, datasets, and variable values for a document. It is a good idea to give

your variables and datasets meaningful names. This makes the exported variable library easier to read, and can also make your Illustrator documents easier to understand.

When Illustrator creates a variable library, it does not save the bindings between variables and objects as part of the data. You should think of the Illustrator file as a template containing primarily information about the *form* of the total document, while the variable library provides the *content*. Separation of form and content allows you to apply different designs to the same information. As long as the Illustrator document into which you import the variable library has a variable with the same name as the variables in the library, Illustrator successfully imports the data. This makes it that much more important to carefully name the objects and variables in your documents so that you can easily match them up later.

EXPORT VARIABLE LIBRARIES

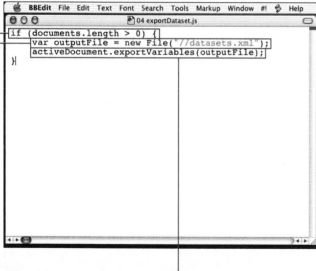

1 Type **if (documents.length > 0) {**.

2 Set a variable equal to **new File();** and place the path to the file you want to create in the parentheses.

3 Type **activeDocument. exportVariables();** with your variable in the parentheses.

4 Open a document with variables in Illustrator.

5 Execute the script.

■ Illustrator creates a variable library file.

Apply It

Variable library files do not contain information about which page items binds to which variable. When you import a variable library, there is a chance that some of the variables in the library will not bind to any object on the page. You can generate a list of variables that are not currently bound to any page item.

TYPE THIS:

```
if (documents.length > 0) {
  var doc = activeDocument;
  var srcFile = File("//variables.xml");
  doc.importVariables(srcFile);
  var unbound = new Array();
  for (var i=0; i<doc.variables.length; i++) {
    if(doc.variables[i].pageItems.length == 0) {
      unbound.push(doc.variables[i]);
    }
  }
}
```

RESULT:

Illustrator creates an array listing all variables that are not bound to a page item.

IMPORT VARIABLE LIBRARIES

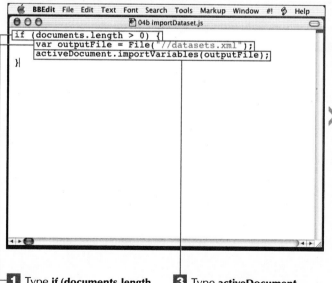

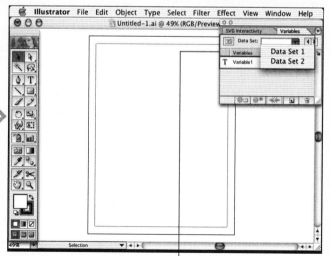

1 Type **if (documents.length > 0) {**.

2 Set a variable equal to **new File();** and place the path to the variable library file in the parentheses.

3 Type **activeDocument. importVariables();** with your variable in the parentheses.

4 Open a document with variables in Illustrator.

5 Execute the script.

■ Illustrator imports a variable library file.

EDIT A VARIABLE LIBRARY BY HAND

Y ou can edit the properties of a variable library file by hand. You can easily accomplish this with a text editor, and you may find if faster than using Illustrator to edit your library. Using a text editor to edit variable library files gives you access to the more developed text manipulation capabilities, such as copy, paste, find, and

replace. Understanding the format of a variable library file also enables you to create the file using a spreadsheet or database. A developer can create a program to export values directly to a variable library file, allowing you to integrate data from almost any source into your designs.

UNDERSTANDING XML

A variable library is a XML file that defines the variable names, variable types, datasets, and values for a document. XML is a way of formatting data that is easy for applications to understand. It is also user friendly in that a person can easily read, understand, and edit XML to fit a particular situation. *XML* stands for *eXtensible Markup Language*, which means that although it has a general set of rules that help to classify a document as XML, you can change the specific content and meaning of the format to meet different needs.

If you are familiar with HTML, XML will look somewhat familiar to you. Information is organized into *tags* or *nodes*. The name of the node is used to define its meaning to the application reading the file. As in HTML, a node can contain *child* nodes to represent a relationship between them.

XML VARIABLE LIBRARY

In the case of an Illustrator variable library, the primary node is the `variableSets`, which in turn contains a node for `variables` and a node for `sampleDataSets`. The child nodes in the `variables` node define both the name and the type of the variables present in the Illustrator document. A variable node represents each variable. You define the name and type of the variable using attributes of the tag. For example, a text string variable named `titleText` would look like this:

Example:

```
<variable varName="titleText" trait=
"textcontent"
category="&ns_flows;"></variable>.
```

You define the type of variable in the `trait` attribute. You must include the `category` attribute, which helps Illustrator understand how to use this information, in any new tags that you add to a document. There are three different category types to go with the four different types of variables.

TRAIT	CATEGORY	DESCRIPTION
textcontent	&ns_flows;	Indicates that this node defines a text string variable.
visibility	&ns_vars;	Indicates that this node defines a visibility variable.
graphdata	&ns_graphs;	Indicates that this node defines a graph data variable.
fileref	&ns_vars;	Indicates that this node defines a file reference variable.

Each of these is actually an entity that Illustrator defines at the top of the XML file. An in-depth explanation of XML entities is outside the scope of the book, but remember to add the correct `trait` and `category` attributes when creating variables by hand.

The `v:sampleDataSet` tag defines each dataset. Each variable in the document has a tag named after the variable it represents, and the variable's tags define the value for this variable in the dataset.

VARIABLE LIBRARY CODE ELEMENTS

The following variable library file defines a single text string
variable named Var1. The variable has a unique value in
each of two datasets, named Data Set 1 and Data Set 2.

VARIABLE SETS NODE

This is the parent node for
all other nodes used to define
Illustrator variable data.

VARIABLES NODE

This is the parent node for
all variables defined in the
document.

**DATASET DEFINITION
NODE**

This node defines a single
dataset and the dataset's
name. The content for each
variable is defined inside
this node.

```
 BBEdit   File  Edit  Text  Font  Search  Tools  Markup  Window  #!   Help
 ○ ○ ○                          05 variables.xml
<?xml version="1.0" encoding="utf-8"?>
<!DOCTYPE svg PUBLIC "-//W3C//DTD SVG 20001102//EN"
  "http://www.w3.org/TR/2000/CR-SVG-20001102/DTD/svg-20001102.dtd" [
  <!ENTITY ns_graphs "http://ns.adobe.com/Graphs/1.0/">
  <!ENTITY ns_vars "http://ns.adobe.com/Variables/1.0/">
  <!ENTITY ns_imrep "http://ns.adobe.com/ImageReplacement/1.0/">
  <!ENTITY ns_custom "http://ns.adobe.com/GenericCustomNamespace/1.0/">
  <!ENTITY ns_flows "http://ns.adobe.com/Flows/1.0/">
<!ENTITY ns_extend "http://ns.adobe.com/Extensibility/1.0/">
]>
<svg>
<variableSets  xmlns="&ns_vars;">
  <variableSet  varSetName="binding1" locked="none">
    <variables>
      <variable  varName="Var1" trait="textcontent" category="&ns_flows;"></variable>
    </variables>
    <v:sampleDataSets  xmlns="&ns_custom;" xmlns:v="&ns_vars;">
      <v:sampleDataSet  dataSetName="Data Set 1">
        <Var1>
          <p>Dataset 1</p>
        </Var1>
      </v:sampleDataSet>
      <v:sampleDataSet  dataSetName="Data Set 2">
        <Var1>
          <p>Dataset 2</p>
        </Var1>
      </v:sampleDataSet>
    </v:sampleDataSets>
  </variableSet>
</variableSets>
</svg>
```

**VARIABLE
DEFINITION NODE**

This node defines a single
variable including the
variable type and its name.

**VARIABLE NODE FOR
THIS DATASET**

This node defines the
value of a particular
variable for this dataset.

DATASETS NODE

This is the parent node for
all datasets defined in the
document.

**VARIABLE VALUE IN
THIS DATASET**

The contents of the
variable for this dataset.

SAVE A DOCUMENT AS PDF AND EPS FROM ILLUSTRATOR

You can save an Illustrator document as an EPS or PDF using JavaScript. Illustrator supports saving documents in three different formats: AI, EPS, and PDF. With JavaScript, you can access the save functionality and create a document in many different formats. This makes it easy to batch process a group of files to another format, such as saving them as PDF for publishing to the Web.

You use the `document.saveAs()` method to save a file from Illustrator. You can call the `document.saveAs()` method using a single parameter to define the file that you want to save the document as. You specify the file using a `File` object. See Chapter 8 for more on saving an active document in Photoshop and Illustrator.

The `document.saveAs()` method can also take an optional second parameter that defines what format you want to save the file as, and the options for the saved file.

There are three types of options objects that you can use in Illustrator: `IllustratorSaveOptions`, `EPSSaveOptions`, and `PDFSaveOptions`. When you choose the File ⇨ Save As menu path with a document open, you can save the file in a number of different formats. After you select a format, a dialog box displays and presents you with a number of options for the file format you have chosen. The `SaveOptions` objects are a way to access those options using JavaScript.

You can create a new options object using the `new` keyword along with the name of the object you want to create, much like when you create a new array. See Chapter 2 for more on creating objects. After you create the object, you can set the specific options for that file type. See Appendix A for a complete list of the possible parameters for each `SaveOptions` object.

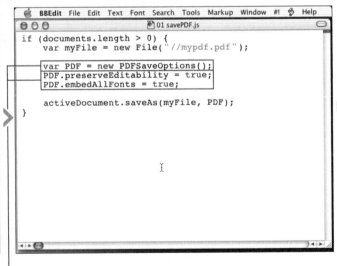

1 Type **if (documents.length > 0) {**.

2 Set a variable equal to a **new File();**, placing the path to the file you want to create in the parentheses.

3 Set a variable equal to **new PDFSaveOptions();**.

4 Set any parameters for the `SaveOptions` object.

Note: See Appendix A for a complete list of parameters.

Apply It

You may find it tedious to create a new SaveOptions object and set the save parameters to the same values over and over again. You can use a function to store common settings for save options. This saves you time and makes your scripts easier to write and maintain. To use a function to store common settings, you must create a function that makes a new SaveOptions object, sets the necessary parameters, and returns the object.

TYPE THIS:

```
function webPDF() {
  var PDF = new PDFSaveOptions();
  PDF.preserveEditability = true;
  PDF.embedAllFonts = true;
  PDF.compressArt = true
  PDF.colorCompression = CompressionQuality.JPEGLOW;
  return PDF;
}
var PDF = webPDF();
```

RESULT:

This function sets the variable PDF to a PDFSaveOptions object with the properties specified in the webPDF function.

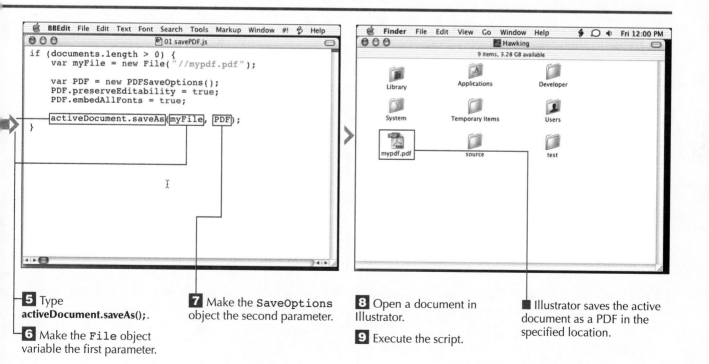

5 Type
activeDocument.saveAs();.

6 Make the File object variable the first parameter.

7 Make the SaveOptions object the second parameter.

8 Open a document in Illustrator.

9 Execute the script.

■ Illustrator saves the active document as a PDF in the specified location.

CREATE AN ILLUSTRATOR EXPORT OBJECT

You can export a document from Illustrator with JavaScript. Illustrator supports a wide number of export formats including JPEG, GIF, PNG, PSD, and SWF. Knowing how to export to a wide range of formats allows you to write powerful scripts for batch processing documents.

You control exporting in Illustrator using an `ExportOptions` object and the `document.exportFile()` method. The `document.exportFile()` method takes three parameters: the destination file of the save operation, a type of file to create, and the options object for the file type. You specify the file destination as a `File` object. You define the type of file to export using an `ExportType` constant. The third parameter defines the options for the selected export file type. You define the options using an `ExportOptions` object. See Chapter 8 for details on creating a `File` object. You can find possible values for the `ExportType` constant in Appendix A.

You can create a new `ExportOptions` object using the `new` keyword along with the name of the object you want to create. After you create the object, you can set the properties of the object that define the export options. See Chapter 2 for more on creating objects.

Each type of `ExportOptions` object has a number of properties specific to the file format with which it is associated. If you select File ⇨ Export within Illustrator, and then choose the type of file to export, a dialog box appears and presents you with the available options for that file type. See Appendix A for a complete list of properties for each `ExportOptions` object.

The Export dialog box in Illustrator supports many more file types than are available with scripting. However, most of the common formats are available. This example creates a JPEG export object.

CREATE AN ILLUSTRATOR EXPORT OBJECT

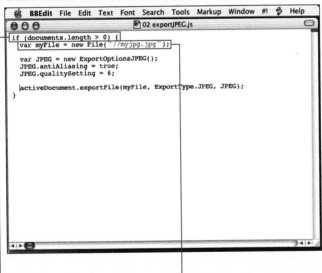

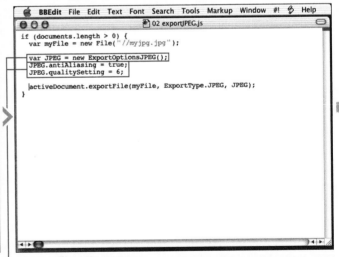

1 Type if **(documents.length > 0) {**.

2 Set a variable equal to a **new File();**, placing the path to the file you want to create in the parentheses.

3 Set a variable equal to **new ExportOptionsJPEG();**.

4 Set any properties for the `ExportOptions` object.

Note: See Appendix A for a complete list of properties.

Extra

With the exception of Photoshop PSD files, when you export a file, Illustrator automatically appends the appropriate extension to the filename.

FILE TYPE	EXTENSION	EXPORT OBJECT NAME
GIF	.gif	ExportOptionsGIF
JPEG	.jpg	ExportOptionsJPEG
PNG (25 bit)	.png	ExportOptionsPNG24
PNG (8 bit)	.png	ExportOptionsPNG8
PSD	none	ExportOptionsPhotoshop
SVG	.svg	ExportOptionsSVG
SWF	.swf	ExportOptionsFlash

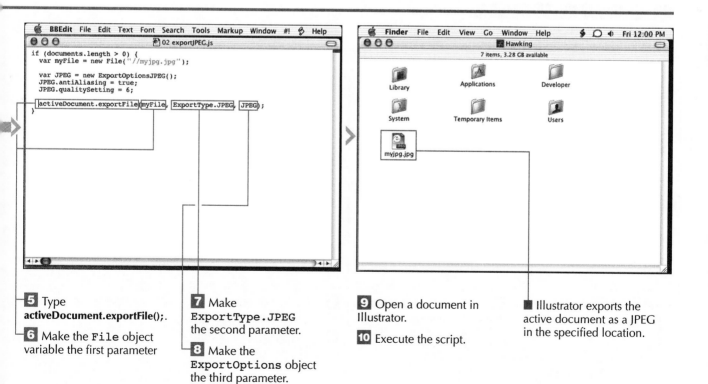

```
if (documents.length > 0) {
  var myFile = new File("//myjpg.jpg");

  var JPEG = new ExportOptionsJPEG();
  JPEG.antiAliasing = true;
  JPEG.qualitySetting = 6;

  activeDocument.exportFile(myFile, ExportType.JPEG, JPEG);
}
```

5 Type **activeDocument.exportFile();**.

6 Make the **File** object variable the first parameter

7 Make **ExportType.JPEG** the second parameter.

8 Make the **ExportOptions** object the third parameter.

9 Open a document in Illustrator.

10 Execute the script.

■ Illustrator exports the active document as a JPEG in the specified location.

SAVE A JPEG FROM PHOTOSHOP

You can save a document to a number of different file formats with Photoshop and JavaScript, including EPS, JPEG, GIF, PNG, PDF, and PICT. With JavaScript, you can access the save functionality and create a document in many different formats. This makes it easy to batch process a group of files to another format, such as saving them as JPEGs for publishing to a Web site.

You use the `document.saveAs()` method to save a file from Photoshop. You can then call the `document.saveAs()` method with a single parameter, which defines the file to which you want to save the document. You specify the file using a `File` object. See Chapter 8 for more on saving an active document in Photoshop and Illustrator.

The `document.saveAs()` method can also take an optional second parameter that defines the format to which you want to save the file as well as the options for the saved

file. Unlike Illustrator, Photoshop uses the `document.saveAs()` method for almost all saving operations. The type of `SaveOptions` object passed to the method determines the type of file to create. When you choose the File ⇨ Save As menu path with a document open, you can save the file in a number of different formats. After you select a format, a dialog box displays and presents you with a number of options for the file format you have chosen. The `SaveOptions` objects are a way to access those options using JavaScript. See Appendix B for a complete list of `SaveOptions` objects and their properties.

You can create a new options object using the `new` keyword along with the name of the object you want to create, much like when you create a new array. After you create the object, you can set the specific options for that file type. See Chapter 2 for more on creating objects.

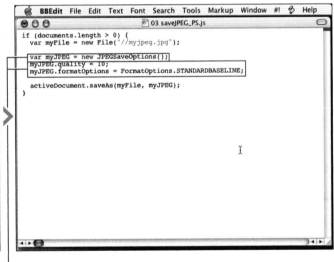

1 Type **if (documents.length > 0) {**.

2 Set a variable equal to a **new File();**, placing the path to the file you want to create in the parentheses.

3 Set a variable equal to **new JPEGSaveOptions();**.

4 Set any parameters for the `SaveOptions` object.

Note: See Appendix B for a complete list of parameters.

Apply It

The `document.saveAs()` method can accept two additional parameters. The third parameter is a `true` or `false` value for saving the document as a copy. When you save a document as a copy, it does not become the active document in Photoshop. If you save a copy, make changes, and save again, you end up with two copies of the original document. Saving as a copy is useful when you need to make changes to a document, but want to save the steps as they progress. Unlike clicking File ⇨ Save as a Copy in Photoshop, Photoshop does not automatically append the word `copy` to the end of the filename when you set save as copy to `true`.

The fourth parameter lets you define how Photoshop should treat the file extension. It takes an `Extension` constant. Using `Extension.LOWERCASE` causes Photoshop to automatically append the correct file extension for the type of file you are creating. When you instruct Photoshop to automatically append the extension, you do not need to specify it as part of the filename when creating the `File` object to which to save.

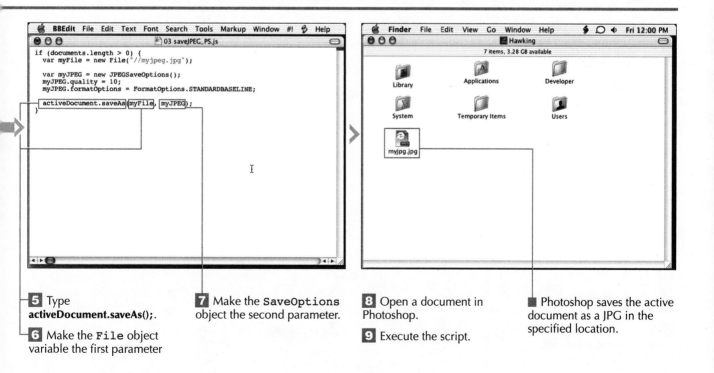

5 Type **activeDocument.saveAs();**.

6 Make the `File` object variable the first parameter

7 Make the **SaveOptions** object the second parameter.

8 Open a document in Photoshop.

9 Execute the script.

■ Photoshop saves the active document as a JPG in the specified location.

PRINT A DOCUMENT FROM ILLUSTRATOR

Y ou can use JavaScript to print a document from
Illustrator. Automating the printing process can help
save time. You can create a script to print an entire
folder of Illustrator files, or loop through every layer in a
document and print each one separately.

You perform printing with JavaScript in Illustrator using the
`document.print()` method. The method accepts a single
parameter. The parameter is a `true` or `false` value that
determines if a Print dialog box displays for the user. If you
select the File ⇨ Print menu path with a document open in
Illustrator, you see the Print Options dialog box. The options
this dialog box presents differ depending on the operating
system and type of printer that you have in use. If you set
the parameter to `false`, Illustrator uses the default printer,
which your system settings determine. If you do not define
the parameter, it defaults to `true` and the dialog box
displays.

Unfortunately, you cannot access many Illustrator-specific
printing options with JavaScript. PostScript type, selection,
source space, and print space are all unavailable when
printing from a script. You cannot configure these options in
JavaScript, AppleScript, or VB Script. Hopefully, a future
version of Illustrator scripting will support more printing
options.

You can configure some of the options available in the
File ⇨ Document Setup ⇨ Printing and Export dialog box.
You set the output resolution for the document using the
`document.outputResolution` property. You can set the
`document.splitLongPaths` option to `true` or `false` to
split paths when printing. You cannot set the Use Printer's
Default Screen option using JavaScript, but you can test the
current value for the option using the
`document.useDefaultScreen` property.

PRINT A DOCUMENT FROM ILLUSTRATOR

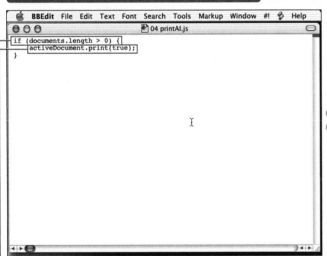

1 Type **if (documents.length > 0) {**.

2 Type
activeDocument.print(true);.

■ You can type
activeDocument.print(false);
to have Illustrator use the
default printer.

3 Open a document in
Illustrator.

4 Execute the script.

■ In this example, Illustrator
opens the Print dialog box.

PRINT A DOCUMENT FROM PHOTOSHOP

You can print a document from Photoshop with JavaScript. You can create a script to print an entire directory of documents, or print each layer set in a document one at a time. Automating the printing process can help save time by quickly performing an otherwise time consuming task.

Printing from Photoshop with JavaScript uses the `document.print()` method. Unlike printing from Illustrator, there is no way to suppress the system Print dialog box. Photoshop does not show the Photoshop Print dialog box when this method is called, but the system dialog box always appears.

If you select the File ⇨ Print menu path with a document open in Photoshop, you see the Print Options dialog box. The options that Photoshop presents differ depending on the operating system and type of printer that you have in use. Despite the drawback of not being able to suppress the

system print dialog box, Photoshop does provide access to a few more printing features as opposed to Illustrator. The `document.print()` method can accept up to four parameters. With these parameters, you can define the PostScript Encoding, Source Space, Print Space, Intent, and Black Point Compensation.

The PostScript Encoding setting is very useful for printing to a variety of different printers on different platforms. This setting allows you to change the format of the data being set to the printer. The default is binary, but you can also use either JPEG or ASCII depending on the needs of your printer. See the Photoshop manual for more details on the differences between the printing types.

Taken together, the print options available with JavaScript allow you to have great control over the outcome of the printing process.

PRINT A DOCUMENT FROM PHOTOSHOP

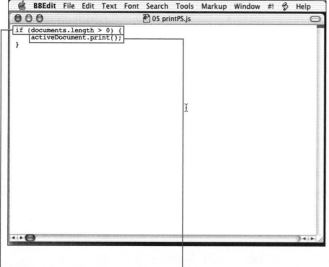 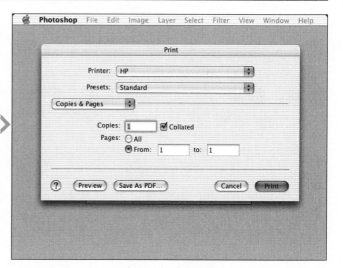

1 Type **if (documents.length > 0) {**.

2 Type **activeDocument.print();**.

3 Open a document in Photoshop.

4 Execute the script.

■ Photoshop opens the Print dialog box.

USING MODULAR SCRIPTING TECHNIQUES

You can build a library of easily reusable code components. Building a code library makes writing scripts easier because it cuts down on the amount of work necessary to write a new script. Rather than re-invent the wheel every item you write a new script, you can reuse parts of earlier scripts.

WRITING REUSABLE CODE

Modular code is the key to building a robust code library. When writing a new script, you should first consider if there are any scripts you have already written that you can modify or rewrite to achieve the task at hand. If you find that you need to write all or most of the script from scratch, you should keep a few concepts in mind when developing the parts of the script.

First, isolate the key steps in the script that could be useful in other contexts. For example, a task may require remembering the current visibility, position, and opacity of all layers in the document so that it can restore these properties before it finishes execution.

Once you have identified these elements, you can begin writing the functions necessary to accomplish each step. Try to write each step so that it can act independently of the other steps in the script. The task of remembering the state of all layers can stand on its own. If written in the right way, the code to accomplish this task will do only that; create a data structure containing the position, visibility, and opacity of every layer.

As you write scripts and encounter new situations for which you do not have a ready solution, you can save the new components and add them to your code library. When writing new functions to add to your library, it is often helpful to establish a general methodology for defining your components. Think of different functions as being members of certain classes,

all of which share ideas about how to use the class. One class, for example, may be loop functions — functions that perform a specific set of actions on a collection of objects. You can create members of this class functions that act on every open document, every layer, every text item, or every page element. Creating a general framework for understanding the requirements of each class of action helps you create script components that are consistent and easy to implement in future scripts.

As you become a more experienced and agile scripter, you can begin to organize these snippets into objects; see Chapter 2 for more information on creating objects, properties, and methods. Organizing your code into an *object-oriented* design greatly enhances your ability to quickly and easily write scripts. Imagine if one of the built-in objects like the `String` object was not a consolidated object, but instead simply a number of seemingly unrelated functions. To continue with the layer states example, you can create an object with a number of methods to generate and manipulate the layer states data. You can use one method to collect and store the information, and use yet another to restore the layers to their saved state.

Batch processing scripts can take particular advantage of modular coding techniques. Many of the key elements of a batch processing script lend themselves to reusable design. For example, all batch processing scripts involve performing the same action or set of actions on a number of objects, whether they are layers, groups, path items, documents, files, or folders.

BATCH PROCESSING

The power of scripting Photoshop and Illustrator is that you can automate repetitive tasks to get work done faster. Many of the tasks that you perform using JavaScript with both Photoshop and Illustrator consist of a series of specific actions that you apply to a number of objects. For example, a script may export every layer in a document to a file in a specific format. You can break down the steps of this script into doing something to each layer, creating an export object, and exporting the document to a file using the export object. Each of these steps is so common that you quite likely need to perform a similar task again and again. When writing the script, you can think specifically of the task at hand and achieve the required goals, or you can break the script into its component parts and write functions to handle each of these specific actions. Perhaps one function performs a specified action on each layer, another creates an export object with the properties you need, and yet another saves the exported document to a specific location on the hard drive.

If you are familiar with AppleScript on the Macintosh, or Visual Basic on Windows, you can use these languages together with JavaScript to modify documents using information from other applications or Web sites. Both of these languages can access information on the Internet and control and retrieve data from other applications. You can then trigger your JavaScript and use the information from these other sources. When a JavaScript is run using AppleScript or Visual Basic, you can pass parameters to the script and access their values using the `Application.arguments` array. See the Photoshop and Illustrator Scripting Reference for more information on running JavaScripts with AppleScript and Visual Basic.

COMMENTS AND DOCUMENTATION

The most difficult part of creating a useful code library is breaking down the steps in a script and translating them into reusable functions. Often an older component does not exactly fit the needs of the new situation. Commenting and documenting your scripts makes it easier to tailor older code components to meet the new requirements. This is especially important when writing scripts that perform a number of complex actions, or gather information from external sources such as a text file. If your script uses an external text file as a source of data, you must include a description of the format in the comments of the script. It is also a good idea to highlight any special conditions that you must have in place for a script to run successfully.

It is a good practice to add comments to each function so that it is clear how a user can utilize the function. You can include a description of what the function does, the types of parameters the function expects, and how the function uses each parameter. For example, if a function expects a document reference, and an array of strings as the two parameters, you should explain this in the function comments. Also, if your function returns a value, you should explain the type of the returned value. See Chapter 2 for more information on how to create comments and document your scripts.

BATCH PROCESS OPEN DOCUMENTS

Y ou can perform the same action on every open document in Photoshop and Illustrator. The first step to creating a code library for batch processing in Photoshop and Illustrator is to make a useful general-purpose function for executing a specified action on every open document. You can easily modify this function to work on layers, art objects, text items, or any other set of items you may need.

Functions in JavaScript are considered a special type of variable. This means that you can copy functions much like you copy a normal variable, simply by setting one variable equal to another. To call a function, you place a set of parentheses after the variable name, with or without parameters. To copy a function, you set a variable equal to the name of another variable without placing the parentheses at the end of the variable name. If you include

the parentheses, you are setting the variable to the return value of the function. See Chapter 2 for more information on creating and calling a function as well as returning values from a function.

A consequence of treating functions like variables is that you can pass a function name as a parameter to another function. Then inside the function receiving the call, you can execute the passed function using the parameter name with parentheses. Passing functions to other functions allows you to write more dynamic scripts.

You can pass a function to the looping functions that you often use in batch processing. This essentially performs as the action on each item in the collection through which you are looping. By changing the "action" function, you can quickly and easily change the behavior of the script.

BATCH PROCESS OPEN DOCUMENTS

```
é BBEdit  File  Edit  Text  Font  Search  Tools  Markup  Window  #!  é  Help
000                    02 loopdocuments.js
function allDocuments(action) {
    for (i=(documents.length - 1); i>=0; i--) {
        activeDocument = documents[i];
        action(activeDocument);
    }
}
```

```
é BBEdit  File  Edit  Text  Font  Search  Tools  Markup  Window  #!  é  Help
000                    02 loopdocuments.js
function allDocuments(action) {
    for (i=(documents.length - 1); i>=0; i--) {
        activeDocument = documents[i];
        action(activeDocument);
    }
}

function savePDF(doc) {
    var PDF = new PDFSaveOptions();
    PDF.preserveEditability = true;
    PDF.embedAllFonts = true;
}
```

1 Create a new function that accepts one parameter for a function reference.

2 Create a `for` loop by typing **for (i=(documents. length - 1); i>=0; i--) {**.

3 Set **activeDocument** equal to **documents[i];**.

4 Type the name of the parameter followed by **(activeDocument);**.

5 Create a new function that accepts one parameter for a document reference.

6 Create a save options object for the format to which you want to export.

7 Set the options for the save options object.

Extra

When looping through documents, you should write your `for` loop to start at the last document and count down, as opposed to a common `for` loop that counts up. This way, if you have closed documents during the loop, the loop does not exit prematurely. Similarly, if you are adding documents during the course of the loop, you should not use the `documents.length` parameter in the looping condition. Each time you add a document, this value changes and your loop will continue forever. You can prevent this by setting a variable equal to `documents.length` and using the variable in the condition.

Many of the scripts in earlier chapters start by setting a variable equal to the active document, and then use this reference variable in the script actions. This makes it easy to turn older scripts into functions that can act on any document. By placing the script in a function body and making the name of the active document reference a parameter, the script becomes a function that acts on whatever document reference the function is passed.

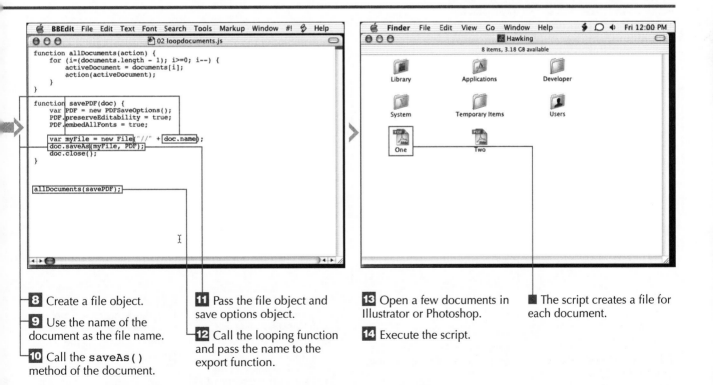

8 Create a file object.

9 Use the name of the document as the file name.

10 Call the `saveAs()` method of the document.

11 Pass the file object and save options object.

12 Call the looping function and pass the name to the export function.

13 Open a few documents in Illustrator or Photoshop.

14 Execute the script.

■ The script creates a file for each document.

BATCH PROCESS A DIRECTORY TREE

You perform an action on every file in a directory. You can use a simple recursive function to retrieve a reference to every file — even those nested in other directories. Using recursion allows you to traverse a directory of any depth with any number of files. Traversing a file structure is a great way to use Photoshop and Illustrator to automate repetitive tasks because it performs operations on a large number of files.

A *recursive* function is one that calls itself during its operation. Recursion offers a type of looping mechanism that can operate on a wider range of structures. When a directory contains other directories, which can in turn contain more directories, a simple loop can only access a single level of elements, such as the top level of folders and files. This greatly reduces the usefulness of a simple loop for more complex multidimensional data structures.

With the example of a directory, a recursive function begins by looping through the first level of files and folders in the directory. You specify the directory through which you loop as a parameter to the function. The function tests each item in the directory to see if it is a file or folder. If it is a folder, the function calls itself and passes the folder as the parameter.

Whenever you use a recursive function you should be aware of the type of data with which you are dealing. If you attempt to traverse a very large directory structure, there is a good chance your script will take a very long time to run, particularly when executing complex actions on each file. You may consider using an alert to communicate to the user that the script could take a long time to execute if the directory is very large.

BATCH PROCESS A DIRECTORY TREE

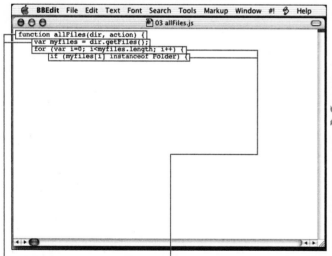

1 Create a new function that accepts two parameters, one for a **Folder** object, one for a function reference.

2 Set a variable to the name of the folder reference, and then type **.getFiles();**.

3 Create a **for** loop to loop through the array.

4 Type **if (myfiles[i] instanceof Folder) {** replacing **myfiles** with your file array.

5 If the condition is **true**, type the function name then type **(new Folder(myfiles[i].fsName), action)**, replacing **action** with the name of the function parameter and **myfiles** with the name of the file array.

6 If the condition is **false**, type the name of the function parameter and pass this item in the files array as the parameter.

Apply It

You can access the current filename and path of each processed file to mirror the directory structure in another location. When batch processing files, you may find it useful to have your script create a mirror of the source directory to place the exported files.

TYPE THIS:

```
function mirrorDir(dir, dest) {
  var myfiles = dir.getFiles();
  var i=0;
  while (i<myfiles.length) {
    if (myfiles[i] instanceof Folder) {
      var newfolder = new Folder(dest.path + "/" + myfiles[i].name + "/");
      newfolder.create();
      mirrorDir(new Folder(myfiles[i].fsName), newfolder);
    }
    i++;
  }
}
```

RESULT:

This function copies the entire directory structure under the directory object passed as the first parameter into the directory object passed as the second parameter.

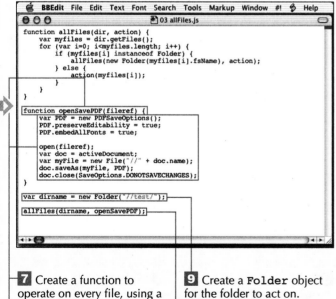

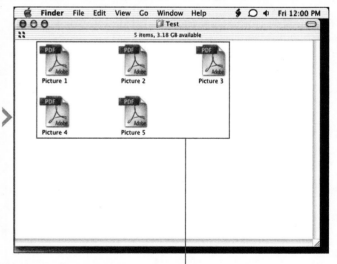

7 Create a function to operate on every file, using a single parameter for the file reference.

8 Type code to open and manipulate the file for the function body.

9 Create a **Folder** object for the folder to act on.

10 Call the looping function and pass the **Folder** object, **action** function.

11 Execute the script in Photoshop or Illustrator.

■ The script performs the action on every file in the folder.

REMOVE UNUSED SYMBOLS, SWATCHES, AND STYLES IN ILLUSTRATOR

You can reduce the size of Illustrator documents by removing unused styles, swatches, brushes, and symbols. All new documents that you create in Illustrator have a default set of swatches, styles, and symbols. This excess information can greatly increase the size of your Illustrator documents. A handy use for a script is to remove all unused instances of these objects and thus reduce the size of the file. This can make sharing the file with co-workers easier and save you time when you need to open or save the file.

Around 140K of each Illustrator document consists of the default objects automatically added to every new Illustrator file. Of course, it is important to only remove unused copies of these objects because the loss of something that your document actually uses can severely impact your artwork. Also keep in mind that symbols can help reduce the overall

file size when you use them properly. Symbols can make your documents easier to manage and modify because they tie multiple instances of an art object to the same master version. To learn how to easily change the entire look and feel of a document simply by changing a single symbol in Illustrator, see Chapter 5.

There is no easy way to retrieve a complete list of currently used symbols, brushes, and so on, in a document. To determine which are in use, you need to loop through every element in the document, and keep track of which, if any, are in use. You can then use this information to remove the appropriate element from its corresponding collection. By making a function to remove each item separately, you can choose to only use what you need given a certain situation.

REMOVE UNUSED SYMBOLS, SWATCHES, AND STYLES IN ILLUSTRATOR

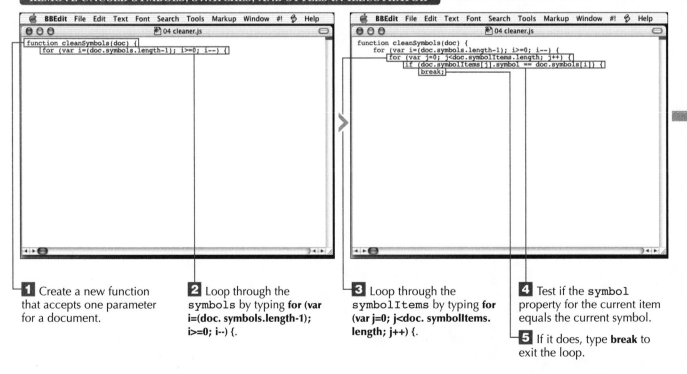

1 Create a new function that accepts one parameter for a document.

2 Loop through the **symbols** by typing **for (var i=(doc. symbols.length-1); i>=0; i--) {**.

3 Loop through the **symbolItems** by typing **for (var j=0; j<doc. symbolItems. length; j++) {**.

4 Test if the **symbol** property for the current item equals the current symbol.

5 If it does, type **break** to exit the loop.

Extra

You can use the same method for removing symbols to remove styles and swatches. You can combine the functions for removing unused swatches, styles, and symbols using the steps in either the section "Batch Process Open Documents" or the section "Batch Process a Directory Tree" to quickly process a large number of files. This sort of cleaning is a good idea for getting documents as small as possible at the end of a project and is ideal for archiving or delivery. Create a single master function that calls each individual "cleaning" function you want to run, and use this as the action for the looping functions.

Using symbols in a document can greatly slow down the amount of time it takes Illustrator to save and manipulate documents. One way to work around this is to resave your document and uncheck the Create PDF Compatible File option in the Illustrator save options dialog box. You can also set this property using the `pdfCompatibility` property of the Illustrator Save Options object. See Chapter 8 for more information on saving with Illustrator.

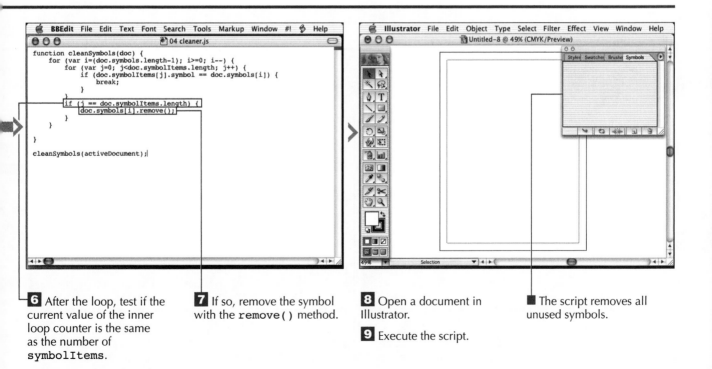

```
function cleanSymbols(doc) {
    for (var i=(doc.symbols.length-1); i>=0; i--) {
        for (var j=0; j<doc.symbolItems.length; j++) {
            if (doc.symbolItems[j].symbol == doc.symbols[i]) {
                break;
            }
        }
        if (j == doc.symbolItems.length) {
            doc.symbols[i].remove();
        }
    }
}

cleanSymbols(activeDocument);
```

6 After the loop, test if the current value of the inner loop counter is the same as the number of `symbolItems`.

7 If so, remove the symbol with the `remove()` method.

8 Open a document in Illustrator.

9 Execute the script.

■ The script removes all unused symbols.

CREATE PATTERNS USING MATH IN ILLUSTRATOR

You can use JavaScript with Illustrator to create patterns and shapes using math. You can generate some wonderful patterns using mathematical equations, which are far too tedious to create by hand. Scripting is a great way to generate these patterns and save time.

First you must find an equation that lends itself to the generation of patterns. The world of geometry is filled with equations that describe beautiful figures, including physics equations that determine the motion of objects. Some of the more interesting patterns are related to the "Golden Ratio" and Fibonacci numbers. The Golden Ratio, used to illustrate the steps in this section, is a number that you often find in the design of natural objects and animals. The most famous examples are the shell of a snail and the pattern made by the position of seed pods in the center of a sunflower. There are a number of wonderful resources of interesting mathematical patterns and equations through search engines such as google.com.

Once you find an equation, it is normally an easy process to convert it into JavaScript syntax. You may need to use mathematical functions like sine, cosine, tangent, and square root. JavaScript's `Math` object provides access to many useful mathematical functions. All of the basic trigonometry functions are available including `Math.sin()`, `Math.cos()`, and `Math.tan()`. A good JavaScript reference contains a complete description of the `Math` object and its methods.

When translating a mathematical pattern to JavaScript, there are many different ways to use the information generated by the equation. What the equation gives you will often be simply a number, or perhaps an x and y coordinate. Even if the initial algorithm does provide a specific type of data, points to draw for example, you can experiment with how you use the values and create some truly wonderful effects.

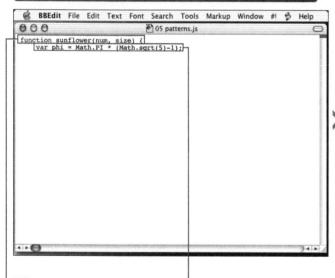

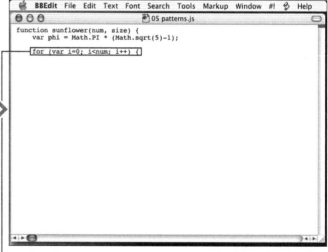

1 Create a new function to generate the pattern.

2 Determine the variables of the equation and define them as parameters.

3 Create a loop to generate a series of values for the pattern.

Note: Many patterns require the use of a loop to generate a series of values from the equation.

Extra

You can make other interesting patterns using the sunflower algorithm — the example for this section — by thinking of new ways to use the generated points. One way is to connect the points to each other in a series, to create a star-like pattern, or perhaps connect every point to every other point to make a complex weave pattern. You can also use the numbers generated for other values, for example, setting the transparency or scale of an object depending on its position in the list of points.

When using mathematical equations to generate patterns or create animations, it is a good idea to play around with the results and experiment with the numbers the equations are generating. You may encounter an equation in one context that creates a very specific type of pattern, and through experimentation discover that is has desirable effects when put to a different purpose.

Another modification you can make on this script is to use the coordinates to set the position of a symbol from the Symbols palette. Placing a symbol for each item keeps down the size of your file and makes it easy to change the repeated item.

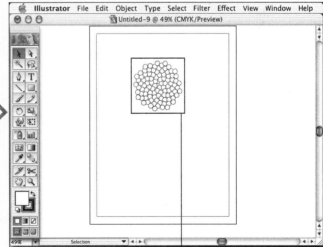

4 Set any variables necessary to calculate the values of the equation.

■ This example uses the value of "The Golden Angle."

■ You can add comments to the script to remind you of the reason for otherwise difficult to understand calculations.

5 Call the function.

6 Open a document in Illustrator.

7 Execute the script.

■ The script creates a pattern.

CREATE A REPORT OF ALL FONTS IN AN ILLUSTRATOR DOCUMENT

You can quickly create a useful report listing all fonts that you use in a document. Font reports are very useful when preparing files to send to a printer or client, or even when sharing documents in the office. Although you may find it difficult to manually keep track of every typeface you use in a project, using scripts to generate reports saves you time and effort.

There are a few ways to create the final product when writing a script to generate a report. One option is to create the report as a text file and use the file system functions to save the file to a disk. See Chapter 8 for more on creating files with JavaScript. The other option is to create the report directly in Illustrator itself. You can open a new document and create text items and add the outcome of the report to the document.

Each method offers different advantages. Writing to a text file is simple and provides for almost universal compatibility. It is safe to assume that everyone to whom you send a text file can open the file and read it. Using Illustrator allows you more creative freedom with typography and layout. You can even create a template document and use your script to fill in the values. Generating the report with Illustrator may limit the number of people that can read the file. An alternative involves exporting the document as a PDF or image file, both of which allow nearly anyone to read the file.

The same basic ideas that apply to creating a font report with Illustrator also work with Photoshop; see p. 94–95 for more information on how to access font names in Photoshop.

CREATE A REPORT OF ALL FONTS IN AN ILLUSTRATOR DOCUMENT

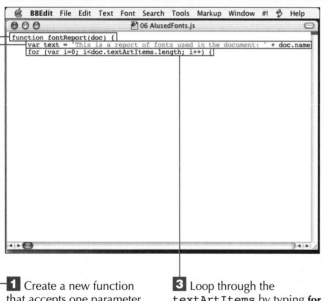

```
function fontReport(doc) {
    var text = "This is a report of fonts used in the document: " + doc.name
    for (var i=0; i<doc.textArtItems.length; i++) {
```

1 Create a new function that accepts one parameter for a document.

2 Create a variable for the results and set it equal to some header text.

3 Loop through the textArtItems by typing **for (var i=0; i<doc.textArtItems. length; i++) {**.

```
function fontReport(doc) {
    var text = "This is a report of fonts used in the document: " + doc.name
    for (var i=0; i<doc.textArtItems.length; i++) {
        var range = doc.textArtItems[i].textRange();
        for (var j=0; j<range.characters.length; j++) {
            if (text.indexOf(range.characters[j].font) < 0) {
```

4 Set a variable equal to the textrange( ) for this text item.

5 Loop through the range.characters by typing **for (var j=0; j<range. characters.length; j++) {**.

6 Test if the results variable contains the name of this character's font.

Apply It

You can alphabetize the list of used fonts in font report. Rather than use a string to store a list of font names, you can add each unique font name to an array. You then use the `Array.sort()` method to place the list in alphabetical order. Finally, you use the `Array.join()` method to change the array into a string for output to Illustrator or a text file. See Chapter 2 for more on arrays.

TYPE THIS:

```
var fontnames = new Array();
for (var i=0; i<doc.textArtItems.length; i++) {
  var range = doc.textArtItems[i].textRange();
  fontnames.push(range.font);
}
fontnames.sort();
var text = fontnames.join("\r");
```

RESULT:

This script creates an alphabetically sorted array of the names of fonts used in the document. The text variable is set to the names of these fonts separated by a return character.

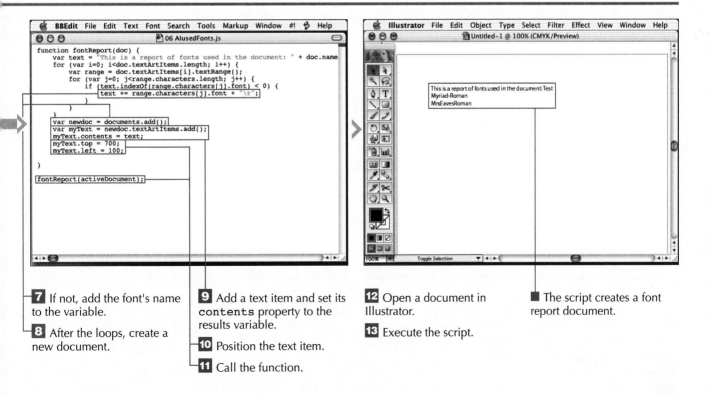

7 If not, add the font's name to the variable.

8 After the loops, create a new document.

9 Add a text item and set its **contents** property to the results variable.

10 Position the text item.

11 Call the function.

12 Open a document in Illustrator.

13 Execute the script.

■ The script creates a font report document.

CREATE A REPORT OF ALL LINKED FILES IN AN ILLUSTRATOR DOCUMENT

Y ou can use scripting to help you bundle documents and assets together for delivery to a client or press. Illustrator supports the use of linked files. You may find it a hassle to make sure that you have collected all necessary image files for a project before sending the project off. Generating a linked file report helps you make sure that you have every file.

When you use the File ➪ Place menu path to insert a vector or bitmap image into an Illustrator document, the placed file does not necessarily embed into the Illustrator document. It is easier to make changes to external image files without the hassle of re-importing the file after you edit it. However, if the Illustrator document and external files are separated, Illustrator cannot locate them and the images may not appear in the document.

You can view linked files in Illustrator using the Links palette. Although all linked files appear in this palette, when using JavaScript, vector art files and bitmap art files are treated differently and are members of different collections. See Chapter 8 for more information on embedding images with JavaScript.

When creating a linked file report, be sure to include the contents of both the `document.placedItems` and `document.rasterItems` collections.

When creating a report, you should take into consideration what type of report file you want to create. See the section "Create a Report of All Fonts in an Illustrator Document" for more information on the differences and advantages of Illustrator versus text file reports. Keeping a separate function for creating an Illustrator or text file report is a great way to keep your script modular and reusable.

CREATE A REPORT OF ALL LINKED FILES IN AN ILLUSTRATOR DOCUMENT

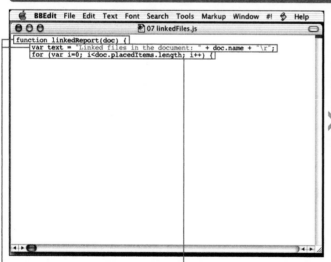

1 Create a new function that accepts one parameter for a document.

2 Create a variable for the results and set it equal to some header text.

3 Loop through the **placedItems** by typing **for (var i=0; i<doc.placedItems. length; i++) {**.

4 Add the filesystem name of the **file** property of the current placed item to the result text.

5 Loop through the **rasterItems** by typing **for (var i=0; i<doc.rasterItems. length; i++) {**.

6 Add the filesystem name of the **file** property of the current raster item to the result text.

Extra

You can modify the script in this section to package required files together for delivery. A useful, and complex, script can collect almost all required files for an Illustrator document. The first step is to save a copy of the Illustrator document. Next, you should create a folder for linked files in the same location as the copy of the document. See Chapter 8 for more information on saving files and creating folders. When you create the folder, you should obtain a list of all linked files and copy them to the new directory. Now that you have the linked files copied to the new location, you must update the Illustrator document so that the placed items are associated with the files in the new location. The fonts in the document are the only remaining element to deliver the file. You can create a font report to help you find the necessary font file. See the section "Create a Report of All Fonts in an Illustrator Document" for more information.

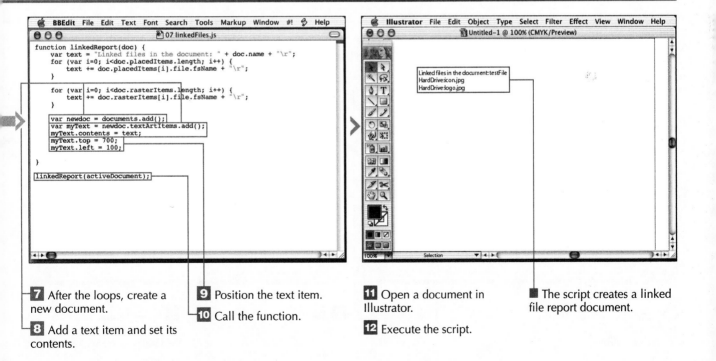

7 After the loops, create a new document.

8 Add a text item and set its contents.

9 Position the text item.

10 Call the function.

11 Open a document in Illustrator.

12 Execute the script.

■ The script creates a linked file report document.

EXPORT FILES FROM DATASETS IN ILLUSTRATOR

Datasets are a powerful way to access the content of your documents and create dynamic designs. As seen in Chapter 9, you can use Illustrator variables and datasets with JavaScript to connect your designs to external data sources. This makes it easy to create a number of different versions of the same design for different purposes or locations.

You can use Illustrator variables to control text items, placed images, graph data, or the visibility of page items. You can then capture the state of all variables in a document into a dataset. A document can contain multiple datasets, with each dataset representing different values for the content of the document.

Datasets allow you to create dynamic documents, documents with a separation between the design and the content. You can use scripting and datasets to easily flow different

content into the same design. Once you configure a document to use variables and datasets to define the contents of a document, you can use JavaScript to cycle through the available datasets and export a new file for each one.

Because a variable library is an XML file, you can couple Illustrator variables and datasets with other programming languages to create truly dynamic documents that retrieve their data from databases or even Web sites. A great way to use datasets with an external data source is to generate an XML file populated with data from an address book or database containing personnel information. You can then use the generated variable library file to create a sheet of mailing labels or business cards for each person. See p. 140–141 for a description of the parts of an Illustrator variable library and how to edit a variable library by hand.

EXPORT FILES FROM DATASETS IN ILLUSTRATOR

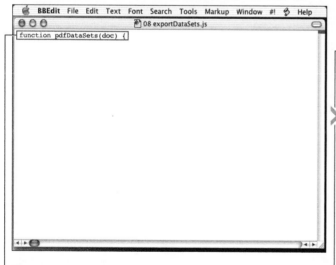

1 Create a new function that accepts one parameter for a document.

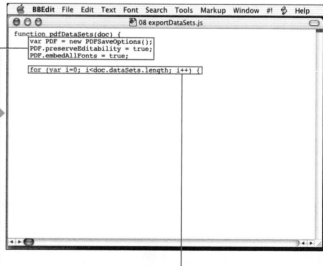

2 Create an export options object.

3 Loop through the **datasets** by typing **for (var i=0; i<doc.dataSets.length; i++).**

Extra

The script illustrated in this section is great for creating title images for a Web site. You can store the values for the titles in the datasets and export them. This makes it easy to change the font or size without creating a lot of extra work updating each image. You can also use visibility variables to export images with a watermark and copyright information overlaid on the image.

You can use hidden or off-screen text items to store additional information about the dataset that you might not need as part of the design. For example, you may want to store the path or filename where you want to export this particular dataset. You can access the value of this variable and use the information it contains to create the export file.

You can also use text areas, variables, and datasets to hold additional information about the current dataset. This serves as a dataset-based metadata, much like the document metadata in Photoshop. See Chapter 3 for more information on Photoshop's document meta-data.

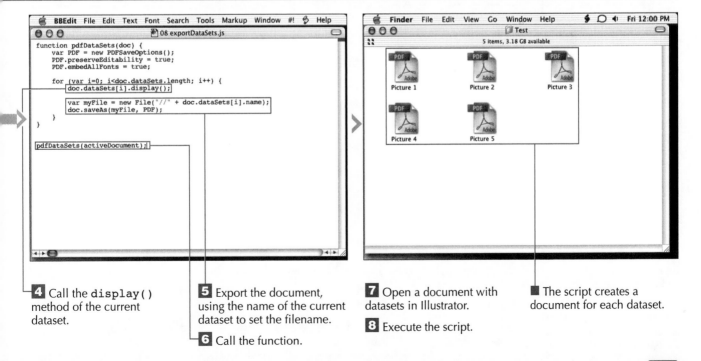

4 Call the `display()` method of the current dataset.

5 Export the document, using the name of the current dataset to set the filename.

6 Call the function.

7 Open a document with datasets in Illustrator.

8 Execute the script.

■ The script creates a document for each dataset.

CREATE MAILING LABELS FROM A TEXT FILE IN ILLUSTRATOR

You can use JavaScript and Illustrator to automate repetitive tasks. You can make common tasks, like generating a sheet of custom designed mailing labels, simpler using Illustrator scripting. You can separate the content of the labels from the design. This makes new labels easier to create and allows other people not as familiar with Illustrator to easily edit and generate their own labels.

The JavaScript file system functions and objects available with Photoshop and Illustrator can open and read the contents of files. Once you have the files open, the JavaScript string method can read the files as a string and manipulate them. See p. 118 for more information on opening text files with JavaScript. The String object has a number of methods that are useful for parsing and interpreting strings of text. See Chapter 2 for more on string functions.

When organizing a text file to use as the source of data, it is important to determine how your script will know where one piece of data ends and another begins. You commonly use a delimiter to make the boundaries between individual pieces of data in a file. You can use multiple delimiters to further subdivide the information.

Once you establish how to format the data, you can create the source file for the operation. This file may serve as an example to people using your script in the future. It is a good idea to use comments in your script to document the correct format for the data source file. You may even want to include a copy of a portion of the source file, surrounded by multi-line comments, at the top of the script itself. That way a quick example of the source file format travels with the script and cannot get lost.

CREATE MAILING LABELS FROM A TEXT FILE IN ILLUSTRATOR

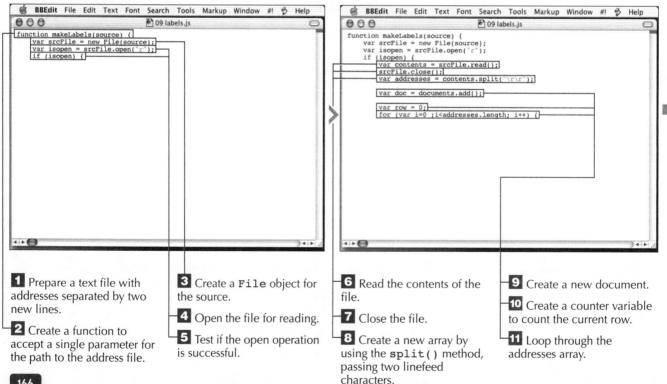

1 Prepare a text file with addresses separated by two new lines.

2 Create a function to accept a single parameter for the path to the address file.

3 Create a `File` object for the source.

4 Open the file for reading.

5 Test if the open operation is successful.

6 Read the contents of the file.

7 Close the file.

8 Create a new array by using the `split()` method, passing two linefeed characters.

9 Create a new document.

10 Create a counter variable to count the current row.

11 Loop through the addresses array.

Extra

The script in this section makes use of the modulo operator (%). The modulo operator returns the remainder from a division operation. For example, ⅔ leaves a remainder of 2. Do not confuse the remainder with part of a division after the decimal point. You use the modulo to determine if a number is even or odd. An even number always divide by 2 without a remainder. This means that `x%2 == 0` is `true` when x is an even number. The modulo is also useful when working with information that needs to appear in rows and looping over values. If the remainder of the current item number and the total number of items in a row equals 0, then you can move on to the next row.

The best way to establish the position of repeated items on the page is to set a variable for the distance between each item. Then, when looping through the data and adding a new object on each pass, you can calculate the position of the current object by multiplying the current value of the loop counter by the spacing variable. For example, a spacing value of 5 places items at 0, 5, 10, 15... until the end of the loop.

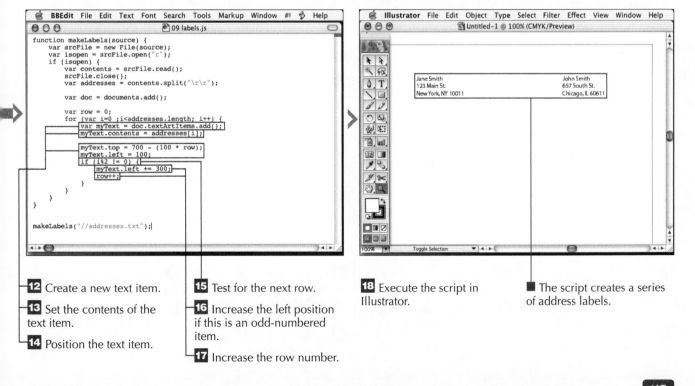

```
function makeLabels(source) {
    var srcFile = new File(source);
    var isopen = srcFile.open("r");
    if (isopen) {
        var contents = srcFile.read();
        srcFile.close();
        var addresses = contents.split("\r\r");

        var doc = documents.add();

        var row = 0;
        for (var i=0 ;i<addresses.length; i++) {
            var myText = doc.textArtItems.add();
            myText.contents = addresses[i];

            myText.top = 700 - (100 * row);
            myText.left = 100;
            if (i%2 != 0) {
                myText.left += 300;
                row++;
            }
        }
    }
}

makeLabels("//addresses.txt");
```

12 Create a new text item.

13 Set the contents of the text item.

14 Position the text item.

15 Test for the next row.

16 Increase the left position if this is an odd-numbered item.

17 Increase the row number.

18 Execute the script in Illustrator.

■ The script creates a series of address labels.

EXPORT ALL VISIBLE LAYERS IN PHOTOSHOP

Y ou can use JavaScript to quickly export only visible layers from a Photoshop document, and thus keep related images together. You can keep a number of images that you want to export individually, for use on a Web site for example, in a single file. Then, when you need to apply a filter, or crop or resize them all, you can save time by making changes to a single file.

Photoshop layers and layer sets are an indispensable tool for creating exciting designs. You can use them to organize a document into different views. When creating different compositions for a design piece, you can place the parts for each composition in a different layer set, and place the shared components in a separate layer set. See Chapter 4 for more information on working with layers in Photoshop. You can then quickly export the compositions and show

them to a client. You do this by writing a JavaScript to toggle the visibility of each layer set and to export the document as an image or PDF. See Chapter 10 for scripts and information on exporting a document from Photoshop.

When writing a script that has a potentially harmful effect on the document, such as changing the visibility of layers, you should take time to save the current state of the document before the script executes. That way, after the script completes its work, you can restore the document to the way it was before you ran the script. Imagine a large document with a number of layers, very carefully setup to show only what a user needs. Then a script runs and the visibility of all layers, except for one, turns off. It can take a very long time to determine which layers were visible and which were hidden before the script ran and restore them by hand.

EXPORT ALL VISIBLE LAYERS IN PHOTOSHOP

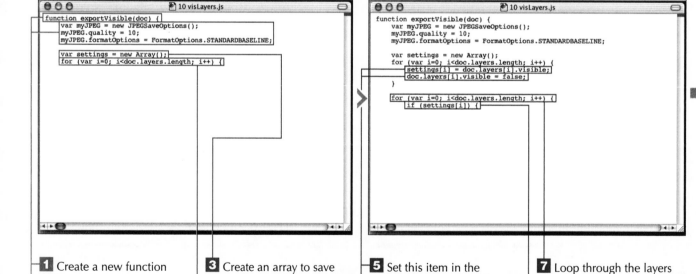

1 Create a new function that accepts one parameter for a document.

2 Create a save options object.

3 Create an array to save the current visibility values.

4 Type **for (var i=0; i<doc. layers.length; i++){**.

5 Set this item in the settings array equal to the value of the visible property for this layer.

6 Set the layer visibility equal to **false**.

7 Loop through the layers again as in step 4.

8 Test if this value in the settings array is **true**.

Extra

You can modify the script in this section to export according to layer sets. Organizing your document into layer sets gives you more control over the layout and keeps your designs easy to modify. To use layer sets instead of layers, replace all instances of `layers` with `layerSets`. This revised script loops through and manipulates only layer sets. See Chapter 4 for more information on layer sets.

You can also adapt this script to work with Illustrator. Keep in mind that the structure of layers in Illustrator can be more complex than Photoshop because every object is on a sub-layer that has its own visible property. Illustrator also has more ways in which to organize art and text in the document. You can easily modify this script to work not only on layers, but also on sub-layers or groups. See Chapter 2 for more information on layers, and Chapter 5 for information on using groups in Illustrator.

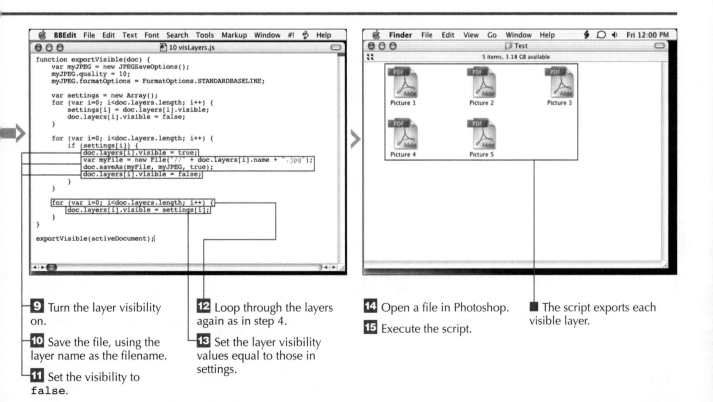

9 Turn the layer visibility on.

10 Save the file, using the layer name as the filename.

11 Set the visibility to `false`.

12 Loop through the layers again as in step 4.

13 Set the layer visibility values equal to those in settings.

14 Open a file in Photoshop.

15 Execute the script.

■ The script exports each visible layer.

CHANGE EVERY FONT IN A PHOTOSHOP DOCUMENT

You can change the font, size, and weight of every text item in a Photoshop document with JavaScript. Sometimes it is necessary to change the type properties of a large number of text items in a document. You may find it much faster and more efficient to use a script rather than to hunt, click, select, and then choose the correct typeface, and so on, from the Character or Paragraph palettes.

Much like the function you use to generate a font report in Illustrator, modifying the font information in a document requires you to loop through every text item in a document and modify that item's properties. See the section "Create a Report of All Fonts in an Illustrator Document" for more on generating a font report. However, the process of doing this in Photoshop is slightly different. In contrast to Illustrator, text in Photoshop exists as a special type of artLayer.

This means that to find all of the text items in a document, you must check every artLayer in a document to see if its kind property is set to LayerKind.TEXT.

Things get more complicated when the document contains layer sets that in turn contain text layers. The artLayers property of the document object only contains a reference to the art layers that are not in a layer set. To access every text item in a document, you can use a recursive function that loops through the layers collection, and calls itself when it finds a layerSet object, and performs some other action when the layer contains text.

For more information on using recursive functions, see the section "Batch Process a Directory Tree in Photoshop and Illustrator" in this chapter, and p. 28–29 in Chapter 2.

see the section "Batch Process a Directory Tree in Photoshop and Illustrator" in this chapter, and p. 28–29 in Chapter 2.

CHANGE EVERY FONT IN A PHOTOSHOP DOCUMENT

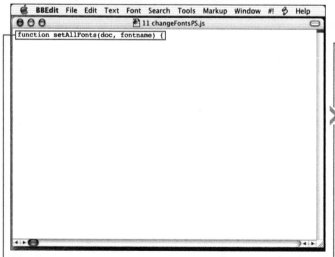

1 Create a new function that accepts two parameters, one for a document and one for the font name.

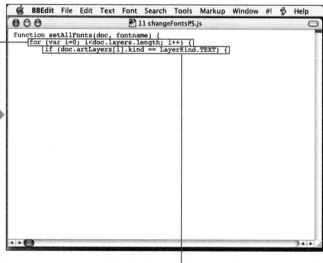

2 Type **for (var i=0; i<doc.layers.length; i++){.**

3 Test if the current layer is a text layer.

Apply It

You can modify the font changing script to only change text items that have specific properties. For example, you can find every text item in a document that uses a specific font and change the font size and weight only for those items. You can also limit your changes to text items that are over a certain size. In this way you can fake text style classes. A script like this might have the effect of only changing text items that you use as the titles or headers in a document.

TYPE THIS:

```
function setLargeFonts(doc, 60, fontname) {
  for (var i=0; i<doc.layers.length; i++) {
    if (doc.artLayers[i].kind == LayerKind.TEXT) {
      if (doc.artLayers[i].textItem.size >= 60) {
        doc.artLayers[i].textItem.font = fontname;
      }
    }
  }
}
setLargeFonts(activeDocument, 60, "ArialMT");
```

RESULT:

This script sets the font of every text item in a Photoshop document with a size larger than 60 to ArialMT.

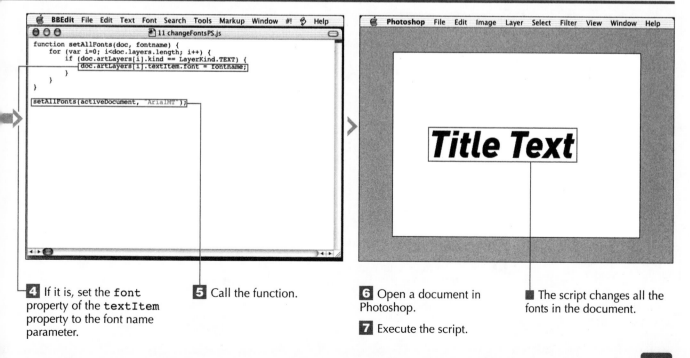

4 If it is, set the `font` property of the `textItem` property to the font name parameter.

5 Call the function.

6 Open a document in Photoshop.

7 Execute the script.

■ The script changes all the fonts in the document.

CREATE AN HTML GALLERY IN PHOTOSHOP

You can use Photoshop and JavaScript to dynamically generate an HTML gallery for use on the Web. HTML galleries are great ways to quickly display a large number of images. You can use them for everything from showing design ideas to a client, to sharing digital vacation pictures with your family.

One way to generate an HTML gallery is to use a text file to define the title, description, and image file for each image you want to appear in the gallery. Your script can parse the text file for the image information, then open and export the image along with some HTML for each image. The main drawback of this method is that it requires a good deal of work and coding to make a file format that is not too difficult for your script to read and understand, while remaining easy enough for a user to edit.

Another option is to organize the files you want to include in a directory, and use the method like the one described in the section "Batch Process a Directory Tree in Photoshop

and Illustrator" to access each image in the directory. Once you know your files, you can label each image with its filename and create a simple proof sheet.

You can improve on this by using the document metadata to generate the description and title for each image. You can access the document metadata using the File ⇨ File Info menu path in Photoshop. For more information on accessing the document metadata in Photoshop, see Chapter 3.

The script in this section does require a limited knowledge of HTML to generate the main page of the gallery. Explanation of the required HTML is beyond the scope of this book. A good resource book on HTML is *HTML: Your visual blueprint for designing effective Web pages*, 2000.

CREATE AN HTML GALLERY IN PHOTOSHOP

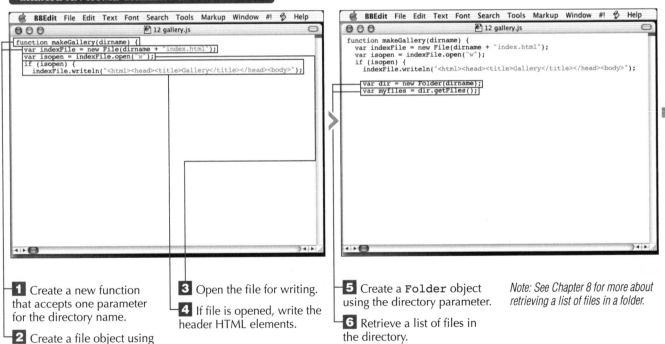

1 Create a new function that accepts one parameter for the directory name.

2 Create a file object using the directory parameter and `"index.html"`.

3 Open the file for writing.

4 If file is opened, write the header HTML elements.

5 Create a `Folder` object using the directory parameter.

6 Retrieve a list of files in the directory.

Note: See Chapter 8 for more about retrieving a list of files in a folder.

Extra

You can make the script in this section more advanced by creating a thumbnail for each image that links to another page showing a full size version of the image. The first step is to create a folder to place all the images and HTML in. Next, you need to open all of the images, save a copy to the new folder, resize them, and save the smaller thumbnails in the new folder. See Chapter 8 for more on saving a file. You can use Photoshop's `document.resizeImage()` method to resize a document. See Chapter 3 for more information on manipulating a document in Photoshop. Once you have copied the full size images to the new folder and created the thumbnail images, the final step is to create the HTML for each image. In addition to the image, you might want to include the filename and some of the file metadata in the HTML. See Chapter 3 for how to access the document metadata. The final step is to create the home page for the gallery. This gallery must include the thumbnails and links to each of the full size pages.

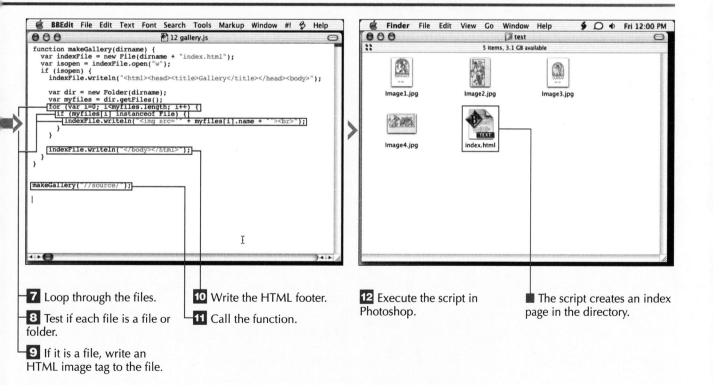

7 Loop through the files.

8 Test if each file is a file or folder.

9 If it is a file, write an HTML image tag to the file.

10 Write the HTML footer.

11 Call the function.

12 Execute the script in Photoshop.

■ The script creates an index page in the directory.

RESIZE ALL IMAGES IN A FOLDER WITH PHOTOSHOP

You can use Photoshop and JavaScript to resize and rename a large number of images. When doing work on the Web, you may find it often necessary to resize and export a large number of images — which is very tedious work. Scripting lets you automate the work and save time.

You can traverse a directory of files and folders using JavaScript. See the section "Batch Process a Directory Tree in Photoshop and Illustrator" for more information on how to use JavaScript to walk through a specified directory structure. As your script moves through the directory and files, it can open each file it encounters and modify it, eventually saving or exporting it to a new location.

One of the most useful actions to execute on a large number of files is to open, resize, and save each image. You may find this very useful for generating a thumbnail version

of images for display on the Web. You can also perform other manipulations to the images, including applying filters or color corrections to each image. Applying the same corrections is useful for adjusting a batch of digital photos all taken under similar conditions, or perhaps for giving an effect such as a sepia tone.

When using a script to traverse a directory structure, you should keep in mind that the script may take a very long time to execute. This is particularly true when working with a large number of files, or a deep directory structure with lots of subfolders. If a script runs for too long, or if you need to cancel the action, you can press command + . on a Mac, or Ctrl + . on a PC, to cancel execution of the script.

RESIZE ALL IMAGES IN A FOLDER WITH PHOTOSHOP

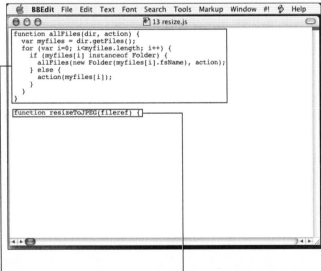

1 Insert the function to loop through files and folders.

Note: See the section "Batch Process a Directory Tree in Photoshop and Illustrator" for more on inserting this function.

2 Create a function to operate on every file using a single parameter for the file reference.

3 Create a save options object.

4 Open the file reference.

5 Call the `resizeImage()` method of the `activeDocument`, passing the current width and height multiplied by a scale factor.

Extra

While looping through the image files in a directory structure, you can add information to the images by editing the document metadata. Metadata is a great way to keep your images organized and easy to find. Many image management applications can access image metadata for searching images based on keywords and descriptions contained in the image file. Metadata is also handy because it is part of the image file, and therefore you are less likely to lose it. See Chapter 3 for more information on editing the document metadata in Photoshop.

You can also use metadata to create a credit watermark on images for use on the Web. While looping through the directory, you can extract copyright or creator information and create a text area on top of the image to show this information. Including a watermark on images destined for display on the Internet is a good idea. This makes it much more difficult for others users to utilize your work for a different purpose you do not intend.

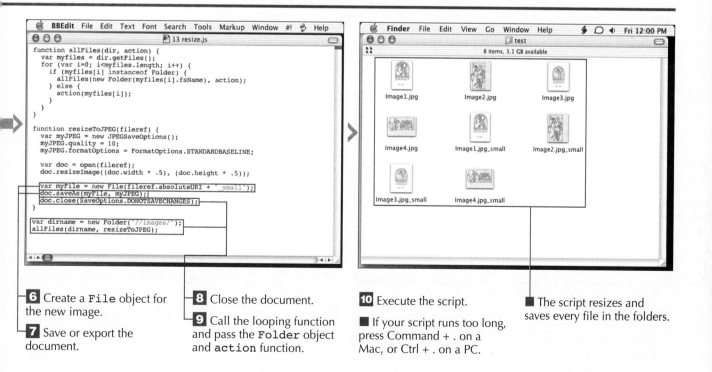

<6> Create a `File` object for the new image.

<7> Save or export the document.

<8> Close the document.

<9> Call the looping function and pass the `Folder` object and `action` function.

<10> Execute the script.

■ If your script runs too long, press Command + . on a Mac, or Ctrl + . on a PC.

■ The script resizes and saves every file in the folders.

RECORD SCRIPTS FOR PHOTOSHOP WITH THE SCRIPTING LISTENER PLUG-IN

You can access items not normally accessible with JavaScript in Photoshop by using the Scripting Listener plug-in. When you enable it, the Scripting Listener plug-in records every action the user takes. Then, when you quit Photoshop, the plug-in writes the results to a text file on the desktop.

The plug-in is part of the installer package that includes scripting support for Photoshop. See Chapter 1 for more information on obtaining and installing scripting support and the utilities that are included with the installer. To install the Scripting Listener plug-In, simply drop it in the Plug-Ins folder in the directory with Photoshop. Remember that running the Scripting Listener plug-in may cause Photoshop to run slower than normal. Also, the plug-in records every action you take and creates very large scripts. Consider not installing the plug-in for day-to-day use, but rather only when you need to record actions.

The Scripting Listener plug-in generates JavaScript code, but it does not look much like code that a person might write to produce similar actions. Nevertheless, you can use this code to design scripts and to build functions in order to execute actions that are otherwise unavailable to JavaScript.

Each action that a user takes with the plug-in installed writes to a file named ScriptingListenerJS.log on the desktop. The plug-in separates each step with comment lines:

```
//  =====================
```

These comments make it easier to locate the part of the script you need. To help you navigate the generated script, you must execute as few actions as possible and remember the steps you performed while recording. Once you locate the desired piece of the script, you can copy and paste it into another script.

RECORD SCRIPTS FOR PHOTOSHOP WITH THE SCRIPTING LISTENER PLUG-IN

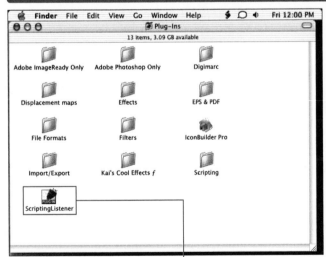

1 Close Photoshop.

2 Copy the ScriptingListener plug-in into the Photoshop Plug-Ins folder.

3 Open Photoshop and execute a few actions.

4 Keep track of what you do for reference.

Extra

The code generated by the Scripting Listener plug-in is very difficult to understand, even for an experienced scripter. There are no major resources online discussing this particular aspect of Photoshop scripting. However, there is very limited documentation on the objects, methods, and properties you see when using Scripting Listener code. The scripting support installer comes with some documentation on JavaScript for Photoshop; this includes the specific code that the Scripting Listener creates. Some of the objects in the code that the Scripting Listener creates include: `ActionDescriptor`, `ActionList`, and `ActionReference`. There are also some key functions like `stringIDToTypeID` and `executeAction` that are described in the section on the Application object.

If you find yourself relying heavily on generated code snippets, you might find it worthwhile to look a bit more closely at this documentation. You will become more familiar with generated code, and be better able to rewrite and modify it for your purposes.

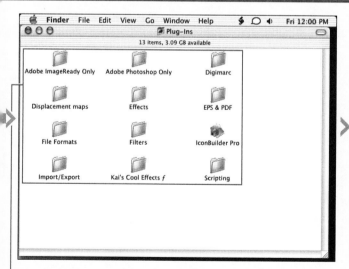

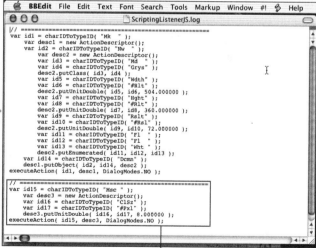

5 Quit Photoshop and remove the ScriptingListener plug-in for the Plug-Ins directory.

6 Open the ScriptingListenerJS.log file on the desktop.

■ The log displays the code for the actions you made in Photoshop.

7 Locate the code sections that correspond to the actions you took while recording.

MAKE SCRIPTING LISTENER CODE INTO FUNCTIONS FOR PHOTOSHOP

You can use the code that the Scripting Listener plug-in generates to create easy to use functions for scripting Photoshop. Although you may often find it difficult to read the code that the Scripting Listener plug-in creates, it is a useful tool for writing powerful scripts in Photoshop.

One of the most common uses for the Scripting Listener plug-in is to script third party plug-ins and filters. For example, you cannot normally access the Filter ⇨ Pixelate ⇨ Mosaic filter using JavaScript. You can use the Scripting Listener to generate the code to run the filter. By looking closely at the script that the Scripting Listener plug-in generates, you can create an easy to use function that provides access to the filter and the parameters the filter requires. See the section "Record Scripts for Photoshop with the Scripting Listener Plug-In" for information on using and installing the plug-in.

When using the Scripting Listener, you should pay close attention to the steps you take and the values you use while recording. You can hunt for the values when setting the properties for filters and plug-ins. This helps you determine what values you can turn into variables for use in a function.

Once you record the actions and generate the ScriptingListenerJS.log file, you can open the file in a text editor. The first step is to locate the required sections of code. After you find the snippets of code you need, you can wrap the entire block of code in a function definition so you can easily reuse the code. The next step is to pick through the code and find the values you specified when recording the script. You can change each of these values into a function parameter.

MAKE SCRIPTING LISTENER CODE INTO FUNCTIONS FOR PHOTOSHOP

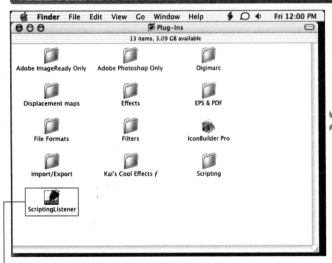

1 Close Photoshop.

2 Copy the ScriptingListener plug-in into the Photoshop Plug-Ins folder.

Note: See the section "Record Scripts for Photoshop with the Scripting Listener Plug-In" for more on copying this plug-in.

3 Open Photoshop and execute a filter.

4 Keep track of what you do and the values you enter.

5 Quit Photoshop and remove the ScriptingListener plug-in for the Plug-Ins directory.

Extra

The code that the Photoshop Scripting Listener plug-in generates is very difficult to read and understand. When you first finish recording a new script, you may want to add to the delimiter comments that the plug-in generates to help label what actions you took at what point in the script. This can make it easier to go though the code later. The more you work with code from the Scripting Listener plug-in, the more familiar and easy-to-read it becomes.

When using the Scripting Listener plug-in to generate code, you should take careful notes of what actions you take and the value of variables you set in each step. Having detailed notes makes it much easier to translate Scripting Listener code into functions. Knowing the specific values for the parameters of filters and actions is the best way to quickly isolate those values and replace them with function parameters or variables.

Make sure to move or rename the log file generated by the Scripting Listener plug-in; if you do not, and go to generate another script, you may overwrite the original script and lose your changes.

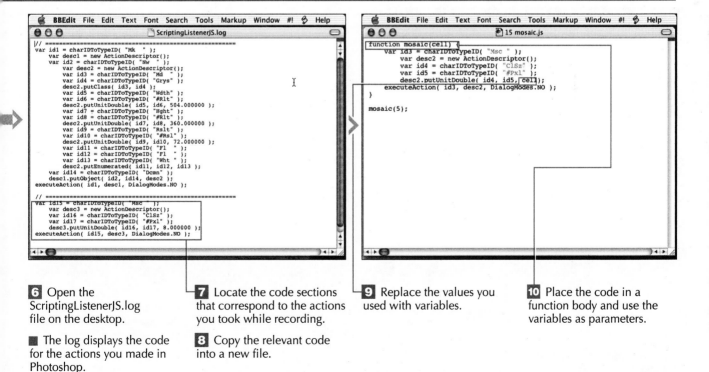

6 Open the ScriptingListenerJS.log file on the desktop.

■ The log displays the code for the actions you made in Photoshop.

7 Locate the code sections that correspond to the actions you took while recording.

8 Copy the relevant code into a new file.

9 Replace the values you used with variables.

10 Place the code in a function body and use the variables as parameters.

USING JAVASCRIPT WITH PHOTOSHOP ACTIONS

You can use JavaScript together with Photoshop Actions. Actions are a great way to quickly automate simple tasks in Photoshop. JavaScript and actions can work together to quickly and easily create complex behaviors for automating tasks. Using actions to trigger a JavaScript is a great way to make commonly used actions easier to get to.

You can view actions in Photoshop via the Actions palette. Photoshop organizes all actions into folders. Photoshop comes with a number of default actions you can use. All of the default actions are in the Default Actions folder. You can use the buttons at the bottom of the palette to create new actions and new folders. See the Photoshop manual for more information about working with actions.

Communication between JavaScript and Photoshop actions can go in either direction. You can use JavaScript to execute actions using the `doAction()` function. The function takes

two parameters, both of which are required to run the correct action. You use the first parameter to specify the name of the action to execute. The second parameter specifies the name of the folder that contains the action. Both parameters are strings, and you must enclose them in quotation marks.

You can also execute JavaScripts using Photoshop actions. You can execute a JavaScript with an action by creating a new action using the buttons in the Actions palette. Next, execute the script normally and stop recording after the script finishes execution. Because there are quite a few steps involved in accessing and running a JavaScript in Photoshop, you can create an action for frequently used scripts and make them easier to execute. An action can execute a script located anywhere on your computer; you do not need to locate it in Photoshop's Presets ⇨ Scripts folder.

USING JAVASCRIPT WITH PHOTOSHOP ACTIONS

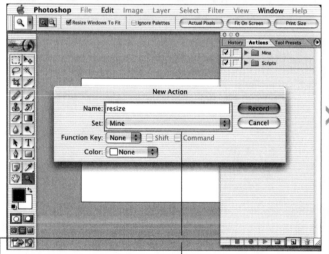

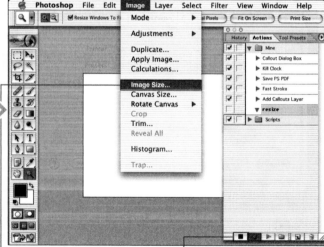

1 Open a Document in Photoshop.

2 Click the Create New button in the Actions palette to begin recording a new action.

3 Name the action and note the name of the folders containing the action.

4 Perform some actions.

5 Stop recording by clicking the Stop button.

Extra

You can also execute a JavaScript using an action. First, open a document in Photoshop. Create an action using the Create New button. Name the action, then execute a JavaScript normally by clicking File ➪ Automate ➪ Scripting. After the script executes, stop recording. The action you created now executes the JavaScript.

One of the most useful features of Photoshop actions is the ability to create *droplets* to execute actions. A droplet is a type of application that executes a Photoshop action on whatever files or folders you drop on its icon. You can make any Photoshop action into a droplet, and you can create droplets using the File ➪ Automate ➪ Create Droplet menu item. A dialog box presents you with a number of different options for creating the droplet. You can also make droplets from actions that execute scripts, which can dramatically improve your workflow by creating a drag-and-drop interface for your scripts.

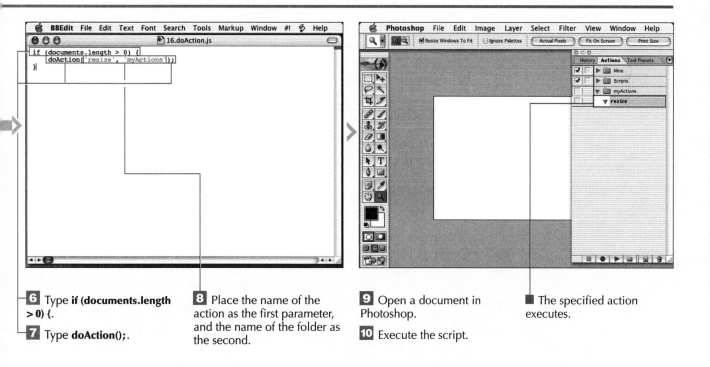

6 Type **if (documents.length > 0) {**.

7 Type **doAction();**.

8 Place the name of the action as the first parameter, and the name of the folder as the second.

9 Open a document in Photoshop.

10 Execute the script.

■ The specified action executes.

DETECT AND HANDLE ERRORS

You can improve the performance of your scripts by writing code to gracefully handle errors. Error handling is one of the most important parts of a script. This is particularly true when writing scripts you intend to distribute to the public. You can write scripts that generate error messages that are meaningful to the user, making your scripts easier to use.

Although you can write scripts with little or no error handling, this limits their usability. For example, if you write a script that makes changes to a specific type of object in a document, such as a specific format to the selected text item, the script might work 100% of the time, given that the currently selected item is a text area. But what if the current selection is a path item, or what if there is no selection at all? If you make the script too specific, you might need to select a particular type of text item, such as an area text item, for the script to work.

HANDLING COMMON ERRORS

An easy way to handle common errors is to verify that your script checks that key objects are present and valid before continuing. Most of the scripts in this book begin by verifying the existence of at least one document before execution; this is an example of a very basic way to avoid errors. If no documents are open, then there is no way to perform any manipulations on the active document.

The most common source of error stems from a user supplying invalid data, such as selecting the wrong type of object, or no object at all. Alternatively, a user may use your script in ways that you, as a programmer, may not have accounted for, such as selecting multiple text items and running a formatting script.

PROVIDE MEANINGFUL ERROR MESSAGES

The basic error handling methods outlined above prevent your scripts from causing runtime errors upon execution. However, your script may leave your user in the dark concerning why the script did not perform as expected. In the example of the text formatting script, if the user selects nothing, the script does not attempt to format the non-existent selection and no errors will occur. But from the user's point of view, the script has run and nothing has happened. This is a potentially confusing situation and the user may be left thinking that script simply did not work.

Providing meaningful error messages when your scripts encounter incorrect data or unexpected problems make your scripts easier to use and debug. Whenever you test for the existence or type of an object before continuing, include an `else` statement in your condition that displays a message explaining why the script cannot continue. For example you can improve the common

conditional used to test for the existence of a document by adding an `else` statement to the conditional that uses the `alert()` function to display a message:

Example:
```
if (documents.length > 0) {
   // execute code
} else {
   alert("There must be document open for this
script to run.");
}
```

See Chapter 2 for more information on the `alert()` function.

When communicating a problem to a user, be mindful of the number of alerts a user may encounter. Too many alerts can make your script very frustrating to use.

ENABLE THE JAVASCRIPT DEBUGGER IN PHOTOSHOP

You can use Photoshop's built in JavaScript debugger to help you find the source of errors and optimize your code. Photoshop includes a useful debugger for JavaScript. The debugger lets you trace the execution of a script as it progresses and helps you catch the source of errors.

You must activate the JavaScript debugger in Photoshop using the File ⇨ Automate ⇨ Scripts... menu path. When running a script normally in Photoshop, you can navigate to this dialog box and choose or browse to the script to execute. See Chapter 1 for more information on running scripts in Photoshop.

Running a script with the JavaScript debugger enabled is as simple as holding down the Option key on Macintosh or Alt key on Windows while activating the Run Script option in the Scripts dialog box. The Run Script option opens the JavaScript debugger, which pauses on the first line of your script. The major drawback of launching the debugger in this

way is that it requires you to locate your script in the Photoshop/Presets/Scripts folder. You cannot use the debugger on a script you browse to using the Browse option.

Extra

You can also use Visual Basic or AppleScript to launch the debugger and execute a JavaScript file. A complete description of AppleScript and Visual Basic is beyond the scope of this book. However each language does contain a `do javascript` function that lets you tell Photoshop to execute a file or string as JavaScript. You can set the `show debugger` property of this command to display the debugger at the beginning of the script, or only when a runtime error occurs. For more about Visual Basics, see *Visual Basic .NET: Your visual blueprint for building versatile programs on the .NET Framework 2002.*

ENABLE THE JAVASCRIPT DEBUGGER IN PHOTOSHOP

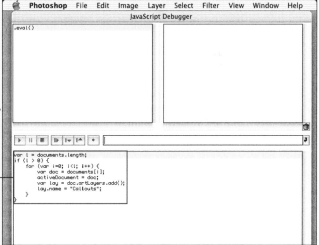

1 Open a new Document in Photoshop.

2 Click File ⇨ Automate ⇨ Scripts.

3 In the dialog box that opens, select a script to debug.

4 Press and hold down the Alt key in Windows, or the Options key on a Macintosh.

5 Click Debug Script.

■ The JavaScript debugger appears showing the script you selected.

ENABLE THE JAVASCRIPT DEBUGGER IN ILLUSTRATOR

You can use Illustrator's built in JavaScript debugger to optimize code and help find the source of errors. The debugger is a powerful tool for writing scripts for Illustrator. With the debugger, you can trace the execution of a script as it progresses and catch the source of errors that a script causes. You can also pause execution of the script and change the value of variables to test their effects on the script. See the section "Using the Debugger" in this chapter for more information.

It is much easier to launch the JavaScript debugger for Illustrator. The major difference between the two methods lies in the way breakpoints interact with the scripting environment. See the section "Using the Debugger to Optimize Code" for more information on breakpoints. To launch the JavaScript debugger, you must place $.bp(); in your script at the point where you want to launch the debugger. The $.bp() indicates that you want to add a breakpoint at this point in the script.

When you execute your script, the debugger appears with your script loaded, and paused at the point where you inserted the breakpoint. JavaScript has already executed all the code up to the line containing the breakpoint. This means that any changes you made to your document and any created variables are ready for you to inspect and use.

The advantage to allowing breakpoints to launch the debugger is that no additional work is necessary when running the script from Illustrator. You do not need to hold any modification keys or store scripts in a special location to launch the JavaScript debugger in Illustrator.

The disadvantage of this method is that you must comment out or remove your breakpoints after you finish debugging the script. Future versions of Illustrator may or may not incorporate a debugger like Photoshop's. This requires you to explicitly launch the debugger for breakpoints to be recognized.

ENABLE THE JAVASCRIPT DEBUGGER IN ILLUSTRATOR

1 Open an Illustrator JavaScript.

2 Add the line **$.bp();** at the point in the script where you want the debugger to appear.

Extra

You can specify what code executes when the Illustrator debugger encounters a breakpoint. Inserting a breakpoint calls a special type of function that you only use for debugging. Sometimes it can be helpful to display a message, change the value of a variable, or even call a function at the same moment the script encounters a breakpoint.

You can specify what code to execute by passing the code as a parameter to the $.bp() function. Just as you pass an argument to any other function, you place the code you want to execute between the parentheses. See p. 26–27 for more information. You must pass the code to the breakpoint function as a string. You enter the code normally, but place "" around the code to make it a string. Entering the code as a string means that you must pay attention to the way quotes interact; you must use single quotes (') inside of double quotes or else the string will break. The debugger then interprets the contents of the string as code and executes it. The following code displays an alert with the message "Launch the Debugger" when JavaScript encounters the breakpoint.

Example:
```
$.bp("alert('Launch the Debugger')");
```

3 Open a new document in Illustrator.

4 Execute the script by clicking File ⇨ Scripts.

■ The JavaScript debugger appears paused at the breakpoint placed in your script.

USING THE DEBUGGER

You can use the JavaScript debugger in Photoshop and Illustrator to find the source of errors and to optimize your code. The basic controls for the JavaScript debugger in Photoshop and Illustrator are the same. Understanding how the debugger works helps you hone in on problems in your scripts.

When the debugger first launches, your script loads and pauses. In the case of Illustrator, the debugger executes all code up to the breakpoint that launched the debugger. In Photoshop, the debugger pauses on the first line of your script.

THE DEBUGGER CONTROLS

The debugger has a series of buttons that allow you to step through the code during the execution of your script. The buttons are located in the center of the debugger window. In addition to the seven buttons, there is also a text field. The text field allows you to type in code to execute while the script is paused. If you type the name of a variable, the value of the variable prints in the debugger output pane.

PAUSE BUTTON

Temporarily stops execution of the script. This button only remains active while the script runs.

STEP OVER BUTTON

Executes the currently selected line then pauses the script. Unlike the Step Into button, if the current line contains a function call, the function executes in its entirety before the script pauses.

RESUME BUTTON

Continues normal execution of the script. If there are any breakpoints set later in the script, execution pauses when the debugger reaches that line of the script.

STEP OUT

Causes a script paused within the body of a function to play through the end of the function and pause on the line after the original function call. If the script is not currently in the body of a function, execution of the script continues as if you had pushed the resume button.

STOP BUTTON

Stops execution of the script. A runtime error generates when the script stops.

STEP INTO BUTTON

Executes the currently selected line of the script then pauses. If the line contains a function call, the debugger "steps into" the function and executes the first line of the function.

ANATOMY OF THE DEBUGGER WINDOW

The debugger window consists of three panes, each displaying different information about your script. The top left pane is called the "Stack Trace View," the top right pane shows the debugging output, and the bottom pane show the currently executing script.

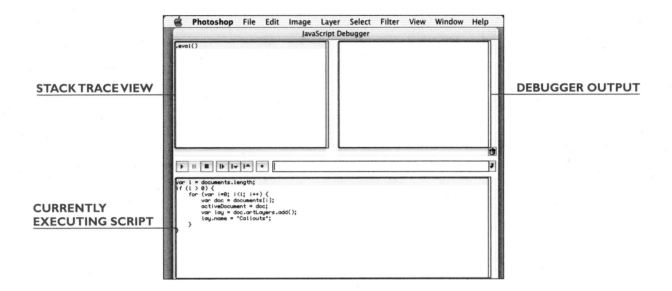

STACK TRACE VIEW

DEBUGGER OUTPUT

CURRENTLY EXECUTING SCRIPT

JavaScript Source View

The JavaScript source view pane shows the source of the JavaScript currently executing. The line of the script under execution is highlighted. This view lets you follow the execution of your script line-by-line. The Photoshop Debugger allows you to double-click a line in the source pane to toggle a breakpoint for that line of the script; breakpoints determine where the execution of code pauses so that you can inspect the current state of the script. You can also set Photoshop breakpoints in your script by placing `debugger;` on the line of your script where you want execution to pause. Photoshop only interprets the `debugger` command if you run the script with the debugger active. See the section "Enable the JavaScript Debugger in Photoshop" for more information.

Stack Trace View

The Stack Trace view displays the current position in the calling hierarchy — in other words, the location of the code currently under execution. If the code currently running is located within a function, the Stack Trace view shows the function call that place the script in its current state. For example, if you have a script with a single function that finds the square of a number, when the script calls this function, the name of the function and the passed parameters appear in this view exactly as it was called in the script.

Debugging Output

The debugging output pane shows the results of any debugger output operations. The debugger allows you to execute parts of scripts interactively. The results of interactive operations appear in this pane.

USING TRY-CATCH STATEMENTS

Yo u can add advanced error handling to your scripts using JavaScript's try...catch statements. Try...catch statements let you provide meaningful error messages to the users of your script. Not only are they useful for debugging scripts, but they also provide useful error messages, which make your scripts feel more professional and ultimately easier to use.

Every try...catch statement block begins with `try {`. The bracket indicates the beginning of a code block. To end a try...catch statement, close the block with `}` then immediately after begin the `catch(err) {` statement. The parameter in the parentheses is passed the text of the error message when an error occurs in the `try` block.

JavaScript attempts to execute any code that appears in the `try` block. If an error occurs when running the script, the error passes to the `catch` block and the code in the `catch` block executes. You can use the parameter to test for the type of error, or simply to display to the user with an `alert()`. If there are no problems with the code in the `try` block, JavaScript ignores the `catch` block.

The error object that the catch statement receives has a number of properties that are useful for narrowing down the cause of the error. In addition to the name of the error, the object also contains the error number, description, line number one which the error occurred, the source of the script, and an error message. You find these values in the `number`, `description`, `line`, `source`, and `message` parameters of the `error` object.

Sometimes you may find it necessary to write scripts for Photoshop or Illustrator that deliberately cause non-fatal errors. You can capture these errors with a try...catch statement. When you do so, JavaScript ignores these errors and does not report them to the user. You commonly use this technique to call the `duplicate()` method of a `LayerSet`. The method throws an error for no reason. You can safely ignore this error by wrapping the code in a try block. In the associated `catch` block, you can simply place a comment to indicate that you are ignoring the error.

USING TRY-CATCH STATEMENTS

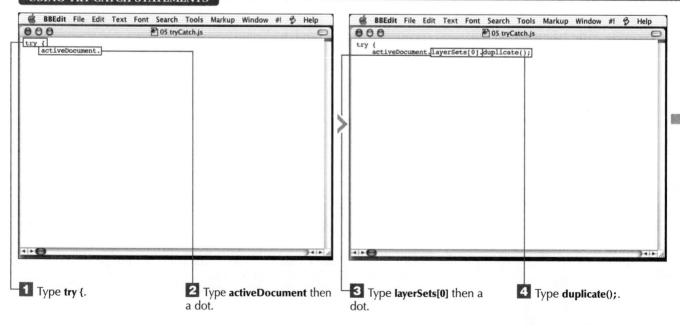

1 Type **try {**.

2 Type **activeDocument** then a dot.

3 Type **layerSets[0]** then a dot.

4 Type **duplicate();**.

Apply It

You can use the `throw` command to throw errors manually in your scripts. Throwing your own errors helps you provide meaningful error messages to the user. It can also make your code easier to manage because you can control at what points the code fails under certain conditions.

TYPE THIS:

```
try {
    throw "An error has occurred.";
} catch (myError) {
    alert(myError);
}
```

RESULT:

An alert box appears and displays the text "An error has occurred."

To get a better idea of how the try...catch statement affects script execution, try running the script under different conditions that you know will cause errors to occur. First, run the script with no document open. This generates an error because there is no `activeDocument`. Next, try running the script on a document without any layer sets. Photoshop generates another type of error because there is no layer set to duplicate. Finally, try removing the try...catch statement and executing the script under the different conditions to see the difference it makes.

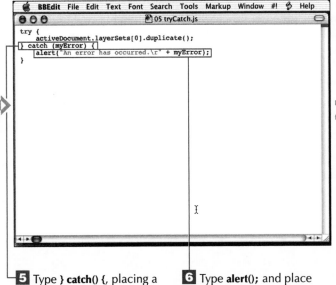

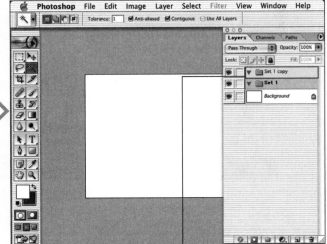

5 Type **} catch() {**, placing a name for the error parameter in the parentheses.

6 Type **alert();** and place the name of the error text parameter in the parentheses.

7 Open a document with a layer set in Photoshop.

8 Execute the script.

■ Photoshop duplicates the Layer Set and no error occurs.

THE APPLICATION OBJECT

When using JavaScript for Illustrator, you do not need to specify the `Application` object to access its properties and methods. You can simply type the name of the function or property.

PROPERTIES

PROPERTY NAME	TYPE	DESCRIPTION
activeDocument	Document object	A reference to the document object of the topmost open document.
documents	Documents collection object	Contains a pointer to a document object for each open document.
preferences	Preference object	The preference setting for Illustrator.
selection	Array	An array of pointers to currently selected objects in the active document.
textFaces	TextFaces collection object	The fonts available to the application.
version	String	Version of Illustrator executing the script.

METHODS

Communication

METHOD NAME	RETURN TYPE	DESCRIPTION
alert(string message)	void	Displays a message box to the user displaying the text and an OK button.
beep()	void	Causes a beep sound.
confirm(string message)	Boolean	Displays a confirmation box containing a message, Yes and No buttons. Returns the user's response, true for yes, false for no.

Application Methods

METHOD NAME	RETURN TYPE	DESCRIPTION
open(File Object filespec [, ColorSpace constant colorspace] [, PDFOpenOptions object options])	Document object	Opens the file that filespec defines, in the color space that colorspace specifies. If the file is a PDF, you can use a PDFOpenOptions object to define PDF specific options.
quit	none	Quits Illustrator. If you have an unsaved document open, the script may prompt the user to save the file.

CONTAINER OBJECTS

The container objects are the three main Illustrator JavaScript objects that contain other types of page items. These include the document, layer, and groupItem objects. Each of these container objects plays a key role in the Illustrator object model hierarchy.

THE DOCUMENTS COLLECTION

Documents is a collection of all open document objects. This collection is accessible from the Application object. You do not need to specify the Application object before accessing its properties and methods.

Properties

PROPERTY NAME	TYPE	DESCRIPTION
length	Number	The number of open documents. This property is read-only.
parent	Object	The Application object.

Methods

METHOD NAME	RETURN TYPE	DESCRIPTION
add([DocumentColorSpace constant colorspace] [, number width] [, number height])	Document object	Creates a new document. The color space, width, and height of the document can be specified.

THE DOCUMENT OBJECT

Properties

PROPERTY NAME	TYPE	DESCRIPTION
activeLayer	Layer object	A reference to the currently selected layer. You can set this property to change the active layer.
compoundPathItems	CompoundPathItems collection	Compound path items contained in the document.
dataSets	Datasets collection	Collection of all datasets in the document.
defaultFillColor	Color object	Controls the default color to fill path items with, only applicable if defaultFilled is true.
defaultFilled	Boolean	If true, all created path items are filled with the color specified in defaultFillColor.
defaultStrokeColor	Color object	Default color for the stroke of all created path items.
defaultStroked	Boolean	If true, all paths are stroked.

CONTAINER OBJECTS (CONTINUED)

Properties *(continued)*

PROPERTY NAME	TYPE	DESCRIPTION
documentColorSpace	DocumentColorSpace constant	A read-only value specifying the color space for the document.
fullName	String	Complete path to the file associated with the document.
geometricBounds	Array of 4 numbers	Bounds of the entire document, including strokes.
gradients	Gradients collection	Collection of all gradients in the document.
groupItems	GroupItems collection	Groups items in the document.
height	Number	Height of the document. This property is read-only.
layers	Layers collection	Collection of layers that this document contains.
name	String	Name of this document.
pageItems	PageItems collection	Collection of page items contained in the document.
pageOrigin	Array of 2 numbers	Zero point of page location relative to the height and width of the document.
parent	Application object	The Application object.
path	String	Path of the file associated with this document excluding the file name.
pathItems	PathItems collection	Path items contained in this document. This includes paths that are a part of a compound path.
placedItems	PlacedItems collection	Placed vectors items in the document.
rasterItems	RasterItems collection	Placed raster items in this document.
rulerOrigin	Array of 2 numbers	Zero point of the coordinate system.
rulerUnits	RulerUnits constant	User's preference setting for default unit of measure.
saved	Boolean	True if you have saved the document since the last change. Also false if you have never saved the document. Note that this behavior differs from Photoshop.
selection	An array of Objects	An array of all selected items in the document.
symbolItems	SymbolItems collection	Collection of placed symbols in the document.
symbols	Symbols collection	Collection of all symbols defined for the document. All symbols appear in the Symbols palette.
textArtItems	TextArtItems collection	All textArtItems contained in the document.
width	Number	The width of the document. This property is read-only.

THE DOCUMENT OBJECT (CONTINUED)

Methods

METHOD NAME	RETURN TYPE	DESCRIPTION
`activate()`	void	Brings the document to the front. You can also achieve this setting using the `activeDocument` property as reference to the document.
`close([SaveOptions object options])`	void	Closes the document. The save options control how the script treats unsaved documents.
`exportFile(File fileobj, ExportType constant exportAs, [, exportOptions])`	void	Exports the document to the file defined by the `File` object to the format that `ExportType` specifies. You can use export options to set further options for some file types. See the "Export Options Objects" section for a list of possible export option types.
`importVariables (File fileobj)`	void	Imports the variable library that the `File` object specifies. The script destroys existing variables in the document.
`print([boolean dialog])`	void	Prints the document. If the parameter is `false`, the application print dialog box opens.
`save()`	void	Saves the document. Returns an error if you have not saved the document before. See `saveAs` for saving documents for the first time.
`saveAs(File fileobj [, options])`	void	Saves the document to the file that the `File` object specifies. If you provide a save options object, the script saves the document in that format with the options that the object defines. You can save files as EPS, Illustrator, or PDF. See the section on Options Objects for more information.

THE LAYERS COLLECTION

`Layers` is a collection of `layer` objects. This
collection is accessible from the `document` object.

Properties

PROPERTY NAME	TYPE	DESCRIPTION
`length`	Number	The number of layers in this collection. This property is read-only.
`parent`	Object	The `document` object that contains this collection.

Methods

METHOD NAME	RETURN TYPE	DESCRIPTION
`add()`	Layer object	Adds a layer to the collection.
`removeAll()`	void	Removes every object in the collection.

CONTAINER OBJECTS (CONTINUED)

Properties

PROPERTY NAME	TYPE	DESCRIPTION
artworkKnockout	KnockoutState constant	What kind of knockout this object creates, if any.
blendingMode	BlendModes constant	Mode to use when compositing an object.
color	RGBColor object	Color of the layer's selection outline.
compoundPathItems	CompoundPathItems collection	Compound path items contained in the layer.
dimPlacedImages	Boolean	Determines whether placed images are dimmed.
graphItems	GraphItems collection	Graph items in the layer.
groupItems	GroupItems collection	Groups in the layer.
hasSelectedArtwork	Boolean	True if any object contained in this layer is part of the current selection. If set to false, all items on this layer are deselected.
isIsolated	Boolean	Determines if the object is isolated.
layers	Layers collection	Collection of sub-layers contained by this layer.
locked	Boolean	Controls if this item is locked.
name	String	The name of this layer, which is the same as the name that appears in the Layers palette.
opacity	Number	Opacity of this object. Valid values are between 0 and 100. This is the same value that appears in the Transparency palette.
pageItems	PageItems collection	Collection of page items contained in the layer.
parent	Document or layer object	The document or layer that contains this layer. This property is read-only.
pathItems	PathItems collection	Path items contained in this layer. Paths that are a part of a compound path are not present in this collection.
placedItems	PlacedItems collection	Placed vectors items in the layer.
rasterItems	RasterItems collection	Placed raster items in this layer.
sliced	Boolean	True if this item is sliced.
symbolItems	SymbolItems collection	Collection of placed symbols in this layer.
textArtItems	TextArtItems collection	All textArtItems contained by the layer.
visible	Boolean	Visibility of the layer. This is the same as the button in the Layers palette.
zOrderPosition	Number	The position of this object in the stacking order of the parent object. You can make the parent a document or layer object. This property is read-only. Use the zOrder method of the object to change the stacking order.

THE LAYER OBJECT (CONTINUED)

Methods

METHOD NAME	RETURN TYPE	DESCRIPTION
moveAfter(object destination)	void	Moves the layer behind the specified object.
moveBefore(object destination)	void	Moves the layer in front of the specified object.
moveToBeginning(object destination)	void	Moves the layer to the front of the specified object.
moveToEnd(object destination)	void	Moves the layer to the back of the specified object.
remove()	void	Removes the layer.
zOrder(ZOrderMethod constant ZOrderMethod)	void	Arranges the item in the parent container's stacking order. You can make the parent a document or layer object. Works like the options in the Object ⇨ Arrange menu.

THE GROUPITEMS COLLECTION

GroupItems is a collection of groupedItem objects.
This collection is accessible from the document
and layers objects.

Properties

PROPERTY NAME	TYPE	DESCRIPTION
length	Number	The number of layers in this collection. This property is read-only.
parent	Object	The document or layer object that contains this collection.

Methods

METHOD NAME	RETURN TYPE	DESCRIPTION
add()	GroupItem object	Adds a groupItem to the collection.
createFromFile (file object file)	GroupItem	Creates a group by placing the contents of the file as a group.
removeAll()	void	Removes every object in the collection.

CONTAINER OBJECTS (CONTINUED)

Properties

PROPERTY NAME	TYPE	DESCRIPTION
artworkKnockout	KnockoutState constant	What kind of knockout this object is used to create, if any.
blendingMode	BlendModes constant	Mode to use when compositing an object.
clipped	Boolean	If true, the top layer of the group is used as a clipping mask, masking the contents of the other layers in the group.
compoundPathItems	CompoundPathItems collection	Compound path items contained in the group.
controlBounds	Array of 4 numbers	Bounds of the object including strokes. This property is read-only.
editable	Boolean	If true, you can edit this item. Read-only.
geometricBounds	Array of 4 numbers	Bounds of the object without strokes. Read-only.
graphItems	GraphItems collection	Graph items in the group.
groupItems	GroupItems collection	Groups in the group.
height	Number	Height of the object.
hidden	Boolean	Determines whether the group is hidden.
isIsolated	Boolean	Determines if the object is isolated.
layers	Layers collection	Collection of sub-layers contained by this group.
left	Number	Left coordinate of the group.
locked	Boolean	Determines if this item is locked.
name	String	Name of this group. Same as the name that appears in the Layers palette.
opacity	Number	Opacity of this object. Valid values are between 0 and 100. This is the same value that appears in the Transparency palette.
parent	Layer or groupItem object	The layer or groupItem that contains this group. This property is read-only.
pathItems	PathItems collection	Path items contained in this group. Paths that are a part of a compound path are not present in this collection.
placedItems	PlacedItems collection	Placed vectors items in the group.
rasterItems	RasterItems collection	Placed raster items in this group.
sliced	Boolean	True if this item is sliced.
symbolItems	SymbolItems collection	Collection of placed symbols in this layer.
textArtItems	TextArtItems collection	All textArtItems contained by the layer.
visible	Boolean	Visibility of the layer. Same as the button in the Layers palette.
zOrderPosition	Number	The position of this object in the stacking order of the parent object. You can make the parent a document or layer object. Read-only. Use the zOrder method of the object to change the stacking order.

Methods

METHOD NAME	RETURN TYPE	DESCRIPTION
duplicate()	GroupItem **object**	Duplicates the groupItem **and returns a reference to the new group.**
moveAfter(object destination)	void	Moves the group behind the specified object.
moveBefore(object destination)	void	Moves the group in front of the specified object.
moveToBeginning(object destination)	void	Moves the group to the front of the specified object.
moveToEnd(object destination)	void	Moves the group to the back of the specified object.
remove()	void	Removes the group.
resize(number xscale, number yscale [, boolean changePosition] [, boolean changeFillPattern] [,boolean changeFillGradient] [,boolean changeStrokePattern] [,number changeLineWidths] [,Transformation constant scaleCenter])	void	Scales the groupItem, xscale is the horizontal scale, yscale is the vertical scale. 100.0 is 100%. If changePosition is false, **the shape of the object does not change and only the gradient, patterns, and strokes are affected.** changeFillPattern **determines if the fill pattern scales with the item, or if the pattern stays the current size and tiles to fill the shape.** changeFillGradient **is like** changeFillPattern **but for gradient fills. If** changeStrokePattern **is** true, **resize affects the dashed line pattern of the stroke.** changeLineWidths **is the percentage to scale the stroke widths, where 100.0 is 100%.** scaleCenter **sets the center point for the resize operation.**
rotate(number Angle [, boolean changePosition] [,boolean changeFillPattern] [,boolean changeFillGradient] [,boolean changeStrokePattern] [Transformation constant rotationCenter])	void	Rotates the item. The new rotation is relative to the current rotation. If the angle is negative, the item rotates clockwise. The rotationCenter parameter defines what point is the center point for the rotation.
zOrder(ZOrderMethod constant ZOrderMethod)	void	Arranges the item in the parent container's stacking order. You can make the parent a document or layer object. Works like the options in the Object ⇨ Arrange menu.

TEXT OBJECTS AND COLLECTIONS

Working with text in Illustrator involves the use of a number of different objects and methods. These include character, textRange, word, paragraph, textArtItem, textFace, textLine, and textPath.

THE CHARACTERS COLLECTION

The Characters collection is a collection of character objects. This collection is accessible from the paragraph, textLine, textRange, and word objects.

Properties

PROPERTY NAME	TYPE	DESCRIPTION
length	Number	The number of characters in this collection. This property is read-only.
parent	Object	The textArtItem object that contains this collection.

Methods

METHOD NAME	RETURN TYPE	DESCRIPTION
add()	Character Object	Adds a character at the end of the collection.
addBefore()	Character Object	Adds a character at the beginning of the collection.
removeAll()	void	Removes every object in the collection.

THE CHARACTER OBJECT

Properties

PROPERTY NAME	TYPE	DESCRIPTION
autoKerning	Boolean	Specifies whether to uses the font's kerning information.
baselineShift	Number	Offset of the text from the baseline.
clipping	Boolean	True if the textArtItem containing this character has a clipping path. This property is read-only.
contents	String	The text contents of this character object.
direction	CharacterDirection constant	The orientation of the characters in a vertical text block.
evenodd	Boolean	Determines if the even-odd rule should be used as the fill type for compound paths.
fillColor	Color object	Fill color of the text.
filled	Boolean	Use to specify whether this text item is filled with color.
fillOverprint	Boolean	Determines if the art under the text fill is overprinted.

PROPERTY NAME	TYPE	DESCRIPTION
font	String	Name of the font used for this character.
kerning	Number	Space between two characters. Units are measured in thousandths of an em.
leading	Number	Vertical leading of the text.
length	Number	Number of characters in this text range item. This property is read-only. It always return 1 for character objects.
note	String	The contents of a note associated with this text item. This property is read-only.
offset	Number	The offset of this text object. The number of characters from the beginning of the parent textArtItem where this text object begins. This property is read-only.
orientation	TextOrientation constant	The orientation of this textArtItem. This property is read-only. Use the textPath item of the textArtItem object to set this property.
paragraph	Paragraph object	The paragraph object that contains this character object.
parent	TextArtItem object	The textArtItem that contains this character.
resolution	Number	Resolution of the object in DPI (dots per inch). This property is read-only.
scaling	Array of 2 numbers	The scaling for this character. The first number in the array is the horizontal scale and the second is the vertical scale.
size	Number	Font size for this text object.
strokeCap	StrokeCap constant	The type of stroke capping to use. See Chapter 5 for more information.
strokeColor	Color object	Stroke color for the text object. The stroke on a text object appears as an outline around the characters.
stroked	Boolean	Determines if the text item has a stroke.
strokeDashes	Array	Array of dash lengths. Set to an empty array to get a solid line. See Chapter 5 for more information of using stroke dashes.
strokeDashOffset	Number	Distance into the dash pattern set by strokeDashes that the dash pattern should begin.
strokeJoin	StrokeJoin constant	The type of joints to be used.
strokeMiterLimit	Number	Determines if the joins are pointed or squared off. This property is only valid when you use mitered joints.
strokeOverprint	Boolean	Determines if the art under the text stroke are overprinted.
strokeWidth	Number	The width of the stroke. The unit is determined by the current preference setting for stroke units.
textLine	TextLine object	The textLine object containing this character. This property is read-only.
textPath	TextPath object	The text path associated with the textArtItem that contains this character. This property is read-only.
tracking	Number	Spacing between multiple characters.
word	Word object	The word object for the word containing this character.

TEXT OBJECTS AND COLLECTIONS (CONTINUED)

THE CHARACTER OBJECT (CONTINUED)

Methods

METHOD NAME	RETURN TYPE	DESCRIPTION
remove()	void	Remove the character.

THE PARAGRAPHS COLLECTION

Paragraphs is a collection of paragraph objects in a text range. This collection is accessible from the textRange object.

Properties

PROPERTY NAME	TYPE	DESCRIPTION
length	Number	The number of paragraphs in this collection. This property is read-only.
parent	Object	The textArtItem object that contains this collection.

Methods

METHOD NAME	RETURN TYPE	DESCRIPTION
add()	Paragraph Object	Adds a paragraph at the end of the collection.
addBefore()	Paragraph Object	Adds a paragraph to the beginning of the collection.
removeAll()	void	Removes every object from the collection.

THE PARAGRAPH OBJECT

Properties

PROPERTY NAME	TYPE	DESCRIPTION
autoKerning	Boolean	Specifies whether to use the font's kerning information.
baselineShift	Number	Offset of the text from the baseline.
clipping	Boolean	True if the textArtItem containing this paragraph has a clipping path. This property is read-only.
contents	String	The text contents of this paragraph object.
defaultTabSize	Number	Default size of tab stops. The General Unit setting in the preferences determines the unit.
desiredLetterSpacing	Number	Preferred letter spacing for the paragraph. 100.0 is normal letter spacing.

THE PARAGRAPH OBJECT (CONTINUED)

PROPERTY NAME	TYPE	DESCRIPTION
desiredWordSpacing	Number	Preferred word spacing for the paragraph. 100.0 is normal word spacing.
direction	Character Direction constant	The orientation of the characters in a vertical text block.
evenodd	Boolean	Determines if the script should use the even-odd rule as the fill type for compound paths.
fillColor	Color object	Fill color of the text.
filled	Boolean	Use to specify whether this text item is filled with color.
fillOverprint	Boolean	Determines if the art under the text fill is overprinted.
firstLineIndent	Number	Size of the indent of the first line. The General Unit setting in the preferences determines the unit.
font	String	Name of the font in use.
hangingPunctuation	Boolean	Determines if punctuation should appear outside of the paragraph margins.
hyphenation	Boolean	Enable hyphenation of this paragraph.
justification	Justification constant	Paragraph justification.
leading	Number	Vertical leading of the text.
leftIndent	Number	Size of the left side indent of the paragraph.
length	Number	Number of characters in the contents of this text range item. This property is read-only.
limitConsecutive Hyphenations	Boolean	If true, limits the number of consecutive hyphenated lines. See maximumConsecutiveHyphenations.
maximumConsecutive Hyphenations	Number	Maximum number of consecutive hyphenated lines. Only valid if limitConsecutiveHyphenations is set to true.
maximumLetterSpacing	Number	Maximum value for letter spacing. 100.0 is normal spacing.
maximumWordSpacing	Number	Maximum value for word spacing. 100.0 is normal spacing.
minimumAfterHyphen	Number	Minimum number of characters to appear after a hyphen.
minimumBeforeHyphen	Number	Minimum number of characters to appear before a hyphen.
minimumLetterSpacing	Number	Minimum value for letter spacing. 100.0 is normal spacing.
minimumWordSpacing	Number	Minimum value for word spacing. 100.0 is normal spacing.
note	String	The contents of a note associated with this text item. Read-only.
offset	Number	The offset of this text object. The number of characters from the beginning of the parent textArtItem where this text object begins. Read-only.

TEXT OBJECTS AND COLLECTIONS (CONTINUED)

Properties *(continued)*

PROPERTY NAME	TYPE	DESCRIPTION
orientation	TextOrientation constant	The orientation of this textArtItem. Read-only. Use the textPath item of the textArtItem object to set this property.
parent	TextArtItem object	The textArtItem that contains this character.
repeatedCharacter Processing	Boolean	Set if repeated character processing should be used.
resolution	Number	Resolution of the object in DPI (dots per inch). This property is read-only.
rightIndent	Number	Size of the right side indent of the paragraph.
scaling	Array of 2 numbers	The scaling for this paragraph. The first number in the array is the horizontal scale and the second is the vertical scale.
size	Number	Font size for this text object.
spaceBefore	Number	Size of space before this paragraph. The General Unit setting in the preferences determines the unit.
strokeCap	StrokeCap constant	The type of stroke capping to use. See Chapter 5 for more information.
strokeColor	Color object	Stroke color for the text object. The stroke on a text object appears as an outline around the characters.
stroked	Boolean	Sets if the text item has a stroke.
strokeDashes	Array	Array of dash lengths. Set to an empty array to get a solid line. See Chapter 5 for more information of using stroke dashes.
strokeDashOffset	Number	Distance into the dash pattern set by strokeDashes that the dash pattern should begin.
strokeJoin	StrokeJoin constant	The type of joints to be used.
strokeMiterLimit	Number	Determines whether the joins are pointed or squared off. This property is only valid when mitered joints are used.
strokeOverprint	Boolean	Determines if the art under the text stroke is overprinted.
strokeWidth	Number	The width of the stroke. The current preference setting for stroke units determines the units.
textLines	TextLines collection object	The collection of lines of this paragraph as textLine objects.
textPath	TextPath object	The text path associated with the textArtItem that contains this character. This property is read-only.
tracking	Number	Spacing between multiple characters.
words	Words collection object	The collection of word objects in this paragraph.

THE PARAGRAPH OBJECT (CONTINUED)

Methods

METHOD NAME	RETURN TYPE	DESCRIPTION
remove()	void	Remove the object from the document.
textRange([number start] [, number end])	TextRange object	Returns a textRange object that references a substring of this paragraph. The range begins at the start character and ends at the end character. All character indexes begin at 0. If you do not specify parameters, the entire range is used. If you do not specify the end, the range continues to the last character.

THE TEXTARTITEMS COLLECTION

TextArtItems is a collection of every textArtItem in the document. This collection is accessible from the document object.

Properties

PROPERTY NAME	TYPE	DESCRIPTION
length	Number	The number of objects in the collection. Read-only.
parent	Object	The document object that contains this collection.

Methods

METHOD NAME	RETURN TYPE	DESCRIPTION
add()	TextArtItem Object	Adds a textArtItem to the document.
removeAll()	void	Removes every textArtItem in the document.

THE TEXTARTITEM OBJECT

Properties

PROPERTY NAME	TYPE	DESCRIPTION
artworkKnockout	KnockoutState constant	What kind of knockout, if any, this object creates.
blendingMode	BlendModes constant	Mode to use when compositing an object.
contents	String	The text contents of this textArtItem.
contentVariable	Variable object	The variable object bound to the text contents of this textArtItem.
controlBounds	Array of 4 numbers	The bounds of the object including stroke width. Read-only.
editable	Boolean	Is this item editable? An item is not editable if its layer is locked. Read-only.

TEXT OBJECTS AND COLLECTIONS (CONTINUED)

Properties _(continued)_

PROPERTY NAME	TYPE	DESCRIPTION
geometricBounds	Array of 4 numbers	The bounds of the object excluding strokes. These are the values that appear in the info palette. Read-only.
height	Number	The height of the textArtItem. You may experience unexpected results when trying to set the height of a textArtItem that does not contain text.
hidden	Boolean	Determines if this object is visible. This is the same as the Visible property in the Layers palette.
isIsolated	Boolean	Determines if the object is isolated.
kind	TextType constant	The kind of textArtItem, in Area Text.
layer	Layer object	The layer that contains this textArtItem. Read-only.
locked	Boolean	Determines whether this textArtItem is locked.
name	String	Name of this textArtItem. Same as the name that appears in the Layers palette.
opacity	Number	Opacity of this object. Valid values are between 0 and 100. This is the same value that appears in the Transparency palette.
parent	Layer or groupItem object	The layer object or groupItem object that contains this textArtItem. Read-only.
position	Array of 2 numbers	Position of the top left corner of the object. The first number is the left position and the second is the top position. Both numbers are always given in points, regardless of the preference settings.
selected	Boolean	Determines whether this item is selected.
selection	TextRange object	A textRange object that refers to the selected text.
sliced	Boolean	True if this item is sliced.
tags	Tags collection	The tags contained by this textArtItem. Read-only.
textPath_ PathItems	PathItems collection	The path items associated with this textArtItem. This property is read-only.
textPaths	TextPaths collection	The text paths associated with this textArtItem. Read-only.
top	Number	Position of the top of this item.
url	String	Sets the value of the Adobe URL tag associated with this textArtItem.

PROPERTY NAME	TYPE	DESCRIPTION
visibilityVariable	Variable **object**	The variable object bound to the visibility of this textArtItem.
visibleBounds	Array of 4 numbers	The visible bound of the textArtItem including stroke widths. This property is read-only.
width	Number	The width of the textArtItem. You might experience unexpected results when trying to set the width of a textArtItem that does not contain text.
wrapped	Boolean	Controls whether the textArtItem wraps around other object. Only valid for area text that you group with another object. See Chapter 7 for more information.
zOrderPosition	Number	The position of this object in the stacking order of the parent object. You can make the parent a layer or groupItem object. Read-only. Use the zOrder method of the object to change the stacking order.

Methods

METHOD NAME	RETURN TYPE	DESCRIPTION
createOutline()	GroupItem **object**	Breaks a text items into a group of path and compound path items.
duplicate()	textArtItem	Creates a duplicate of the object.
moveAfter(object target)	void	Moves the item behind the target object.
moveBefore(object target)	void	Moves the item in front of the target object.
moveToBeginning (object target)	void	Moves the item to the front of the target object.
moveToEnd(object target)	void	Moves the item to the bottom of the target object.
remove()	void	Remove the object.
resize(number xscale, number yscale [, boolean changePosition] [, boolean changeFillPattern] [, boolean changeFill Gradient] [, boolean changeStrokePattern] [, number changeLineWidths] [, Transformation constant scaleCenter])	void	Scales the textArtItem, xscale is the horizontal scale, yscale is the vertical scale. 100.0 is 100%. If changePosition is false, the shape of the object does not change and only the gradient, patterns, and strokes are affected. changeFillPattern determines if the fill pattern should scale with the item, or if the pattern should stay the current size and tile to fill the shape. changeFillGradient is like changeFillPattern but for gradient fills. If changeStrokePattern is true, resizing affects the dashed line pattern of the stroke. changeLineWidths is the percentage to scale the stroke widths, where 100.0 is 100%. scaleCenter sets the center point for the resize operation.

TEXT OBJECTS AND COLLECTIONS (CONTINUED)

Methods

METHOD NAME	RETURN TYPE	DESCRIPTION
rotate(number Angle [, boolean changePosition] [, boolean changeFill Pattern] [, boolean change FillGradient] [, boolean changeStrokePattern] [Transformation constant rotationCenter])	void	Rotates the item. The new rotation is relative to the current rotation. If the angle is negative, the item rotates clockwise. The rotationCenter parameter defines what point is the center point for the rotation.
textRange([number start] [, number end])	TextRange object	Returns a textRange object that references a substring of the textArtItem. The range begins at the start character and ends at the end character. All character indexes begin at 0. If you do not specify parameters, the entire range is used. If you do not specify an end, the range continues to the last character.
zOrder(ZOrderMethod constant ZOrderMethod)	void	Arranges the item in the parent container's (document, layer, or group) stacking order. Works like the options in the Object ⇨ Arrange menu.

THE TEXTFACES COLLECTION

TextFaces is a collection of every currently available font face.
This collection is available from the Application object.

Properties

PROPERTY NAME	TYPE	DESCRIPTION
length	Number	The number of objects in the collection. Read-only.
parent	Object	The Application object that contains this collection.

THE TEXTFACE OBJECT

An object representing a currently available font.

Properties

PROPERTY NAME	TYPE	DESCRIPTION
name	String	The name of the font. Read-only.
parent	Object	The Application object that contains this collection.

THE TEXTLINES COLLECTION

`TextLines` **is a collection of lines of text in a text range. This collection is accessible from the** `textRange` **and** `paragraph` **objects.**

Properties

PROPERTY NAME	TYPE	DESCRIPTION
`length`	Number	The number of lines in this collection. Read-only.
`parent`	Object	The `textArtItem` object that contains this collection. Note that the parent is the `textArtItem` object, not the `textRange` object.

Methods

METHOD NAME	RETURN TYPE	DESCRIPTION
`removeAll()`	void	Removes every object from the collection.

THE TEXTLINE OBJECT

You cannot create lines of text. When you change the contents of a text item, Illustrator creates new `textLines` **after it reflows the new text.**

Properties

PROPERTY NAME	TYPE	DESCRIPTION
`autoKerning`	Boolean	Specifies whether to use the font's kerning information.
`baselineShift`	Number	Offset of the text from the baseline.
`characters`	`Characters` collection	The `characters` collection for this line of text.
`clipping`	Boolean	`True` if the `textArtItem` containing this `textLine` has a clipping path. Read-only.
`contents`	String	The text contents of this `textLine` object.
`direction`	`CharacterDirection` constant	The orientation of the characters in a vertical text block.
`evenodd`	Boolean	Determines if the even-odd rule should be used as the fill type for compound paths.
`fillColor`	`Color` object	Fill color of the text.
`filled`	Boolean	Use to specify whether this text item is filled with color.
`fillOverprint`	Boolean	Determines if the art under the text fill is overprinted.
`font`	String	Name of the font in use.
`leading`	Number	Vertical leading of the text.
`length`	Number	Number of characters in the contents of this text range item. Read-only.

TEXT OBJECTS AND COLLECTIONS (CONTINUED)

Properties *(continued)*

PROPERTY NAME	TYPE	DESCRIPTION
note	String	The contents of a note associated with this text item. Read-only.
offset	Number	The offset of this `text` object. The number of characters from the beginning of the parent `textArtItem` where this `text` object begins. Read-only.
orientation	TextOrientation constant	The orientation of this `textArtItem`. Read-only. Use the `textPath` item of the `textArtItem` object to set this property.
paragraph	Paragraph object	The `paragraph` object that contains this `textLine`. Read-only.
parent	TextArtItem object	The `textArtItem` that contains this character.
resolution	Number	Resolution of the object in DPI (dots per inch). Read-only.
scaling	Array of 2 numbers	The scaling for this line. The first number in the array is the horizontal scale and the second is the vertical scale.
size	Number	Font size for this `text` object.
strokeCap	StrokeCap constant	The type of stroke capping to use. See Chapter 5 for more information.
strokeColor	Color object	Stroke color for the `text` object. The stroke on a `text` object appears as an outline around the characters.
stroked	Boolean	Determines whether the text item has a stroke.
strokeDashes	Array	Array of dash lengths. Set to an empty array to get a solid line. See Chapter 5 for more information of using stroke dashes.
strokeDashOffset	Number	Distance into the dash pattern set by `strokeDashes` that the dash pattern should begin.
strokeJoin	StrokeJoin constant	The type of joints to be used.
strokeMiterLimit	Number	Determines whether the joins are pointed or squared off. This property is only valid when you use mitered joints.
strokeOverprint	Boolean	Determines if the art under the text stroke is overprinted.
strokeWidth	Number	The width of the stroke. The current preference setting for stroke units determines the unit.
textPath	TextPath object	The text path associated with the `textArtItem` that contains this character. Read-only.
tracking	Number	Spacing between multiple characters.

THE TEXTLINE OBJECT (CONTINUED)

Methods

METHOD NAME	RETURN TYPE	DESCRIPTION
remove()	void	Removes the object from the document.
textRange([number start] [, number end])	TextRange object	Returns a textRange object that references a substring of this line. The range begins at the start character and ends at the end character. All character indexes begin at 0. If you do not specify parameters, the entire range is used. If you do not specify an end, the range continues to the last character.

THE TEXTPATHS COLLECTION

TextPaths is a collection of all textPaths associated with a textArtItem. This collection is accessible from the textArtItem object.

Properties

PROPERTY NAME	TYPE	DESCRIPTION
length	Number	The number of objects in the collection. Read-only.
parent	TextArtItem Object	The textArtItem object that contains this collection.

Methods

METHOD NAME	RETURN TYPE	DESCRIPTION
add()	TextPath Object	Adds a textPath to the textArtItem to which the collection belongs.
removeAll()	void	Removes all but two textPaths from the textArtItem. All textArtItems have at least one path associated with them. If you have created a textPath using textPaths.add(), this method removes all but two textPaths in the textArtItem. You can use the remove() method of the textPath item to remove it.

TEXT OBJECTS AND COLLECTIONS (CONTINUED)

The textPath object controls the orientation of a textArtItem
and provides access to the path item of path and area text.

Properties

PROPERTY NAME	TYPE	DESCRIPTION
matrix	Matrix object	The transformation matrix for this textPath.
orientation	Orientation object	The orientation of the text item, see the orientation object for possible values.
parent	TextArtItem object	The textArtItem with which this object is associated.
textPathObject	PathItem object	If the textArtItem is area or path text, this is the pathItem associated with the textArtItem.
textPathOffset	Number	Valid only for path text. Defines the offset of the text along the path. Units are points on the path; for example, 2 starts the text at the second path point. Path points are counted beginning with 0.

Methods

METHOD NAME	RETURN TYPE	DESCRIPTION
remove()	none	Removes this textPath.

TextPath_PathItems is a collection of every
pathItem associated with area text and path text. This
collection is accessible from the textArtItem object.

Properties

PROPERTY NAME	TYPE	DESCRIPTION
length	Number	The number of objects in the collection. Read-only.
parent	TextArtItem object	The textArtItem object that contains this collection.

The `textRange` object refers to a specific section of text in a `textArtItem`.

Properties

PROPERTY NAME	TYPE	DESCRIPTION
autoKerning	Boolean	Specifies whether to use the font's kerning information.
baselineShift	Number	Offset of the text from the baseline.
clipping	Boolean	True if the textArtItem containing this character has a clipping path. Read-only.
contents	String	The text contents of this character object.
direction	CharacterDirection constant	The orientation of the characters in a vertical text block.
evenodd	Boolean	Determines if the even-odd rule is used as the fill type for compound paths.
fillColor	Color object	Fill color of the text.
filled	Boolean	Use to specify whether this text item is filled with color.
fillOverprint	Boolean	Determines if the art under the text fill is overprinted.
font	String	Name of the font in use for this character.
kerning	Number	Space between to characters. Units are measured in thousandths of an em.
leading	Number	Vertical leading of the text.
length	Number	Number of characters in this text range item. Read-only.
note	String	The contents of a note associated with this text item. Read-only.
offset	Number	The offset of this text object. The number of characters from the beginning of the parent textArtItem where this text object begins. Read-only.
orientation	TextOrientation constant	The orientation of this textArtItem. Read-only. Use the textPath item of the textArtItem object to set this property.
paragraphs	Paragraphs collection	Collection of all paragraph objects contained in this textRange.
parent	TextArtItem object	The textArtItem that contains this textRange.
resolution	Number	Resolution of the object in DPI (dots per inch). Read-only.
scaling	Array of 2 numbers	The scaling for this textRange. The first number in the array is the horizontal scale and the second is the vertical scale.
size	Number	Font size for this text object.
strokeCap	StrokeCap constant	The type of stroke capping to use. See Chapter 5 for more information.
strokeColor	Color object	Stroke color for the text object. The stroke on a text object appears as an outline around the characters.
stroked	Boolean	Determines whether the text item has a stroke.
strokeDashes	Array	Array of dash lengths. Set to an empty array to get a solid line. See Chapter 5 for more information of using stroke dashes.

TEXT OBJECTS AND COLLECTIONS (CONTINUED)

Properties *(continued)*

PROPERTY NAME	TYPE	DESCRIPTION
strokeDashOffset	Number	Distance into the dash pattern set by strokeDashes that the dash pattern should begin.
strokeJoin	StrokeJoin constant	The type of joints in use.
strokeMiterLimit	Number	Determines whether the joins are pointed or squared off. This property is only valid when you use mitered joints.
strokeOverprint	Boolean	Determines if the art under the text stroke is overprinted.
strokeWidth	Number	The width of the stroke. The current preference setting for stroke units determines the unit.
textLines	TextLines collection	Collection of every textLine contained in this textRange. Read-only.
textPath	TextPath object	The text path associated with the textArtItem that contains this textRange. Read-only.
tracking	Number	Spacing between multiple characters.
words	Words collection	Collection of all words contained by this textRange.

Methods

METHOD NAME	RETURN TYPE	DESCRIPTION
deleteRange()	void	Deletes the textRange from the textArtItem.
remove()	void	Removes the item from the document.

THE WORDS COLLECTION

Words is a collection of word objects. This
collection is accessible from the paragraph
and textRange objects.

Properties

PROPERTY NAME	TYPE	DESCRIPTION
length	Number	The number of characters in this collection. Read-only.
parent	Object	The textArtItem object that contains this collection.

Methods

METHOD NAME	RETURN TYPE	DESCRIPTION
add()	Character object	Adds a word at the end of the collection.
addBefore()	void	Adds a word at the beginning of the collection.
removeAll()	void	Removes every object in the collection.

THE WORD OBJECT

Properties

PROPERTY NAME	TYPE	DESCRIPTION
autoKerning	Boolean	Specifies whether to use the font's kerning information.
baselineShift	Number	Offset of the text from the baseline.
characters	Characters collection	Collection of characters in this word.
clipping	Boolean	True if the textArtItem containing this character has a clipping path. Read-only.
contents	String	The text contents of this character object.
direction	CharacterDirection constant	The orientation of the characters in a vertical text block.
evenodd	Boolean	Determines if the even-odd rule is used as the fill type for compound paths.
fillColor	Color object	Fill color of the text.
filled	Boolean	Use to specify whether this text item is filled with color.
fillOverprint	Boolean	Determines if the art under the text fill is overprinted.
font	String	Name of the font in use for this character.
leading	Number	Vertical leading of the text.
length	Number	Number of characters in this text range item. Read-only.
note	String	The contents of a note associated with this text item. Read-only.
offset	Number	The offset of this text object. The number of characters from the beginning of the parent textArtItem where this text object begins. Read-only.
orientation	TextOrientation constant	The orientation of this textArtItem. Read-only. Use the textPath item of the textArtItem object to set this property.
paragraph	Paragraph object	The paragraph object that contains this word.
parent	TextArtItem object	The textArtItem that contains this character.
resolution	Number	Resolution of the object in DPI (dots per inch). Read-only.

TEXT OBJECTS AND COLLECTIONS (CONTINUED)

Properties *(continued)*

PROPERTY NAME	TYPE	DESCRIPTION
scaling	Array of 2 numbers	The scaling for this character. The first number in the array is the horizontal scale and the second is the vertical scale.
size	Number	Font size for this text object.
strokeCap	StrokeCap constant	The type of stroke capping to use. See Chapter 5 for more information.
strokeColor	Color object	Stroke color for the text object. The stroke on a text object appears as an outline around the characters.
stroked	Boolean	Determines whether the text item has a stroke.
strokeDashes	Array	Array of dash lengths. Set to an empty array to get a solid line. See Chapter 5 for more information of using stroke dashes.
strokeDashOffset	Number	Distance into the dash pattern set by strokeDashes that the dash pattern should begin.
strokeJoin	StrokeJoin constant	The type of joints in use.
strokeMiterLimit	Number	Determines whether the joins are pointed or squared off. This property is only valid when you use mitered joints.
strokeOverprint	Boolean	Determines if the art under the text stroke is overprinted.
strokeWidth	Number	The width of the stroke. The current preference setting for stroke units determines the unit.
textPath	TextPath object	The text path associated with the textArtItem that contains this word. Read-only.
tracking	Number	Spacing between multiple characters.

Methods

METHOD NAME	RETURN TYPE	DESCRIPTION
remove()	void	Removes the character.
textRange([number start] [, number end])	TextRange object	Returns a textRange object that references a substring of this line. The range begins at the start character and ends at the end character. All character indexes begin at 0. If you do not specify parameters, the entire range is used. If you do not specify an end, the range continues to the last character.

EXPORT OPTIONS OBJECTS

JavaScript for Illustrator makes use of a number of options objects for specifying how documents are open, saved, and exported. You must create each object using the New keyword. See Chapter 2 for information on creating objects in JavaScript.

OPEN OPTIONS OBJECTS

Used with the open method of the Application object.

PDFOpenOptions

Properties

PROPERTY NAME	TYPE	DESCRIPTION
pageToOpen	Number	Specifies the page of the PDF document that Illustrator will open.

SAVE OPTIONS OBJECTS

Used with the saveAs method of the document object.

EPSSaveOptions

Properties

PROPERTY NAME	TYPE	DESCRIPTION
cmykPostScript	Boolean	Determines whether CMYK PostScript should be used.
compatibility	Compatibility constant	Version of file to save.
embedAllFonts	Boolean	Determines whether fonts should be included in the file.
embedLinkedFiles	Boolean	Determines whether linked filed should be included in the file.
flatternOutput	OutputFlattening constant	Specifies how transparency should be handled for older file formats.
includeDocumentThumbnails	Boolean	Determines whether a thumbnail of the document should be included with the file.
japaneseFileFormat	Boolean	Determines whether the file should be saved as a Japanese version.
postScript	PostScriptLevel constant	Sets the PostScript level for the file.
preview	EPSPreview constant	Format for the EPS preview.

IllustratorSaveOptions

Properties

PROPERTY NAME	TYPE	DESCRIPTION
compatibility	Compatibility constant	Version of Illustrator document to create.
compressed	Boolean	If true, the file compresses. Only available for Illustrator versions 10 and up.
embedAllFonts	Boolean	Determines whether fonts should be embedded in the file.
embedICCProfile	Boolean	Determines whether the ICC color profile should be included in the file.
embedLinkedFiles	Boolean	Determines whether linked files should be embedded and included in the file.
flattenOutput	OutputFlattening constant	Specifies how transparency should be handled for older file formats.
fontSubsetThreshold	Number	Sets a threshold of the percentage of characters used in the document. If the percentage is higher, the script includes the entire font; if it is lower, it only includes a subset.
japaneseFileFormat	Boolean	If true, saves the file in Japanese version format.
pdfCompatibility	Boolean	Determines whether the file should be saved as a PDF compatible document.

IllustratorSaveOptions

Properties

PROPERTY NAME	TYPE	DESCRIPTION
colorCompression	Compression Quality constant	Specifies the type of bitmap color compression.
colorDownsampling	Number	Color downsampling resolution in dots per inch. A value of 0 specifies no downsampling.
compatibility	PDFCompatibility constant	Version of PDF document to create.
compressArt	Boolean	Determines whether paths and text should compress.
embedAllFonts	Boolean	Determines whether fonts embed in the file.
embedICCProfile	Boolean	Determines whether the ICC color profile should be included in the file.
fontSubsetThreshold	Number	Sets a threshold of the percentage of characters used in the document. If the percentage is higher, the script includes the entire font; if it is lower, it only includes a subset.

PROPERTY NAME	TYPE	DESCRIPTION
generateThumbnails	Boolean	If true, thumbnail images will generate and save with the file.
grayscaleCompression	CompressionQuality **constant**	Specifies the grayscale compression quality.
grayscaleDownsampling	Number	Downsampling resolution. If 0, no downsampling occurs.
monochromeCompression	MonochromeCompressionQuality **constant**	Specifies the compression quality for monochrome bitmaps.
monochromeDownsampling	Number	Downsampling resolution. If 0, no downsampling occurs.
preserveEditablity	Boolean	If true, the document remains editable in Illustrator.

EXPORT OPTIONS OBJECTS

Used with the exportFile **method of the** document **object.**

ExportOptionsFlash

Properties

PROPERTY NAME	TYPE	DESCRIPTION
artBoardClipping	Boolean	If true, the script clips the artwork in the document to the artboard.
curveQuality	Number	Quality of the curves in the document. Specified as a number between 0 and 10, with a default of 7.
exportStyle	FlashExportStyle **constant**	Sets the way the script treats the layers in the document when exporting, either as a single flash file, treating layers as frames in the single flash file, or saving each layer as a separate file.
frameRate	Number	Sets the frame rate of the flash movie. Must be a number between 1 and 120.
generateHTML	Boolean	If true, the script creates an HTML file along with the flash movie.
imageFormat	FlashImageFormat **constant**	Defines how bitmap images export.
jpegMethod	FlashJPEGMethod **constant**	Sets the JPEG method for the movie.
looping	Boolean	Determines whether the file should loop on playback.
readOnly	Boolean	Determines whether the file is read-only.
replacing	SaveOptions **constant**	Determines what action Illustrator takes when attempting to export a file to a location where one with the same name already exists.
resolution	Number	Resolution in pixels per inch, between 72 and 2400.

EXPORT OPTIONS OBJECTS (CONTINUED)

ExportOptionsGIF

Properties

PROPERTY NAME	TYPE	DESCRIPTION
antiAliasing	Boolean	If true, the exported image is anti-aliased.
artBoardClipping	Boolean	If true, the script clips the artwork in the document to the artboard.
colorCount	Number	A number from 2 to 256 specifying the number of colors in the GIF's color table.
colorDither	ColorDitherMethod constant	Sets the method for dithering the exported image.
colorReduction	ColorReductionMethod constant	Method for reducing the number of colors in an image.
ditherPercent	Number	Percentage of how much the colors are dithered.
horizontalScale	Number	Horizontal scaling factor of the exported image.
infoLossPercent	Number	Percentage of information that can acceptably lose during export.
interlaced	Boolean	Determines whether the image is interlaced.
matte	Boolean	If true, the script mats the artboard with a color.
matteColor	RGBColor object	Color to use for matting if the matte property is set to true.
saveAsHTML	Boolean	If true, the script creates a HTML file along with the image.
transparency	Boolean	Determines whether the image should use transparency.
verticalScale	Number	Vertical scaling factor for the exported image.
webSnap	Number	Sets how strongly Illustrator should alter the colors in the image to make it Web safe. 100 percent ensures a completely Web safe image.

ExportOptionsJPEG

Properties

PROPERTY NAME	TYPE	DESCRIPTION
antiAliasing	Boolean	If true, the exported image is anti-aliased.
artBoardClipping	Boolean	If true, the script clips the artwork in the document to the artboard.
blurAmount	Number	A number between 0 and 2 to set the amount of blur to apply to the image. More blur results in a smaller image.

PROPERTY NAME	TYPE	DESCRIPTION
horizontalScale	Number	Horizontal scaling factor of the exported image.
matte	Boolean	If true, the script mats the artboard with a color.
matteColor	RGBColor object	Color to use for matting if you set the matte property to true.
optimization	Boolean	If true, the image is optimized for Web viewing.
qualitySetting	Number	Quality value of the JPEG. A number between 0 and 100, with 100 being the best.
saveAsHTML	Boolean	If true, the script creates a HTML file along with the image.
verticalScale	Number	Vertical scaling factor for the exported image.

ExportOptionsPhotoshop

Properties

PROPERTY NAME	TYPE	DESCRIPTION
antiAliasing	Boolean	If true, the exported image is anti-aliased.
compoundShapes	Boolean	If true, compound shapes export as Photoshop shape layers.
editableText	Boolean	If true, exported text items remains editable in Photoshop.
embedICCProfile	Boolean	Determines whether you want the ICC color profile included in the file.
hiddenLayers	Boolean	Determines if hidden layers are preserved in the Photoshop file.
imageColorSpace	ImageColorSpace constant	Sets the color space of the exported file.
imageMap	Boolean	If the document is RGB and this property is true, image maps is preserved for Image Ready.
nestedLayers	Boolean	If true, nested layers are preserved in the file.
resolution	Number	Number between 72 and 2400 for the resolution in dots per inch.
slices	Boolean	If true, slice data is preserved.
warnings	Boolean	If true, a dialog box displays for conflicts.
writeLayers	Boolean	Set if you want to preserve layers in the export.

ExportOptionsPNG24

Properties

PROPERTY NAME	TYPE	DESCRIPTION
antiAliasing	Boolean	If true, the exported image is anti-aliased.
artBoardClipping	Boolean	If true, the script clips the artwork in the document to the artboard.
horizontalScale	Number	Horizontal scaling factor of the exported image.
matte	Boolean	If true, the script mats the artboard with a color.
matteColor	RGBColor object	Color to use for matting if the matte property is set to true.

EXPORT OPTIONS OBJECTS (CONTINUED)

Properties *(continued)*

PROPERTY NAME	TYPE	DESCRIPTION
saveAsHTML	Boolean	If `true`, the script creates a HTML file along with the image.
transparency	Boolean	Sets if the image should use transparency.
verticalScale	Number	Vertical scaling factor for the exported image.

ExportOptionsPNG8

Properties

PROPERTY NAME	TYPE	DESCRIPTION
antiAliasing	Boolean	If `true`, the exported image is anti-aliased.
artBoardClipping	Boolean	If `true`, the script clips the artwork in the document to the artboard.
colorCount	Number	A number from 2 to 256 specifying the number of colors in the GIF's color table.
colorDither	ColorDitherMethod constant	Sets the method for dithering the exported image.
colorReduction	ColorReductionMethod constant	Method for reducing the number of colors in an image.
ditherPercent	Number	Percentage of how much the script dithers colors.
horizontalScale	Number	Horizontal scaling factor of the exported image.
interlaced	Boolean	Determines whether the image is interlaced.
matte	Boolean	If `true`, the script mats the artboard with a color.
matteColor	RGBColor object	Color to use for matting if the matte property is set to `true`.
saveAsHTML	Boolean	If `true`, the script creates a HTML file along with the image.
transparency	Boolean	Determines whether the image should use transparency.
verticalScale	Number	Vertical scaling factor for the exported image.
webSnap	Number	Sets how strongly Illustrator should alter the colors in the image make them Web safe, with 100 percent ensuring a completely Web safe image.

COMMON FEATURES OF PAGE ITEMS

Many of the non-text items that appear in Illustrator documents share a number of common methods and properties. These items include path items, compound paths, placed items, and symbols. All of these common features are listed here.

Properties

PROPERTY NAME	TYPE	DESCRIPTION
artworkKnockout	KnockoutState constant	What kind of knockout this object creates, if any.
blendingMode	BlendModes constant	Mode to use when compositing an object.
controlBounds	Array of 4 numbers	The bounds of the object including stroke width. Read-only.
editable	Boolean	Is this item editable? An item is not editable if you lock its layers. Read-only.
geometricBounds	Array of 4 numbers	The bounds of the object excluding strokes. These are the values that appear in the info palette. Read-only.
height	Number	The height of the object.
hidden	Boolean	Determines if this object is visible. This is the same as the Visible property in the Layers palette.
isIsolated	Boolean	Determines if the object is isolated.
layer	Layer object	The layer that contains this object. Read-only.
left	Number	Left position of the object.
locked	Boolean	Sets if you have this object locked.
name	String	Name of this object. Same as the name that appears in the Layers palette.
opacity	Number	Opacity of this object. Valid values are between 0 and 100. This is the same value that appears in the Transparency palette.
parent	Object	The parent object for this item.
position	Array of 2 numbers	Position of the top left corner of the object. The first number is the left position and the second is the top position. Both numbers always display in points, regardless of the preference settings.
selected	Boolean	Determines whether this item is selected.
sliced	Boolean	True if this item is sliced.
top	Number	Position of the top of this item.
visibilityVariable	Variable object	The variable object bound to the visibility of this textArtItem.
visibleBounds	Array of 4 numbers	The visible bound of the object including stroke widths. Read-only.
width	Number	The width of the object.

APPENDIX
COMMON FEATURES OF
PAGE ITEMS (CONTINUED)

Properties *(continued)*

PROPERTY NAME	TYPE	DESCRIPTION
zOrderPosition	Number	The position of this object in the stacking order of the parent object. You can make the parent a `layer` or `groupItem` object. Read-only. Use the `zOrder` method of the object to change the stacking order.

Methods

METHOD NAME	RETURN TYPE	DESCRIPTION
duplicate()	Same as the duplicated object	Creates a duplicate of the object.
moveAfter(object target)	void	Moves the item behind the target object.
moveBefore(object target)	void	Moves the item in front of the target object.
moveToBeginning(object target)	void	Moves the item to the front of the target object.
moveToEnd(object target)	void	Moves the item to the bottom of the target object.
remove()	void	Removes the object.
resize(number xscale, number yscale [, boolean changePosition] [, boolean changeFillPattern] [, boolean changeFillGradient] [, boolean changeStrokePattern] [, number changeLineWidths] [, Transformation constant scaleCenter])	void	Scales the object, xscale is the horizontal scale, yscale is the vertical scale. 100.0 is 100%. If shape of the `changePosition` is `false`, the object does not change and only the gradient, patterns, and strokes are affected. `changeFillPattern` determines if the fill pattern scales with the item, or if the pattern stays the current size and tiles to fill the shape. `changeFillGradient` is like `changeFillPattern` but for gradient fills. If `changeStrokePattern` is `true`, a resize affects the dashed line pattern of the stroke. `changeLineWidths` is the percentage to scale the stroke widths, where 100.0 is 100%. `scaleCenter` sets the center point for the resize operation.
rotate(number Angle [, boolean changePosition] [, boolean changeFillPattern] [, boolean changeFillGradient] [, boolean changeStrokePattern] [Transformation constant rotationCenter])	void	Rotates the item. The new rotation is relative to the current rotation. If the angle is negative, the item rotates counterclockwise. The `rotationCenter` parameter defines what point to use as the center point for the rotation.
zOrder(ZOrderMethod constant ZOrderMethod)	void	Arranges the item in the parent container's (`document`, `layer`, or `group`) stacking order. Works like the options in the Object ⇨ Arrange menu.

PATH ITEMS

The path item is one of the most basic elements of artwork in Illustrator. In addition to the path item itself, you need the `pathPoint` object to perform many manipulations on paths.

THE PATHITEMS COLLECTION

A collection of all path items in the parent object. You can assess this collection from the `compoundPathItem`, `document`, `groupItem`, and `layer` objects.

Properties

PROPERTY NAME	TYPE	DESCRIPTION
length	Number	The number of objects in the collection.
parent	Object	The parent container of this object.

Methods

METHOD NAME	RETURN TYPE	DESCRIPTION
add()	PathItem object	Creates a new `pathItem` in the parent object.
ellipse([number top] [, number left] [, number width] [, number height] [, boolean reversed] [, boolean inscribed])	PathItem object	Creates a new elliptical path item in the parent object. All parameters are optional, but if you do not supply any, you cannot predict the ellipse's location and size.
polygon([number xcenter] [, number ycenter] [, number radius] [, number sides] [, boolean reversed])	PathItem object	Creates a polygon path item in the parent object. Analogous to the polygon drawing tool.
rectangle([number top] [, number width] [, number width] [, number height] [, boolean reversed])	PathItem object	Creates a rectangle path item in the parent object.
removeAll()	void	Removes all `pathItems` from the parent.
roundedRectangle([number top] [, number width] [, number width] [, number height] [, number horizontalCornerRadius] [, number verticalCornerRadius] [, boolean reversed])	PathItem object	Creates a rectangle with rounded corners in the parent object. The `horizontalCornerRadius` and `verticalCornerRadius` parameters control the corner rounding.

PATH ITEMS (CONTINUED)

Methods *(continued)*

METHOD NAME	RETURN TYPE	DESCRIPTION
star([number xcenter] [, number ycenter] [, number radius] [, number innerRadius] [, number points] [, boolean reversed])	PathItem **object**	Creates a star path item in the parent object. Radius defines the size of the star and innerRadius defines the distance from the center of the inner points of the star. Note that you use the size of a star to define the star's radius, not the width. The total size of the star is twice the number that the radius parameter specifies.

THE PATHITEM OBJECT

This object also contains the methods and properties listed in the section "Common Features of Page Items."

Properties

PROPERTY NAME	TYPE	DESCRIPTION
clipping	Boolean	If true, this path is used as a clipping path.
closed	Boolean	If true, this is a closed path.
evenodd	Boolean	Determines whether the even-odd rule fills in compound paths. See Chapter 5 for more on compound paths.
fillColor	Color **object**	Fill color of the text.
filled	Boolean	Use to specify whether this text item is filled with color.
fillOverprint	Boolean	Determines if the art under the path fill is overprinted.
pathPoints	PathPoints **collection**	Collection of path points in this path.
polarity	PolarityValues **constant**	Polarity of the path.
selectedPathPoints	PathPoints **collection**	A collection of all selected points on the path.
strokeCap	StrokeCap **constant**	The type of stroke capping to use. See Chapter 5 for more information.
strokeColor	Color **object**	Stroke color for the object.
stroked	Boolean	Determines whether the path item has a stroke.
strokeDashes	Array	Array of dash lengths. Set to an empty array to get a solid line. See Chapter 5 for more information of using stroke dashes.
strokeDashOffset	Number	Distance into the dash pattern set by strokeDashes that the dash pattern should begin.

PROPERTY NAME	TYPE	DESCRIPTION
strokeJoin	StrokeJoin constant	The type of joints to use.
strokeMiterLimit	Number	Determines whether the joins are pointed or squared off. This property is only valid when you use mitered joints.
strokeOverprint	Boolean	Determines if the art under the text stroke is overprinted.
strokeWidth	Number	The width of the stroke. The current preference setting for stroke determines the units.

Methods

METHOD NAME	RETURN TYPE	DESCRIPTION
setEntirePath(array)	void	Defines the position of every pathPoint on the path. You specify each point in the array as an array of two numbers, for the x and y positions of the point. See Chapter 5 for more information.

THE PATHPOINTS COLLECTION

A collection of all path points for a specific path item.
You access this collection from the pathItem object.

Properties

PROPERTY NAME	TYPE	DESCRIPTION
length	Number	The number of objects in the collection.
parent	PathItem object	The parent pathItem of this collection.

Methods

METHOD NAME	RETURN TYPE	DESCRIPTION
add()	PathPoint object	Creates a new pathPoint in the parent pathItem.
removeAll()	void	Although this mehod is listed in Adobe's documentation, it always returns an error and does not successfully remove any path points. Use a for loop and the remove() method of the pathPoint object to delete pathPoints. Remember that all paths must have at least two pathPoints.

PATH ITEMS (CONTINUED)

A series of `pathPoint` objects defines every path. Each `pathPoint` is in turn defined by its position, or anchor, and the position of its handles, defined by the left and right direction properties.

Properties

PROPERTY NAME	TYPE	DESCRIPTION
anchor	Array of two numbers	Position of the path point in the document.
leftDirection	Array of two numbers	Position on the page of the left direction handle.
parent	PathItem object	The `pathItem` that contains this path point.
pointType	PointType constant	Sets the type of the path point. You can make each point either a curve or a corner.
rightDirection	Array of two numbers	Position on the page of the right direction handle.
selected	PathPointSelection constant	This property allows you to set the selection of the path point's anchor or either of its handles. You can also use this property to deselect the point.

Methods

METHOD NAME	RETURN TYPE	DESCRIPTION
remove ()	void	Removes this path point from the parent path.

ILLUSTRATOR SCRIPTING CONSTANTS

Many properties and methods require a specific type of value defined by a scripting constant. The value for the constant is provided by typing the constant name, a dot, and then the value you want to use.

CONSTANT NAME	VALUES	DESCRIPTION
BlendModes	COLORBLEND, COLORBURN, COLORDODGE, DARKEN, DIFFERENCE, EXCLUSION, HARDLIGHT, HUE, LIGHTEN, LUMINOSITY, MULTIPLY, NORMAL, OVERLAY, SATURATIONBLEND, SCREEN, SOFTLIGHT	Specifies the blend mode used for an object. Same values that appear in the Blending Mode menu in the Transparency palette.
CharacterDirection	KUMIMOJI, NORMAL, ROTATED	Sets the orientation of the characters in a vertical text area.
ColorDithetMethod	DIFFUSION, NOISE, NOREDUCTION, PATTERNDITHER	Dither method used with the GIF and PNG8 export options objects.
ColorModel	PROCESS, REGISTRATION, SPOT	Used with the spot color object to specify the color model for the color. See the Illustrator JavaScript reference for more on the spot color object.
ColorReductionMethod	ADAPTIVE, PERCEPTUAL, SELECTIVE, WEB	Method used for reducing the number of colors for PNG8 and GIF export options objects.
ColorType	CMYK, GRADIENT, GRAY, NONE, PATTERN, RGB, SPOT	Sets the type with a color specification object.
Compatibility	ILLUSTRATOR10, ILLUSTRATOR3, ILLUSTRATOR4, ILLUSTRATOR5, ILLUSTRATOR6, ILLUSTRATOR7, ILLUSTRATOR8, ILLUSTRATOR9	Version of the file created when using the document.saveAs() method when creating an Illustrator or EPS file.
CompressionQuality	AUTOMATIC, JPEGHIGH, JPEGLOW, JPEGMAXIMUM, JPEGMEDIUM, JPEGMINIMUM, NONE, ZIP4BIT, ZIP8BIT	Quality setting for bitmap images when creating a PDF. Used with the PDFSaveOptions object.
CropOptions	JAPANESE, STANDARD	Document's cropping style.
DocumentColorSpace	CMYK, RGB	Specifies the color space when creating a new document using the documents.add() method.
DocumentType	EPS, ILLUSTRATOR, PDF	File format used when saving a file.
EPSPreview	BWMACINTOSH, BWTIFF, COLORMACINTOSH, COLORTIFF, NONE, TRANSPARENTCOLORTIFF	Format for the image preview when creating an EPS document. Used with the EPSSaveOptions object.
ExportType	FLASH, GIF, JPEG, Photoshop, PNG24, PNG8, SVG	Specifies the type of file to export with the exportFile() method.

ILLUSTRATOR SCRIPTING
CONSTANTS (CONTINUED)

CONSTANT NAME	VALUES	DESCRIPTION
FlashExportStyle	ASFLASHFILE, LAYERSASFILES, LAYERSASFRAMES	Specifies how Illustrator treats layers when exporting a file to SWF. ASFLASHFILE creates a one frame SWF with each Illustrator layer on a separate layer. LAYERSASFILES saves each Illustrator layer as a separate SWF file. And LAYERSASFRAMES creates a SWF file with one frame for each Illustrator layer. You can use this to create animations in Illustrator. Use with the ExportOptionsFlash object.
FlashImageFormat	LOSSLESS, LOSSY	Format for bitmap images when creating an SWF file. Use this with the ExportOptionsFlash object.
FlashJPEGMethod	OPTIMIZED, STANDARD	Method you use with JPEG images when exporting a file as SWF. Use with the ExportOptionsFlash object.
GradientType	LIINEAR, RADIAL	Sets the type of a gradient.
ImageColorSpace	CMYK, GRAYSCALE, RGB	Possible color space for an exported Photoshop file.
Justification	ALLLINES, CENTER, FULLINES, LEFT, RIGHT, UNKNOWN	Use to specify the alignment of a paragraph of text. Use with the paragraph object.
KnockoutState	DISABLED, ENABLED, INHERITED, UNKNOWN	Sets the type of knockout to use. Use with the artworkKnockout property of most page items.
MonochromeCompression	CCIT3, CCIT4, MONOZIP, NONE, RUNLENGTH	Compression type for monochrome bitmaps. Use with the PDFSaveOptions object when creating a PDF document.
OutputFlattening	PRESERVEAPPEARENCE, PRESERVEPATHS	Specifies how Illustrator flattens transparency when saving a file to EPS and Illustrator versions before 10.
PathPointSelection	ANCHORPOINT, LEFTDIRECTION, LEFTRIGHTPOINT, NOSELECTION, RIGHTDIRECTION	Sets which part of a path point is selected.
PDFCompatibility	ACROBAT4, ACROBAT5	Use with the PDFSaveOptions object to set the version of a PDF file.
PointType	CORNER, SMOOTH	Specifies whether a path point is a corner or a smooth curve.
PolarityValues	NEGATIVE, POSITIVE	Use to set the polarity of a path item.
PostScriptLevel	LEVEL1, LEVEL2, LEVEL3	Sets the PostScript compatibility level for an EPS document. Use when creating an EPS file with the EPSSaveOptions object.

CONSTANT NAME	VALUES	DESCRIPTION
RasterLinkState	DATAFROMFILE, DATAMODIFIED, NODATA	Use to test the status of a linked raster item. See the `RasterItem` object in the Illustrator JavaScript Reference for more information.
RulerUnits	CENTIMETERS, INCHES, MILLIMETERS, PICAS, POINTS, QS, UNKNOWN	Possible units of measure for the rulers of a document.
SaveOptions	DONOTSAVECHANGES, PROMPTTOSAVECHANGES, SAVECHANGES	Use to specify how Illustrator treats documents that you have not saved since the last change when using the `document.close()` method.
ScreenMode	DESKTOP, FULLSCREEN, MULTIWINDOW	Use to set the mode of a document view setting.
StrokeCap	BUTTENDCAP, PROJECTINGENDCAP, ROUNDENDCAP	Possible types of line capping for path items and text art items. Same as the available settings in the Stroke palette.
StrokeJoin	BEVELENDJOIN, MITERENDJOIN, ROUNDEDJOIN	Possible types of joints for a path or text art item. Same as the possible settings in the stroke palette.
SVGCSSPropertyLocation	ENTITIES, PRESENTATIONATTRIBUTES, STYLEATTRIBUTES, STYLEELEMENTS	Use when creating an SVG document to specify where CSS properties are located. Use with the `ExportOptionsSVG` object.
SVGDocumentEncoding	ASCII, UTF16, UTF8	Used with the `ExportOptionsSVG` object to specify how to encode the text in an SVG document.
SVGFontSubsetting	ALLGLYPHS, COMMONENGLISH, COMMONROMAN, GLYPHSUSED, GLYPHSUSEDPLUSENGLISH, GLYPHSUSEDPLUSROMAN, NONE	Use with the `ExportOptionsSVG` object to specify what font glyphs are included with the SVG document.
TabStopAlignment	CENTER, DECIMAL, LEFT, RIGHT, UNKNOWN	Use with a `paragraph` object to set the alignment of tab stops.
TextOrientation	HORIZONTAL, VERTICAL	Use to set the orientation of text in a text art item.
TextType	AREATEXT, PATHTEXT, POINTTEXT	Possible types of `textArtItem` objects. See Chapter 7 for more information.
Transformation	BOTTOM, BOTTOMLEFT, BOTTOMRIGHT, CENTER, DOCUMENTORIGIN, LEFT, RIGHT, TOP, TOPLEFT, TOPRIGHT	Use with the `rotate()`, `resize`, and `transform` methods of page items to set the center point for the operation.
UserInteractionLevel	DISPLAYALERTS, DONTDISPLAYALERTS	Sets the how Illustrator interacts with the user.
VariableKind	GRAPH, IMAGE, TEXTUAL, UNKNOWN, VISIBILITY	Use with a `variable` object to set or test the type of the variable.
ZOrderMethod	BRINGFORWARD, BRINGTOFRONT, SENDBACKWARD, SENDTOBACK	Use with the `zOrder()` method of page items, layers, groups, and text art items to change the stacking order of objects. The values and resulting behaviors are the same as those in the Object ⇨ Arrange menu.

THE APPLICATION AND PREFERENCES OBJECTS

When using JavaScript for Photoshop, you do not need to specify the `Application` object to access its properties and methods. You can simply type the name of the function or property.

THE APPLICATION OBJECT

Properties

PROPERTY NAME	TYPE	DESCRIPTION
activeDocument	Document object	Returns a document object for the topmost open document.
arguments	Array	An array of the arguments passed to the script when executed using Visual Basic or AppleScript.
backgroundColor	SolidColor object	Sets the current background color. This is the color that appears in the Tools palette, not the background color of a particular document.
colorSettings	String	Name of the current color settings. These are the settings available in the Photoshop ⇨ Color Settings dialog.
displayDialogs	DialogModes constant	Determines how Photoshop communicates with the user.
documents	Documents collection object	Contains a document object for each open document.
foregroundColor	SolidColor object	Sets the current foreground color.
freeMemory	Number	Amount of unused memory available to Photoshop.
name	String	Name of the application. As of Photoshop 7. This does not include the version number.
path	File object	Path to the location of the Photoshop application.
preferences	Preferences object	The preference settings for Photoshop.
scriptingVersion	String	Currently installed scripting version.
version	String	Version number of the Photoshop application executing the script.

Methods

METHOD NAME	RETURN TYPE	DESCRIPTION
alert(string message)	void	Displays a message to the user displaying the text and an OK button.
beep()	void	Causes a beep sound.

THE APPLICATION OBJECT (CONTINUED)

METHOD NAME	RETURN TYPE	DESCRIPTION
confirm(string message)	Boolean	Displays a confirmation box containing a message, Yes and No buttons. Returns the user's response, true for yes, false for no.
doAction(string actionName, string folderName)	Executes a Photoshop action.	You specify the name of the action with actionName. folderName is the name of the folder containing the action.
open(File fileref [, Options object options])	Document object	Opens the file that fileref specifies. Some file types Open allow you to further specify options using an options object. See the section "Open Options Objects" for possible objects.

THE PREFERENCES OBJECT

You use this object to access and set the user's Photoshop preferences. You can find most of these preferences in the Photoshop ⇨ Preferences menu. However, some are located in the preference settings for the palette associated with the setting.

Properties

PROPERTY NAME	TYPE	DESCRIPTION
additionalPluginFolder	File object	The location of the additional plug-ins folder. This is available at the Photoshop ⇨ Preferences ⇨ Plug-Ins & Scratch Disks menu.
appendExtension	SaveBehavior constant	Defines how Photoshop treats file extensions when saving.
askBeforeSavingLayerTIFF	Boolean	Determines if the user is prompted when saving a layered document as a TIFF.
autoUpdateOpenDocuments	Boolean	If true, documents that you have open in Photoshop update if you altered them in another application.
beepWhenDone	Boolean	If true, Photoshop beeps when it completes a command.
colorChannelsInColor	Boolean	If true, each channel displays in its color in the Channels palette.
colorPicker	ColorPicker constant	Defines what color picker Photoshop should use.
columnGutter	Number	Size of column gutter when using Crop and Image Size. Unit is in points.

THE APPLICATION AND PREFERENCES OBJECTS (CONTINUED)

Properties *(continued)*

PROPERTY NAME	TYPE	DESCRIPTION
columnWidth	Number	Width of gutter when using Crop and Image Size. Unit is in points.
createFirstSnapshot	Boolean	Sets if Photoshop should automatically create a snapshot in the History palette when Photoshop creates a new document.
dynamicColorSlider	Boolean	If true, the color you change with a color slider updates as the slider moves.
exportClipboard	Boolean	If true, Photoshop makes the content of the clipboard available to other applications.
fullSizePreview	Boolean	Should Photoshop save a full-size preview of the image?
gamutWarningOpacity	Number	Opacity for out of gamut areas.
gridSize	GridSize constant	Sets the size of the grid.
gridStyle	GridLineStyle constant	Sets the style used when Photoshop draws the grid.
gridSubDivisions	Number	Sets how many divisions are made between major grid lines.
guideStyle	GuideLineStyle constant	Sets the style you use when drawing guide lines.
iconPreview	Boolean	If true, Photoshop creates an icon preview for saved documents.
imageCacheForHistograms	Boolean	Determine if Photoshop uses a cache for histogram data.
imageCacheLevels	Number	Sets the number of levels of cache data Photoshop uses.
imagePreviews	SaveBehavior constant	Sets how Photoshop should behave with regard to previews when saving a file.
interpolation	ResampleMethod constant	Interpolation method Photoshop uses when scaling or resizing images.
keyboardZoomResizesWindows	Boolean	Determines whether a user resizes the window of documents or zooms using keyboard commands.
macOSThumbnail	Boolean	If true, Photoshop creates a Mac OS thumbnail when saving images.
maxRAMuse	Number	Maximum percentage of available memory Photoshop should use. You must make this a number between 5 and 100.
maximizeCompatibility	Boolean	If true, Photoshop always creates a composite when saving a PSD file.

THE PREFERENCES OBJECT (CONTINUED)

PROPERTY NAME	TYPE	DESCRIPTION
nonLinearHistory	Boolean	If true, Photoshop does not force a chronological progression on states in the History palette.
numberOfHistoryStates	Number	Sets how many history states Photoshop should remember. You must make this a number between 1 and 100.
otherCursors	OtherPainting Cursors constant	Sets how Photoshop draws non-painting cursors.
paintingCursors	PaintingCursors constant	Sets how Photoshop should draw painting cursors.
pixelDoubling	Boolean	If true, Photoshop displays a reduced resolution image when moving objects. This makes dragging objects faster.
pointSize	PointType constant	Determines how Photoshop interprets point sizes.
recentFileListLength	Number	Number of items shown in the File ⇨ Open Recent menu.
redoKey	RedoKey constant	Sets what key command Photoshop uses for the redo command.
rulerUnits	Units constant	Unit of measure for all rulers and scripting commands.
savePaletteLocations	Boolean	If true, Photoshop remembers the location of all palettes.
showAsianTextOptions	Boolean	Sets if Asian text options display.
showEnglishFontNames	Boolean	If true, fonts with names using non-roman characters display using their English names.
showSliceNumber	Boolean	If true, Photoshop displays the number of each slice when drawing slice lines.
showToolTips	Boolean	If true, Photoshop displays tool tips for tools, settings and options.
smartQuotes	Boolean	Determines whether smart or curly quotes are used in text items.
typeUnits	TypeUnits constant	Unit Photoshop uses when setting the size of text items.
useAdditionalPluginFolder	Boolean	If true, Photoshop looks for a plug-in in the alternative plug-in folder.
useDiffusionDither	Boolean	If true, Photoshop uses diffusion dithering on displays that do not support True Color (32 bit).
useLowerCaseExtension	Boolean	If true, file extensions are lowercase on saved files.
useShiftKeyForToolSwitch	Boolean	If true, you must use the Shift key to switch between grouped tools.
useVideoAlpha	Boolean	If true, Photoshop uses video alpha mode.
windowsThumbnail	Boolean	If true, Photoshop creates a Windows thumbnail for saved files.

DOCUMENT AND RELATED OBJECTS

Y ou use the document object in almost every script. It provides access to a particular document. In addition to the document object and documents collection, there are other document-level objects such as the selection object, and options objects required for changing the color mode of a document.

THE DOCUMENTS COLLECTION

Properties

PROPERTY NAME	TYPE	DESCRIPTION
length	Number	The number of currently open documents.

Methods

METHOD NAME	RETURN TYPE	DESCRIPTION
add([number width] [, number height] [, number resolution] [, string name] [, NewDocumentMode constant mode] [, DocumentFill constant fill])	Document object	Creates a new document. You can set features of the document using the optional parameters. If you do not supply parameters, Photoshop creates the document using its default settings.

THE DOCUMENT OBJECT

Properties

PROPERTY NAME	TYPE	DESCRIPTION
activeChannels	Array	An array of Channel objects for active channels in the document. See the Photoshop JavaScript Reference for more on the Channel object.
activeHistoryBrushSource	HistoryState object	A reference to the current state in the History palette that you use with the history brush. See the Photoshop JavaScript Reference for more on the HistoryState object.
activeHistoryState	HistoryState object	A reference to the currently active history state.
activeLayer	ArtLayer or layerSet object	A reference to the currently selected layer.
artLayers	ArtLayers collection	A collection of all artLayer objects in the document.
backgroundLayer	ArtLayer object	A reference to the background layer of the document. This property is only valid for documents with a background layer. Read-only.

PROPERTY NAME	TYPE	DESCRIPTION
bitsPerChannel	BitsPerChannelType constant	The number of bits in each channel.
channels	Channels collection	A collection of all channels in the document. See the Photoshop JavaScript Reference for more on the Channel object and Channels collection.
colorProfileName	String	Name of the color profile associated with a document. This property is only valid for documents using a color profile.
colorProfileType	ColorProfile constant	The type of color profile in use for the document.
componentChannels	Array	An array of all color component channels for a document.
fullName	File object	A File object that refers to the file of a document. Read-only.
height	Number	Height of the document. Read-only.
historyStates	HistoryStates collection	A collection of history states for a document. See the Photoshop JavaScript Reference for more on the historyState object.
info	DocumentInfo object	A reference to the document info for a document.
layerSets	LayerSets collection	A collection of all layer sets in a document.
layers	Layers collection	A collection of all art layers and layer sets at the top level of the document. This collection does not include layers that are inside layer sets.
managed	Boolean	True if a workgroup server manages the document.
modified	Boolean	True if you have modified the document since the last save.
name	String	The name of the document.
path	Folder object	A Folder object referring to the folder containing the document.
quickMaskMode	Boolean	If true, or set to true, the document is in quick mask mode.
resolution	Number	Resolution of the document in pixels per inch. Read-only.
saved	Boolean	True if you have saved the document since the last change. This property is also true for new documents that you have not yet saved.
selection	Selection object	The selection object representing the selection of the document.
width	Number	The width of the document. Read-only.

DOCUMENT AND RELATED OBJECTS (CONTINUED)

THE DOCUMENT OBJECT (CONTINUED)

Methods

METHOD NAME	RETURN TYPE	DESCRIPTION
`changeMode(ChangeMode constant newMode [, Mode Options options])`	void	Changes the mode of the document to the mode that `newMode` defines. You can specify additional options for Bitmap and Index modes using a `BitmapConversionOptions` or `IndexedConversionOptions` object.
`close([SaveOptions constant options])`	void	Closes the document. You can specify how Photoshop treats unsaved documents using the `options` parameter.
`convertProfile(string profileName, intent constant intent [, boolean BlackPoint] [, boolean dither])`	void	Converts the color profile of the document.
`crop(array bounds [, number angle] [, number width] [, number height] [, number resolution])`	none	Crops the document using the supplied parameters. See Chapter 3 for more information on cropping a document.
`duplicate()`	Document object	Makes a duplicate of the document.
`exportDocument(file destination, [, ExportType constant type] [, Export Options options])`	void	Exports the document to the file specified by `destination` to the specified type with any provided options. You can make the `options` parameter any of the `SaveOptions` objects.
`flatten()`	void	Flattens all layers in a document.
`flipCanvas(Direction constant direction)`	void	Flips the document either horizontally or vertically, set by direction.
`importAnnotations(file fileref)`	void	Imports the annotations from `fileref`.
`mergeVisibleLayers()`	void	Flattens all visible layers in the document.
`paste([boolean into])`	ArtLayer	Pastes the contents of the clipboard into the document. If the into parameter is `true`, the clipboard pastes into the current selection.
`print([PrintEncoding constant encoding] [, SourceSpaceType constant space] [, string printSpace] [, Intent constant intent] [, boolean blackPoint])`	void	Prints the document using the supplied parameters.

METHOD NAME	RETURN TYPE	DESCRIPTION
`rasterizeAllLayers()`	**void**	**Converts the contents of every layer to rasterized format. All text and shape layers are no longer editable.**
`resizeCanvas([number width] [, number height] [, AnchorPosition constant anchor])`	**void**	**Resizes the canvas of the document to the size specified by height and width. The anchor position determines where Photoshop adds the additional area.**
`resizeImage([number width] [, number height] [, number resolution] [, ResampleMethod constant resample])`	**void**	**Resizes the document to width, height and resolution. You use the resample parameter to specify what method to use in determining the new size.**
`revealAll()`	**void**	**Changes the size of the document to show areas of clipped images.**
`rotateCanvas(number angle)`	**void**	**Rotates the document.**
`save()`	**void**	**Saves the document, valid only for documents that you have already saved.**
`saveAs(file fileref [, options] [, boolean ascopy] [, Extension constant extension])`	**void**	**Saves the document into the file that `fileref` specifies. You can set options for the new file using one of the `SaveOptions` objects. The extension parameter specifies how Photoshop handles the file extension.**
`splitChannels()`	**Array of documents**	**Creates a new document for each channel in the document. Returns an array of references to the new documents.**
`trap(number width)`	**void**	**Applies a trap to a CMYK document.**
`trim([TrimType type] [, boolean top] [, boolean left] [, boolean bottom] [, boolean right])`	**void**	**Trims the document using the specified `trim` method. You can optionally set whether a side is trimmed.**

All of the properties of this object correspond to the options in the File ⇨ Document Info dialog box.

Properties

PROPERTY NAME	TYPE	DESCRIPTION
`author`	**String**	**The name of the document's author.**
`authorPosition`	**String**	**The name of the document's author position.**
`caption`	**String**	**A caption for the image.**

DOCUMENT AND RELATED OBJECTS (CONTINUED)

Properties *(continued)*

PROPERTY NAME	TYPE	DESCRIPTION
captionWriter	String	Author of the document's caption.
category	String	Category for this document.
city	String	City information.
copyrightNotice	String	Copyright line for the document.
copyrighted	CopyrightedType constant	Type of copyright.
country	String	Country information.
creationDate	String	Date of the document's creation.
credit	String	Credit line for the document.
exif	Array	An array of arrays containing the exif information for images that you create with a digital camera. The first item in each array is the name of the property and the second is the value. Read-only.
headline	String	Headline text for the document.
instructions	String	Instruction text for the document.
jobName	String	Name of the job to which this document belongs.
keywords	Array	An array of all keywords for this document.
ownerUrl	String	Internet address for the owner of the document.
provinceState	String	Province or state information for the document.
source	String	Source information.
supplementalCategories	Array	An array of other categories for the document.
title	String	Title of the document.
transmissionReference	String	Transmission reference for the document.
urgency	Urgency constant	The urgency value for the document, specified as an urgency constant.

Methods

METHOD NAME	RETURN TYPE	DESCRIPTION
clear()	void	Clears the contents of the selection.
contract(number by)	void	Contracts the selection a given amount of pixels.

METHOD NAME	RETURN TYPE	DESCRIPTION
`copy([boolean merge])`	void	Copies the contents of the selection to the clipboard. If the merge parameter is `true`, Photoshop copies the merged contents of all layers.
`cut()`	void	Clears the selection and adds its contents to the clipboard.
`deselect()`	void	Removes the selection.
`expand(number by)`	void	Expands the selection by a specified amount.
`feather(number by)`	void	Feathers the edges of the selection a specified amount.
`fill(fillWith [, ColorBlendMode constant mode] [, number opacity] [, boolean transparency])`	void	Fills the selection with the object that `fillWith` specifies. Valid objects are `color` objects and history states. You can also specify a blend mode and opacity for the fill. If transparency is `true`, transparency is preserved.
`grow(number tolerance, boolean antialias)`	void	Expands the selection to include all adjacent pixels that fall within the tolerance range. This includes sections that you can also anti-alias.
`invert()`	void	Inverts the selection.
`load(channel from, [, SelectionType constant combination] [, boolean inverting])`	void	Loads a selection from the specified `channel` object.
`resize([number horizontal] [, number vertical] [, AnchorPosition constant anchor])`	void	Resizes the contents of the selection to the specified size. The anchor position determines in which direction the selection resizes.
`resizeBoundry([number horizontal] [, number vertical] [, AnchorPosition constant anchor])`	void	Resizes the boundary of the selection without affecting the selection contents.
`rotate(number angle [, AnchorPosition constant anchor])`	void	Rotates the contents of the selection. The anchor determines the center point for the rotation.
`rotateBoundry(number angle [, AnchorPosition constant anchor])`	void	Rotates the boundary of the selection without changing the contents.
`select(array shape [, SelectionType constant type] [, number feather] [, boolean antialias])`	void	Selects a part of a document. You define the area for a selection as an array of point arrays. You can optionally set the type of selection, feather amount, and if you want to anti-alias the selection.

DOCUMENT AND RELATED OBJECTS (CONTINUED)

THE SELECTION OBJECT (CONTINUED)

Methods *(continued)*

METHOD NAME	RETURN TYPE	DESCRIPTION
selectAll()	void	Sets the selection to the entire area of the document.
selectBorder(number width)	void	Sets the selection to the border of the current selection with the specified width.
similar(number tolerance, boolean antialias)	void	Includes all pixels in the document that fall within the tolerance level.
smooth(number radius)	void	Smooths the current selection.
store(channel into [, SelectionType constant combination])	void	Saves the current selection to the specified channel.
stroke(Color object color, number width [, StrokeLocation constant location] [, ColorBlendMode constant mode] [, number opacity] [, boolean transparency])	void	Strokes the selection with the specified color. You can set the location of the stroke to inside, outside, or center. You can also set the color blend and specify if you want to preserve transparency.
translate([number deltax] [, number deltay])	void	Moves the selection contents relative to the current selection location.
translateBoundry([number deltax] [, number deltay])	void	Moves the selection boundary relative to the current selection location without affecting the selection contents.

THE INDEXEDCONVERSIONOPTIONS OBJECT

You use this object to set options when changing the document mode to Indexed. You must create it using the New keyword. See Chapter 2 for more information on creating objects.

Properties

PROPERTY NAME	TYPE	DESCRIPTION
colors	Number	Specifies the number of colors in the target palette.
dither	Dither constant	Sets the type of dither to use.
ditherAmount	Number	Percent of dither when using diffusion dithering. Must be a number between 1 and 100.
forced	ForcedColors constant	Specifies if the target palette should be forced to a specific set of colors.
matte	MatteType constant	Sets the type of matte to use.
palette	Palette constant	Specifies what type of palette to use.
preserveExactColors	Boolean	If true, Photoshop uses the exact colors in the image when possible.
transparency	Boolean	If true, the image retains transparent areas.

THE INDEXEDCONVERSIONOPTIONS OBJECT

You use this object to set options when changing the document mode to Bitmap. You must create it using the New keyword. See Chapter 2 for more information on creating objects.

Properties

PROPERTY NAME	TYPE	DESCRIPTION
angle	Number	Angle to use for the Halftone Screen conversion method.
frequency	Number	Frequency when using Halftone Screen conversion method.
method	BitmapConversionType constant	Bitmap conversion method to use.
patternName	String	Name of pattern to use with the Custom Pattern conversion method.
resolution	Number	Resolution for the result, in pixels per inch.
shape	BitmapHalfToneType constant	Shape to use with the Halftone Screen conversion method.

LAYER AND TEXT OBJECTS

One of the most fundamental elements of a Photoshop document is the layer. All documents are comprised of art layers and layers sets. Layer sets let you organize your documents while art layers contain artwork and text. Photoshop creates all text by converting an art layer into a special type of text layer.

THE ARTLAYERS COLLECTION

The `artLayers` collection contains a reference to all `artLayers` in the parent object. You can access this collection from the document and `layerSet` objects. In the case of the document `layerSets` collection, the art layers contained inside of layer sets are not included.

Properties

PROPERTY NAME	TYPE	DESCRIPTION
length	Number	The number of `artLayers` in the parent object.
parent	`Document` or `layerSet` object	The parent container of this collection.

Methods

METHOD NAME	RETURN TYPE	DESCRIPTION
add()	`artLayer` object	Creates a new art layer in the parent object. You can make the parent either a `document` or `layerSet` object.
removeAll()	none	Removes all `artLayers` from the parent.

THE ARTLAYER OBJECT

The `artLayer` is the most fundamental element of a Photoshop document. Art layers contain all artwork, images, and text.

Properties

PROPERTY NAME	TYPE	DESCRIPTION
allLocked	Boolean	Sets if the layer is locked.
blendMode	BlendMode constant	Sets the blend mode for the layer. This is the same as the drop-down menu in the Layers palette.
fillOpacity	Number	The opacity of filled areas in the layer. You must make this a number between 0 and 100.

PROPERTY NAME	TYPE	DESCRIPTION
grouped	Boolean	True if you group the layer with the layer below it.
isBackgroundLayer	Boolean	True if the layer is the background layer.
kind	LayerKind constant	Sets the type of layer. You can have normal or type layers.
linkedLayers	Array	An array of all layers that are linked with this layer.
name	String	The name of the layer as appears in the Layers palette.
opacity	Number	Opacity of the entire layer.
parent	Document or layerSet object	The parent object that contains this layer.
pixelsLocked	Boolean	Determines if pixels in the layer are locked.
positionLocked	Boolean	Determines if the position of the layer is locked.
textItem	TextItem object	The text item associated with this layer. This property is only valid for text layers.
transparentPixelsLocked	Boolean	Determines if transparent areas of the document are locked.
visible	Boolean	Sets if the layer is visible.

Methods

METHOD NAME	RETURN TYPE	DESCRIPTION
adjustBrightnessContrast (number brightness, number contrast)	void	Adjusts the brightness and contrast of a layer. You must make the values between –100 and 100.
adjustColorBalance([array shadows] [, array midtones] [, array highlights] [, boolean luminosity])	void	Adjusts the color balance of the layer. The shadows, midtones, and highlights parameters each take an array of 3 numbers with values between –100 and 100. The values set the red, green, and blue values. You can set the luminosity parameter to preserve luminosity.
adjustCurves(array shape)	void	Adjust the curves of a layer. The shape parameter is an array of arrays, each representing a point on the curve. You only apply the adjustment to the selected channels.
adjustLevels(number inputRangeStart, number inputRangeEnd, number inputRangeGamma, number outputRangeStart, number outputRangeEnd)	void	Adjusts the levels of the selected channels on the layer.
applyAddNoise(number amount, NoiseDistribution constant distribution, boolean monochromatic)	void	Applies the Add Noise filter to the layer.

LAYER AND TEXT OBJECTS (CONTINUED)

Methods

METHOD NAME	RETURN TYPE	DESCRIPTION
applyBlur()	void	Applies the Blur filter to the layer.
applyBlurMore()	void	Applies the Blur More filter to the layer.
applyClouds()	void	Applies the Clouds filter.
applyCustomFilter(array characteristics, number scale, number offset)	void	Applies a custom filter to the layer. The characteristics parameter is a 25-member array specifying the matrix for the filter action.
applyDeInterlace(EliminateFields constant eliminate, CreateFields constant create)	void	Applies the De-Interlace filter to the layer.
applyDespeckle()	void	Applies the Despeckle filter.
applyDifferenceClouds()	void	Applies the Difference Clouds filter.
applyDiffuseGlow(number graininess, number glowAmount, number clearAmount)	void	Applies the Diffuse Glow filter.
applyDisplace(number horizontalScale, number verticalScale, DisplacementMapType constant map, UndefinedAreas constant undefinedAreas, File displacementMapFile)	void	Applies the Displace filter to the layer.
applyDustAndScratches(number radius, number threshold)	void	Applies the Dust and Scratches filter.
applyGaussianBlur(number radius)	void	Applies the Gaussian Blur filter.
applyGlassEffect(number distortion, number smoothness, number scaling [, boolean invert] [, TextureType constant texture] [, File textureFile])	void	Applies the Glass Effect filter.
applyHighPass(number radius)	void	Applies the High Pass filter.
applyLensFlare(number brightness, array flareCenter, LensType constant lensType)	void	Applies the Lens Flare filter. The flareCenter parameter is an array of two numbers specifying the x and y position of the flare center.
applyMaximum(number radius)	void	Applies the Maximum filter.
applyMedianNoise(number radius)	void	Applies the Median Noise filter.
applyMinimum(number radius)	void	Applies the Minimum filter.
applyMotionBlur(number angle, number radius)	void	Applies the Motion Blur filter.
applyNTSC()	void	Applies the NTSC filter.

THE ARTLAYER OBJECT (CONTINUED)

METHOD NAME	RETURN TYPE	DESCRIPTION
applyOcenRipple(number size, number magnitude)	void	Applies the Magnitude filter.
applyOffset(number horizontal, number vertical, OffsetUndefinedAreas constant undefinedAreas)	void	Applies the Offset filter.
applyPinch(number amount)	void	Applies the Pinch filter.
applyPolarCoordinates(PolarConversionType constant)	void	Applies the Polar Coordinates filter.
applyRadialBlur(number amount, RadialBlurMethod constant blurMethod, RadialBlurQuality constant)	void	Applies the Radial Blur filter.
applyRipple(number amount, RippleSize constant size)	void	Applies the Ripple filter.
applySharpen()	void	Applies the Sharpen filter.
applySharpenEdges()	void	Applies the Sharpen Edges filter.
applySharpenMore()	void	Applies the Sharpen More filter.
applyShear(array curve, UndefinedAreas constant undefinedAreas)	void	Applies the Shear filter.
applySmartBlur(number radius, number threshold, SmartBlurQuality constant quality, SmartBlurMode constant mode)	void	Applies the Smart Blur filter.
applySpherize(number amount, SpherizeMode constant mode)	void	Applies the Spherize filter.
applyStyle(string name)	void	Applies a style to the layer. The parameter specifies the name of the style.
applyTextureFill(File texture)	void	Applies a texture to the layer.
applyTwirl(number angle)	void	Applies the Twirl filter.
applyUnSharpMask(number amount, number radius, number threshold)	void	Applies the Unsharp Mask filter.
applyWave(number generator, number minWavelength, number maxWavelength, number minAmplitude, number maxAmplitude, number horizontalScale, number verticalScale, WaveType constant waveType, UndefinedAreas constant undefinedAreas, number |randomSeed)	void	Applies the Wave filter to the layer. The parameters correspond to the options available in the Filter dialog box.
applyZigZag(number amount, number ridges, ZigZagType constant style)	void	Applies the ZigZag filter.

LAYER AND TEXT OBJECTS (CONTINUED)

Methods *(continued)*

METHOD NAME	RETURN TYPE	DESCRIPTION
autoContrast()	void	Applies the Image ⇨ Adjustments ⇨ Auto Contrast option to the image.
autoLevels()	void	Applies the Image ⇨ Adjustments ⇨ Auto Levels option to the image.
clear()	void	Deletes the contents of the layer.
copy(boolean merge)	void	Copies the contents of the layer. If the merge parameter is true, the merged contents of every visible layer are copied.
cut()	void	Copies, then removes the contents of the layer.
desaturate()	void	Applies the Image ⇨ Adjustments ⇨ Desaturate option to the image.
duplicate()	ArtLayer object	Makes a duplicate copy of the layer.
equalize()	void	Applies the Image ⇨ Adjustments ⇨ Equalize option to the image.
invert()	void	Inverts the layer.
link(layer with)	void	Links the layer with another layer.
merge()	ArtLayer object	Merges the layer into the layer below it. The script removes the layer from the document and returns it with a reference to the layer with which it merged.
mixChannels(boolean monochrome, Channel output)	void	Applies the Image ⇨ Adjustments ⇨ Mix Channels action to the layer.
moveAfter(object destination)	void	Moves the artLayer behind the specified object. You can make the destination an artLayer or layerSet.
moveBefore(object destination)	void	Moves the artLayer in front of the specified object. You can make the destination an artLayer or layerSet.
moveToBeginning(object destination)	void	Moves the artLayer to the front of the specified object. You can make the destination a document or layerSet.
moveToEnd(object destination)	void	Moves the artLayer to the back of the specified object. You can make the destination a document or layerSet.
posterize(number levels)	void	Posterizes the image.

THE ARTLAYER OBJECT (CONTINUED)

METHOD NAME	RETURN TYPE	DESCRIPTION
rasterize(RasterizeType constant method)	void	Rasterizes the specified content of the layer.
remove()	void	Removes the artLayer from the document.
resize([number horizontal] [, number vertical] [, AnchorPosition constant Anchor])	void	Resizes the artLayer and its contents to the specified size. You use the anchor parameter to set the direction of the resize.
rotate(number angle [, AnchorPosition constant anchor])	void	Rotates the artLayer a specified number of degrees. You can use the anchor parameter to set the center point for the rotation.
selectiveColor(AdjustmentReference constant method, [, array reds] [, array yellows] [, array greens] [, array cyans] [, array blues] [, array magentas] [, array whites] [array neutrals] [, array blacks])	void	Applies the Image ⇨ Adjustments ⇨ Selective color action to the layer. Each color is an array of three numbers between −100 and 100 for the value of each color pair.
threshold(number level)	void	Applies a threshold to the layer.
translate([number xdelta] [, number ydelta])	void	Moves the artLayer relative to its current position.
unlink()	void	Unlinks the artLayer from any other layers

THE LAYERSETS COLLECTION

The layerSets collection contains a reference to all layerSets in a document. As of Photoshop 7, you cannot nest layer sets, so you can only access this collection from the document object.

Properties

PROPERTY NAME	TYPE	DESCRIPTION
length	Number	The number of layerSets in the document.
parent	Document object	A reference to the document that contains this collection.

Methods

METHOD NAME	RETURN TYPE	DESCRIPTION
add()	layerSet object	Creates a new layer set in the document.
removeAll()	void	Removes all layerSets from the document.

LAYER AND TEXT OBJECTS (CONTINUED)

THE LAYERSET OBJECT

The `layerSet` object represents a layer set in a document. You can create new layer sets using the `layerSets` collection's `add` method.

Properties

PROPERTY NAME	TYPE	DESCRIPTION
allLocked	Boolean	Locks all layers in the layer set.
artLayers	ArtLayers collection	A collection of all `artLayer` objects in the layer set.
blendMode	BlendMode constant	Sets the blend mode for all art layers in the layer set.
enabledChannels	Array	An array of channel objects that are enabled for the layer set.
layers	Layers collection	A collection of all layers in the layer set.
linkedLayers	Array	An array of all linked layers in the layer set.
name	String	The name of the layer set as it appears in the Layers palette.
opacity	Number	Opacity of the layer set. You apply this value in addition to the opacity of the individual art layer's opacity.
parent	Document object	The parent document for the layer set.
visible	Boolean	Sets the visibility of the layer set and its contents.

Methods

METHOD NAME	RETURN TYPE	DESCRIPTION
duplicate()	layerSet object	Creates a duplicate of the layer set in the document.
link(Layer object layer)	void	Links the `layerSet` with the layer.
merge()	artLayer object	Merges the contents of the layer set into a new art layer. Returns a reference to the new `artLayer`.
moveAfter(object destination)	void	Moves the `layerSet` behind the specified object. You can make the destination an `artLayer` or `layerSet`.
moveBefore(object destination)	void	Moves the `layerSet` in front of the specified object. You can make the destination an `artLayer` or `layerSet`.
moveToBeginning (object destination)	void	Moves the `layerSet` to the front of the specified object. You can make the destination a document or `layerSet`.
moveToEnd(object destination)	void	Moves the `layerSet` to the back of the specified object. You can make the destination a document or `layerSet`.
remove()	void	Removes the `layerSet` from the document.
resize([number horizontal] [,number vertical] [, AnchorPosition constant Anchor])	void	Resizes the `layerSet` and its contents to the specified size. The anchor parameter sets the direction of the resize.

THE LAYERSET OBJECT (CONTINUED)

METHOD NAME	RETURN TYPE	DESCRIPTION
rotate(number angle [, AnchorPosition constant anchor])	void	Rotates the layerSet a specified number of degrees. You can use the anchor parameter to set the center point for the rotation.
translate([number xdelta] [, number ydelta])	void	Moves the layerSet relative to its current position.
unlink()	void	Unlinks the layerSet from any other layers.

THE LAYERS COLLECTION

The layers collection contains a reference to all layerSet and artLayer objects. You can access this collection from the document and layerSet objects.

Properties

PROPERTY NAME	TYPE	DESCRIPTION
length	Number	The number of layerSet and artLayer objects in the parent object.
parent	Document object	A reference to the document or layerSet that contains this collection.

Methods

METHOD NAME	RETURN TYPE	DESCRIPTION
removeAll()	void	Removes all layerSet and artLayer objects from the parent object.

THE TEXTITEM OBJECT

The textItem object provides access to the contents and setting of the text contained by a layer. This object is accessible from every artLayer.

Properties

PROPERTY NAME	TYPE	DESCRIPTION
alternateLigatures	Boolean	Determines if Photoshop should use an alternate ligature set for the text item.
antiAliasMethod	AntiAlias constant	Sets how strongly Photoshop anti-aliases text.
autoKerning	Boolean	If true, Photoshop uses the font's built-in kerning information.
autoLeadingAmount	Number	Percentage of auto-leading amount.
baselineShift	Number	Amount of offset from the baseline. The document ruler unit determines the unit.
capitalization	Case constant	Sets how the script capitalizes the text.

LAYER AND TEXT OBJECTS (CONTINUED)

Properties *(continued)*

PROPERTY NAME	TYPE	DESCRIPTION
color	SolidColor **object**	Sets the color of the text item.
contents	**String**	The contents of the text item.
desiredGlyphScaling	**Number**	Scaling percentage for glyph items.
desiredLetterScaling	**Number**	Scaling percentage for letters.
desiredWordScaling	**Number**	Scaling percentage for words.
direction	Direction **constant**	Direction of the text, either horizontal or vertical.
fauxBold	**Boolean**	Set if you use the faux bold style.
fauxItalic	**Boolean**	Set if you use the faux italic style.
firstLineIndent	**Number**	Sets the indent of the first line of each paragraph.
font	**String**	PostScript name of the font to use.
hangingPunctuation	**Boolean**	Set if you use hanging punctuation.
height	**Number**	Height of a paragraph text item. Valid only for paragraph text.
horizontalScale	**Number**	Percentage to scale text items horizontally.
hyphenLimit	**Number**	Sets the maximum number of consecutive hyphens.
hyphenateAfterFirst	**Number**	Minimum number of letters that must occur before a hyphen.
hyphenateBeforeLast	**Number**	Minimum number of letters that must appear after a hyphen.
hyphenateCapitalWords	**Boolean**	Determines whether capitalized words are hyphenated.
hyphenateWordsLongerThan	**Number**	Tells Photoshop to hyphenate words that are longer than this amount.
hyphenation	**Boolean**	Determines whether you use hyphenation.
justification	Justification **constant**	Sets the paragraph justification.
kind	TextType **constant**	Sets the type of the text item, either point text or paragraph text.
language	Language **constant**	Sets the default language for the text item.
leading	**Number**	Amount of leading for the text item.
leftIndent	**Number**	Amount of left indention.
ligatures	**Boolean**	Determines whether you use ligatures for the text item.
maximumGlyphScaling	**Number**	The maximum scaling for glyph items in justified text.
maximumLetterScaling	**Number**	The maximum scaling for letters in justified text.

PROPERTY NAME	TYPE	DESCRIPTION
maximumWordScaling	Number	The maximum scaling for words in justified text.
minimumGlyphScaling	Number	The minimum scaling for glyph items in justified text.
minimumLetterScaling	Number	The minimum scaling for letters in justified text.
minimumWordScaling	Number	The minimum scaling for words in justified text.
noBreak	Boolean	If `true`, Photoshop does not insert breaks in text items.
parent	artLayer	The parent `artLayer` of this text item.
position	Array of 2 numbers	The position in the document of the text. The first item in the array is the x-position, the second item is the y-position.
rightIndent	Number	Amount of indent from right side.
size	Number	Font size.
spaceAfter	Number	How much space to insert after a text item.
spaceBefore	Number	Amount of space before a text item.
strikeThru	Boolean	Determines whether the text has the strikethrough style.
textComposer	TextComposer	Type of text composing engine to use.
tracking	Number	Sets the spacing between multiple characters.
underline	Boolean	Determines whether you have underlined text.
useAutoLeading	Boolean	If `true`, Photoshop uses the font's leading information.
verticalScale	Number	Vertical scaling applied to the text item.
warpBend	Number	A number between −100 and 100 for the degree of warp bend style to apply.
warpDirection	Direction constant	Direction of the warp effect.
warpHorizontalDistortion	Number	Percentage between −100 and 100 of the horizontal amount for the warp effect.
warpStyle	WarpStyle constant	Sets the type of warp effect to use.
warpVerticalDistortion	Number	Percentage between −100 and 100 of the vertical amount for the warp effect.
width	Number	Width of a paragraph text item.

Methods

METHOD NAME	RETURN TYPE	DESCRIPTION
convertToShape()	void	Converts the text item and its layer into a fill layer with a clipping path.
createPath()	void	Creates a work path from the text item.

SAVE OPTIONS OBJECTS

When saving a document from Photoshop, you specify the type of file to create and the options for each file type using a save options object. You can also set options for exporting a file to Illustrator using the `ExportOptionsIllustrator` object.

THE BMPSAVEOPTIONS OBJECT

Settings for creating a BMP file.

Properties

PROPERTY NAME	TYPE	DESCRIPTION
alphaChannels	Boolean	If `true`, Photoshop preserves alpha channels in the document.
depth	`BMPDepthType` constant	Specifies the bit depth for the image.
flipRowOrder	Boolean	Sets if the row order is flipped.
osType	`OperatingSystem` constant	Sets the target operating system for the image, either Windows or OS/2.
rleCompression	Boolean	Specifies if RLE compression is used for the image.

THE EPSSAVEOPTIONS OBJECT

Settings for creating an EPS file.

Properties

PROPERTY NAME	TYPE	DESCRIPTION
embedColorProfile	Boolean	If `true`, the document color profile is included with the document.
encoding	`SaveEncoding` constant	Sets the type of encoding to use on the document.
halftoneScreen	Boolean	Determines whether a halftone screen is included with the document.
interpolation	Boolean	If `true`, interpolation is used on images.
preview	`Preview` constant	Specifies the type of preview to include with the document.
psColorManagement	Boolean	Determines whether PostScript color management is used.
transferFunction	Boolean	If `true`, transfer functions are included in the document.
transparentWhites	Boolean	When saving a bitmap document, this option causes white spaces to become transparent.
vectorData	Boolean	Set if you want to include vector data in the file.

THE GIFSAVEOPTIONS OBJECT

Settings for creating a GIF file.

Properties

PROPERTY NAME	TYPE	DESCRIPTION
colors	Number	Number of colors to use in the GIF color table.
dither	Dither constant	Dither method to use when reducing colors.
ditherAmount	Number	Percentage of dither to allow. Must be between 1 and 100.
forced	ForcedColors constant	Sets if you want to force the colors to a specific color table.
interlaced	Boolean	If true, the GIF is interlaced.
matte	MatteType constant	Type of matte to apply to the image.
palette	Palette constant	Type of palette to use in the image.
preserveExactColors	Boolean	Determines whether Photoshop attempts to use the exact colors in the document.
transparency	Boolean	If true, the GIF retains transparent spaces.

THE JPEGSAVEOPTIONS OBJECT

Settings for creating a JPEG file.

Properties

PROPERTY NAME	TYPE	DESCRIPTION
embedColorProfile	Boolean	Determines whether the active color profile embeds in the file.
formatOptions	FormatOptions	Sets the format for the JPEG file.
matte	MatteType	Sets the type of matte to use.
quality	Number	Sets the quality of the image. You must make this a number between 1 and 12, with 12 being the best quality.
scans	Number	When creating a progressive scan JPEG, this sets the number of scans to use. You must make this a number between 3 and 5.

THE PDFSAVEOPTIONS OBJECT

Settings for creating a PDF file.

Properties

PROPERTY NAME	TYPE	DESCRIPTION
alphaChannels	Boolean	Set if you want to preserve alpha channels.
annotations	Boolean	If true, Photoshop preserves annotations in the PDF.
downgradeColorProfile	Boolean	If true, the embedded color profile downgrades to level 2.

SAVE OPTIONS OBJECTS (CONTINUED)

Properties

PROPERTY NAME	TYPE	DESCRIPTION
embedColorProfile	Boolean	Set if you want to embed the color profile.
embedFonts	Boolean	If true and if you include vector data, Photoshop embeds font information in the document.
encoding	PDFEncoding constant	Specifies the encoding type for the PDF.
interpolation	Boolean	If true, images are interpolated in the document.
jpegQuality	Number	Sets the quality of JPEG images in the document. You must make this a number between 1 and 12. This property is only valid for PDF documents using JPEG encoding.
layers	Boolean	If true, Photoshop preserves the layer data.
spotColors	Boolean	If true, Photoshop saves spot colors in the document.
transparency	Boolean	If true, Photoshop preserves transparency.
useOutlines	Boolean	If true and if you include vector data, Photoshop converts fonts to outlines before saving the document.
vectorData	Boolean	If true, Photoshop includes vector data in the file.

THE PICTFILESAVEOPTIONS OBJECT

Settings for creating a PICT file.

Properties

PROPERTY NAME	TYPE	DESCRIPTION
alphaChannels	Boolean	Set to preserve alpha channels.
compression	PICTCompression constant	Specifies the compression method to use for the file.
embedColorProfile	Boolean	Set to embed the color profile.
resolution	PICTBitsPerPixels	Sets the color depth for the document.

THE PNGSAVEOPTIONS OBJECT

Settings for creating a PNG file.

Properties

PROPERTY NAME	TYPE	DESCRIPTION
interlaced	Boolean	If true, the image is interlaced.

THE PHOTOSHOPSAVEOPTIONS OBJECT

Settings for creating a Photoshop PSD file.

Properties

PROPERTY NAME	TYPE	DESCRIPTION
alphaChannels	Boolean	Set to preserve alpha channels.
annotations	Boolean	If true, Photoshop preserves annotations in the file.
embedColorProfile	Boolean	Set to embed the color profile.
layers	Boolean	If true, Photoshop preserves the layer data.
spotColors	Boolean	If true, Photoshop saves spot colors in the document.

THE RAWSAVEOPTIONS OBJECT

Settings for creating a Raw format image file.

Properties

PROPERTY NAME	TYPE	DESCRIPTION
bitsPerChannel	Number	Bit depth for each channel, either 8 or 16.
byteOrder	ByteOrder constant	Specifies the byte order for images with 16 bits per channel.
channelNumber	Number	Number of channels in the image.
headerSize	Number	Size of header.
height	Number	Height of the image.
interleaveChannels	Boolean	If true, the channels in the image are interleaved.
retainHeader	Boolean	Set if you want to retain the header when saving.
width	Number	Width of the image.

SAVE OPTIONS OBJECTS (CONTINUED)

You use these settings to create a TIFF image file.

Properties

PROPERTY NAME	TYPE	DESCRIPTION
alphaChannels	Boolean	Set to preserve alpha channels.
annotations	Boolean	If true, Photoshop preserves annotations in the image.
byteOrder	ByteOrder constant	Sets the byte order for the image.
embedColorProfile	Boolean	If true, the color profile embeds in the image.
imageCompression	TIFFEncoding constant	Sets the type of image compression to use.
jpegQuality	Number	Quality of compression when you use JPEG compression. You must make this a number between 1 and 12.
layerCompression	LayerCompression constant	Sets the type of compression to use if the image includes layers.
layers	Boolean	Set if you want to preserve Photoshop layers in the image.
spotColors	Boolean	If true, Photoshop includes spot colors in the image file.
transparency	Boolean	If true, Photoshop retains image transparency.

You use these settings to export to an Illustrator document format.

Properties

PROPERTY NAME	TYPE	DESCRIPTION
path	IllustratorPathType constant	Specifies what type of paths in the image export.
pathname	String	Specifies the name of the path to export when using named paths.

OPEN OPTIONS OBJECTS

You can specify options for opening certain types of files. Open options objects do the work of many of the dialog boxes you might see when opening some file formats in Photoshop.

THE EPSOPENOPTIONS OBJECT

You use the `EPSOpenOptions` object to specify options when opening an EPS file.

Properties

PROPERTY NAME	TYPE	DESCRIPTION
antiAlias	Boolean	Set if you want to anti-alias vectors.
constrainProportions	Boolean	Constrains the proportions of the EPS file.
height	Number	Height of the image after importing.
mode	OpenDocumentMode constant	Controls the color mode for the document.
resolution	Number	The resolution of the image in pixels per inch.
width	Number	Width of the image after importing.

THE PDFOPENOPTIONS OBJECT

You use the `PDFOpenOptions` object to specify options when opening a PDF file.

Properties

PROPERTY NAME	TYPE	DESCRIPTION
antiAlias	Boolean	Set to anti-alias vectors.
constrainProportions	Boolean	Constrains the proportions of the EPS file.
height	Number	Height of the image after importing.
mode	OpenDocumentMode constant	Sets the color mode for the document.
page	Number	Specifies which page of the PDF file to import.
resolution	Number	The resolution of the image in pixels per inch.
width	Number	Width of the image after importing.

OPEN OPTIONS OBJECTS

THE PHOTOCDOPENOPTIONS OBJECT

You use the `PhotoCDOpenOptions` **object to specify options when opening a PhotoCD format file.**

Properties

PROPERTY NAME	TYPE	DESCRIPTION
colorProfileName	**String**	Name of the color profile to use when opening the image.
colorSpace	`PhotoCDColorSpace` **constant**	Color space to use for the image.
orientation	`Orientation` **constant**	Orientation of the image.
pixelSize	`PhotoCDSize`	Specifies the size of the imported image.
resolution	**Number**	The resolution of the image in pixels per inch.

THE RAWFORMATOPENOPTIONS OBJECT

You use the `RawFormatOpenOptions` **object to specify options when opening a Raw format file.**

Properties

PROPERTY NAME	TYPE	DESCRIPTION
bitsPerChannel	**Number**	Bit depth for each channel, either 8 or 16.
byteOrder	`ByteOrder` **constant**	Specifies the byte order for images with 16 bits per channel.
channelNumber	**Number**	Number of channels in the image.
headerSize	**Number**	Size of header.
height	**Number**	Height of the image.
interleaveChannels	**Boolean**	If `true`, the channels in the image are interleaved.
retainHeader	**Boolean**	Set to retain the header.
width	**Number**	Width of the image.

COLOR OBJECTS

When working with color in Photoshop, you need to use a number of different types of color objects to achieve the desired result. In addition to the objects that correspond to each different color model, you use the SolidColor object to set the color of text and other objects.

Properties

PROPERTY NAME	TYPE	DESCRIPTION
cmyk	CMYKColor **object**	Specifies the CMYK values for the color object.
gray	GrayColor **object**	Specifies the gray color values for the color object.
hsb	HSBColor **object**	Specifies the HSB color values for the color object.
lab	LabColor **object**	Specifies the Lab color values for the color object.
model	ColorModel **constant**	Specifies what type of color model this color object is using.
nearestWebColor	RGBColor **object**	Contains an RGB color object representing the closest Web-safe color for this color object's current color. Read-only.
rgb	RGBColor **object**	Specifies the RGB color values for the color object.

Methods

METHOD NAME	RETURN TYPE	DESCRIPTION
isEqual(SolidColor object color)	Boolean	Returns true if the current color and the previous color of this object are visually equivalent.

Properties

PROPERTY NAME	TYPE	DESCRIPTION
black	Number	Black value between 0 and 100.
cyan	Number	Cyan value between 0 and 100.
magenta	Number	Magenta value between 0 and 100.
yellow	Number	Yellow value between 0 and 100.

COLOR OBJECTS (CONTINUED)

THE GRAYCOLOR OBJECT

Properties

PROPERTY NAME	TYPE	DESCRIPTION
gray	Number	Gray value between 0 and 100.

THE HSBCOLOR OBJECT

Properties

PROPERTY NAME	TYPE	DESCRIPTION
brightness	Number	Brightness value between 0 and 100.
hue	Number	Hue value between 0 and 100.
saturation	Number	Saturation value between 0 and 100.

THE LABCOLOR OBJECT

Properties

PROPERTY NAME	TYPE	DESCRIPTION
a	Number	The a value. Must be between –128 and 127.
b	Number	The b value. Must be between –128 and 127.
l	Number	The l value. Must be between 0 and 100.

THE RGBCOLOR OBJECT

Properties

PROPERTY NAME	TYPE	DESCRIPTION
red	Number	The red value. Must be between 0 and 255.
green	Number	The green value. Must be between 0 and 255.
blue	Number	The blue value. Must be between 0 and 255.
hexValue	Number	The hexadecimal representation of this color object's color.

PHOTOSHOP SCRIPTING CONSTANTS

M any properties and methods require a specific type of value defined by a scripting constant. The value for the constant is provided by typing the constant name, a dot, and then the value you want to use.

CONSTANT NAME	VALUES	DESCRIPTION
AdjustmentReference	ABSOLUTE, RELATIVE	Use with the selective color method of the `layer` object.
AnchorPosition	BOTTOMCENTER, BOTTOMLEFT, BOTTOMRIGHT, MIDDLECENTER, MIDDLELEFT, MIDDLERIGHT, TOPCENTER, TOPLEFT, TOPRIGHT	Use to specify the anchor position for rotation and resizing methods.
AntiAlias	CRISP, NONE, SHARP, SMOOTH, STRONG	Use to set the amount of anti-aliasing for text items.
BMPDepthType	BMP_A1R5G5B5, BMP_A4R4G4B4, BMP_A8R8G8B8, BMP_R5G6B5, BMP_R8G8B8, BMP_X1R5G5B5, BMP_X4R4G4B4, BMP_X8R8G8B8, EIGHT, FOUR, ONE, SIXTEEN, THIRTYTWO, TWENTYFOUR	Use to set the bit depth when creating BMP images.
BitmapConversionType	CUSTOMPATTERN, DIFFUSIONDITHER, HALFTHRESHOLD, HALFTONESCREEN, PATTERNDITHER	Use to set the type of conversion to apply when changing a document to Bitmap mode.
BitmapHalfToneType	CROSS, DIAMOND, ELLIPSE, LINE, ROUND, SQUARE	The type of halftone to use when converting a document to Bitmap mode.
BitsPerChannelType	EIGHT, ONE, SIXTEEN	Use to set the number of bits per channel in a document.
BlendMode	COLORBLEND, COLORBURN, COLORDODGE, DARKEN, DIFFERENCE, DISSOLVE, EXCLUSION, HARDLIGHT, HUE, LIGHTEN, LINEARBURN, LINEARDODGE, LINEARLIGHT, LUMINOSITY, MULTIPLY, NORMAL, OVERLAY, PASSTHROUGH, PINLIGHT, SATURATION, SCREEN, SOFTLIGHT, VIVIDLIGHT	The blend mode to apply to an `artLayer` or `layerSet`.
ByteOrder	IBM, MACOS	Use to set the byte order when opening Raw format images or creating TIFF images.
Case	ALLCAPS, NORMAL, SMALLCAPS	Use to set the capitalization of text items.
ChangeMode	BITMAP, CMYK, GRAYSCALE, LAB, INDEXEDCOLOR, MULTICHANNEL, RGB	Use to change the mode of a document.
ChannelType	COMPONENT, MASKEDAREA, SELECTEDAREA, SPOTCOLOR	Use to set a type for a channel.

PHOTOSHOP SCRIPTING
CONSTANTS (CONTINUED)

CONSTANT NAME	VALUES	DESCRIPTION
ColorBlendMode	BEHIND, CLEAR, COLOR, COLORBURN, COLORDODGE, DARKEN, DIFFERENCE, DISSOLVE, EXCLUSION, HARDLIGHT, HUE, LIGHTEN, LINEARBURN, LINEARDODGE, LINEARLIGHT, LUMINOSITY, MULTIPLY, NORMAL, OVERLAY, PINLIGHT, SATURATION, SCREEN, SOFTLIGHT, VIVIDLIGHT	Use to set the blend mode when stroking or filling a selection.
ColorModel	CMYK, GRAYSCALE, HSB, LAB, NONE, RGB	Use to specify what color model a SolidColor object is using.
ColorPicker	ADOBE, APPLE, PLUGIN, WINDOWS	Use to specify what color picker to use.
ColorProfile	CUSTOM, NONE, WORKING	Use to set the type of color profile for a document.
CopyrightedType	COPYRIGHTEDWORK, PUBLICDOMAIN, UNMARKED	The copyright code for the document.
CreateFields	DUPLICATION, INTERPOLATION	For use with the De-interlace filter.
DialogModes	ALL, ERROR, NO	Use to set how often Photoshop shows dialogs.
Direction	HORIZONTAL, VERTICAL	Use to set the direction of text.
DisplacementMapType	STRETCHTOFIT, TILE, DITHER, DIFFUSION, NOISE, NONE, PATTERN	Use with the displace filter.
DocumentFill	BACKGROUNDCOLOR, TRANSPARENT, WHITE	Use to specify the background color mode for new documents.
DocumentMode	BITMAP, CMYK, DUOTONE, GRAYSCALE, INDEXEDCOLOR, LAB, MULTICHANNEL, RGB	
EliminateFields	EVENFIELDS, ODDFIELDS	Use with the Interlace filter.
ExportType	ILLUSTRATORPATHS	Use to export files to Illustrator format.
Extension	LOWERCASE, NONE, UPPERCASE	Use to set how Photoshop handles extensions when saving files.
ForcedColors	BLACKWHITE, NONE, PRIMARIES, WEB	Use to force colors to a specific color table when creating GIF files.
FormatOptions	OPTIMIZEDBASELINE, PROGRESSIVE, STANDARDBASELINE	Use to set the formatting options when creating JPEG files.
GridLineStyle	DASHED, DOTTED, SOLID	Use to set the type of line in the grid preferences.
GridSize	LARGE, MEDIUM, NONE, SMALL	Use to set the size of the grid in the preferences.

CONSTANT NAME	VALUES	DESCRIPTION
GuideLineStyle	DASHED, SOLID	Use to set the type of guide line.
IllustratorPathType	ALLPATHS, DOCUMENTBOUNDS, NAMEDPATH	Use to specify what type of paths are exported to Illustrator.
Intent	ABSOLUTECOLORIMETRIC, PERCEPTUAL, RELATIVECOLORIMETRIC, SATURATION	Use when converting the document color space or printing a document.
Justification	CENTER, CENTERJUSTIFIED, FULLYJUSTIFIED, LEFT, LEFTJUSTIFIED, RIGHT, RIGHTJUSTIFIED	Use to set the justification of paragraphs in text items.
Language	BRAZILLIANPORTUGUESE, CANADIANFRENCH, DANISH, DUTCH, ENGLISHUK, ENGLISHUSA, FINNISH, FRENCH, GERMAN, ITALIAN, NORWEGIAN, NYNORSKNORWEGIAN, OLDGERMAN, PORTUGUESE, SPANISH, SWEDISH, SWISSGERMA	Possible languages for text items.
LayerCompression	RLE, ZIP	Layer compression method for saving layer TIFF files.
LayerKind	BRIGHTNESSCONTRAST, CHANNELMIXER, COLORBALANCE, CURVES, GRADIENTFILL, GRADIENTMAP, HUESATURATION, LEVELS, INVERSION, NORMAL, PATTERNFILL, POSTERIZE, SELECTIVECOLOR, SOLIDFILL, TEXT, THRESHOLD	Sets the type of a layer. The TEXT value allows you to add text to the layer.
LensType	PRIME105, PRIME35, ZOOMLENS	Lens type for Lens Flare filter.
MatteType	BACKGROUND, BLACK, FOREGROUND, NETSCAPE, NONE, SEMIGRAY, WHITE	Use to set the matte when creating JPEG and GIF files.
NewDocumentMode	BITMAP, CMYK, GRAYSCALE, LAB, RGB	Sets the color mode of new documents.
NoiseDistribution	GAUSSIAN, UNIFORM	Use with the Apply Noise filter.
OffsetUndefinedAreas	REPEATEDGEPIXELS, SETTOBACKGROUND, WRAPAROUND	Use with the artLayer. applyOffset() method.
OpenDocumentMode	CMYK, GRAYSCALE, LAB, RGB	Use to specify the mode to open PDF and EPS documents.
OpenDocumentType	ACROBATTOUCHUPIMAGE, ALIASPIX, BMP, COMPUSERVEGIF, ELECTRICIMAGE, EPS, EPSPICTPREVIEW, EPSTIFFPREVIEW FILMSTRIP, JPEG, PCX, PDF, PHOTOCD, PHOTOSHOP, PHOTOSHOPDCS_1, PHOTOSHOPDCS_2, PHOTOSHOPEPS, PHOTOSHOPPDF, PICTFILEFORMAT, PICTRESOURCEFORMAT, PIXAR, PNG, PORTABLEBITMAP, RAW, SCITEXCT, SGIRGB, SOFTIMAGE, TARGA, TIFF, WAVEFRONTRLA, WIRELESSBITMAP	Use to specify the type of file Photoshop is opening up.

PHOTOSHOP SCRIPTING
CONSTANTS (CONTINUED)

CONSTANT NAME	VALUES	DESCRIPTION
OperatingSystem	OS2, WINDOWS	Use specify the operating system type for bitmap images.
Orientation	LANDSCAPE, PORTRAIT	Use when opening PhotoCD images to specify the orientation of the image.
OtherPaintingCursors	PRECISEOTHER, STANDARDOTHER	Use to set the preferences option for non-painting cursors.
PDFEncoding	JPEG, PDFZIP	Specifies image encoding for PDF files.
PICTBitsPerPixels	EIGHT, FOUR, SIXTEEN, THIRTYTWO, TWO	Use to set the bit depth of PICT images.
PICTCompression	NONE, JPEGHIGHPICT, JPEGLOWPICT, JPEGMAXIMUMPICT, JPEGMEDIUMPICT	Use to specify a compression type for PICT images.
PaintingCursors	BRUSHSIZE, PRECISE, STANDARD	Use to set the preference for painting cursor style.
Palette	EXACT, LOCALADAPTIVE, LOCALPERCEPTUAL, LOCALSELECTIVE, MACOSPALETTE, MASTERADAPTIVE, MASTERPERCEPTUAL, MASTERSELECTIVE, PREVIOUSPALETTE, UNIFORM, WEBPALETTE, WINDOWSPALETTE	Use when creating GIF images.
PhotoCDColorSpace	LAB16, LAB8, RGB16, RGB8	Specifies the color space for PhotoCD images.
PhotoCDSize	EXTRALARGE, LARGE, MAXIMUM, MEDIUM, MINIMUM, SMALL	Specifies the image quality for PhotoCD images.
PointType	POSTSCRIPT, TRADITIONAL	Use to set the point size preference.
PolarConversionType	POLARTORECTANGULAR, RECTANGULARTOPOLAR	Use with the Polar Coordinates filter.
Preview	EIGHTBITTIFF, MACOSEIGHTBIT, MACOSJPEG, MACOSMONOCHROME, MONOCHROMETIFF, NONE	Use to specify a preview type when saving EPS documents.
PrintEncoding	ASCII, BINARY, JPEG	Use to specify the encoding when printing a document.
RadialBlurMethod	SPIN, ZOOM	Use with the Radial Blur filter.
RadialBlurQuality	BEST, DRAFT, GOOD	Use with the Radial Blur filter.
RasterizeType	ENTIRELAYER, FILLCONTENT, LAYERCLIPPINGPATH, LINKEDLAYERS, SHAPE, TEXTCONTENTS	Use to rasterize a layer.
RedoKey	COMMANDSHIFTZ, COMMANDY, COMMANDZ	Use to set the Redo key preference.

CONSTANT NAME	VALUES	DESCRIPTION
ResampleMethod	BICUBIC, BILINEAR, NEARESTNEIGHBOR, NONE	Resample method options when resizing an image.
RippleSize	LARGE, MEDIUM, SMALL	Use with the Ripple filter.
SaveBehavior	ALWAYSSAVE, ASKWHENSAVING, NEVERSAVE	Use to set the default extension preference.
SaveEncoding	ASCII, BINARY, JPEGHIGH, JPEGLOW, JPEGMAXIMUM, JPEGMEDIUM	Use to specify the encoding when saving EPS documents.
SaveOptions	DONOTSAVECHANGES, PROMPTTOSAVECHANGES, SAVECHANGES	Use to specify Photoshop's behavior when closing an unsaved document.
SelectionType	DIMINISH, EXTEND, INTERSECT, REPLACE	Use when creating, loading, or saving selections.
SmartBlurMode	EDGEONLY, NORMAL, OVERLAYEDGE	Use with the Smart Blur filter.
SmartBlurQuality	HIGH, LOW, MEDIUM	Use with the Smart Blur filter.
SourceSpaceType	DOCUMENT, PROOF	Use when printing documents.
SpherizeMode	HORIZONTAL, NORMAL, VERTICAL	Use with the Spherize filter.
StrokeLocation	CENTER, INSIDE, OUTSIDE	Use to specify the location along the selection border of a stroke.
TIFFEncoding	JPEG, NONE, TIFFLZW, TIFFZIP	Use to set the encoding for TIFF files.
TargaBitsPerPixels	SIXTEEN, THIRTYTWO, TWENTYFOUR	Use to set the depth when saving Targa images.
TextComposer	ADOBEEVERYLINE, ADOBESINGLELINE	Possible types of text composers.
TextType	PARAGRAPHTEXT, POINTTEXT	Use to set the type of a text item.
TextureType	BLOCKS, CANVAS, FILE, FROSTED, TINYLENS	Use with the Texturize filter.
TrimType	BOTTOMRIGHT, TOPLEFT, TRANSPARENT	Use when trimming a document.
TypeUnits	MM, PIXELS, POINTS	Possible values for the type unit preference.
UndefinedAreas	REPEATEDGEPIXELS, WRAPAROUND	Use with the Displace, Offset, Shear, and Wave filters.
Units	CM, INCHES, MM, PERCENT, PICAS, PIXELS, POINTS	Possible ruler units.
Urgency	FOUR, HIGH, LOW, NONE, NORMAL, SEVEN, SIX, THREE, TWO	Possible urgency settings for a document's info.
WarpStyle	ARC, ARCH, ARCLOWER, ARCUPPER, BULGE, FISH, FISHEYE, FLAG, INFLATE, NONE, RISE, SHELLLOWER, SHELLUPPER, SQUEEZE, TWIST, WAVE	Use with the Warp filter.
WaveType	SINE, SQUARE, TRIANGULAR	Use to set the wave type with the Wave filter.
ZigZagType	AROUNDCENTER, OUTFROMCENTER, PONDRIPPLES	Use with the ZigZag filter.

APPENDIX

WHAT'S ON THE CD-ROM

The CD-ROM included in this book contains many useful files and programs. Before installing any of the programs on the disc, make sure that you do not already have a newer version of the program already

installed on your computer. For information on installing different versions of the same program, contact the program's manufacturer.

SYSTEM REQUIREMENTS

To use the contents of the CD-ROM, your computer must have the following hardware and software:

For Windows 9x, Windows 2000, Windows NT4 (with SP 4 or later), Windows Me, or Windows XP:
- PC with a Pentium processor running at 120 Mhz or faster
- At least 32 MB of total RAM installed on your computer; for best performance, we recommend at least 64 MB
- A CD-ROM drive

For Macintosh:
- Mac OS computer with a 68040 or faster processor running OS 9.0 or later
- At least 32 MB of total RAM installed on your computer; for best performance, we recommend at least 64 MB

AUTHOR'S SOURCE CODE

These files contain all the sample code from the book. You can browse the files directly from the CD-ROM, or you can copy them to your hard drive and use them as the basis for your own projects. To find the files on the CD-ROM, open the Samples folder.

ACROBAT VERSION

The CD-ROM contains an e-version of this book that you can view and search using Adobe Acrobat Reader. You cannot print the pages or copy text from the Acrobat files. The CD-ROM includes an evaluation version of Adobe Acrobat Reader.

INSTALLING AND USING THE SOFTWARE

For your convenience, the software titles appearing on the CD-ROM are listed alphabetically.

Acrobat Reader
For Windows 95/98/NT/2000 and Mac OS. Freeware.

Adobe Acrobat Reader allows you to view the online version of this book. For more information on using Acrobat Reader, see the section "Using the E-Version of this Book" in this Appendix. For more information about Acrobat Reader and Adobe Systems, see www.adobe.com.

Adobe Photoshop Scripting Plug-In
For Windows 95/98/NT/2000 and Mac OS. Freeware.

The Photoshop Scripting Support Plug-in allows you script Photoshop using JavaScript, Visual Basic on Windows, and

AppleScript on Mac OS. See Chapter 1 for more information on how to install the plug-in.

Adobe Illustrator

For Windows 95/98/NT/2000 and Mac OS. Trial version.

Adobe Illustrator is a powerful graphics and Illustrator application. This demo version allows you to get familiar with the application. For more information on Adobe Illustrator please visit the Adobe Web site at www.adobe.com.

BBEdit

For Mac OS. Freeware.

BBEdit is a powerful text editor for the Macintosh. It is full of features that make scripting and text editing a breeze including multiple clipboards and powerful search and replace features.

UltraEdit 32

For Windows 95/98/NT/2000. Shareware.

UltraEdit is a great text editor for Windows. It offers search and replace and multiple document views.

TROUBLESHOOTING

The programs on the CD-ROM should work on computers with the minimum of system requirements. However, some programs may not work properly.

The two most likely problems for the programs not working properly include not having enough memory (RAM) for the programs you want to use, or having other programs running that affect the installation or running of a program. If you receive error messages such as Not enough memory or Setup cannot continue, try one or more of the methods below and then try using the software again:

- Turn off any anti-virus software

- Close all running programs

- In Windows, close the CD-ROM interface and run demos or installations directly from Windows Explorer

- Have your local computer store add more RAM to your computer

If you still have trouble installing the items from the CD-ROM, call the Wiley Publishing Customer Service phone number: 800-762-2974 (outside the U.S.: 317-572-3994). You can also contact Wiley Publishing Customer Service by e-mail at techsupdum@wiley.com.

USING THE E-VERSION OF THIS BOOK

You can view *Adobe Scripting: Your visual blueprint for scripting in Photoshop and Illustrator* on your screen using the CD-ROM included at the back of this book. The CD-ROM allows you to search the contents of each chapter of the book for a specific word or phrase. The CD-ROM also provides a convenient way of keeping the book handy while traveling.

You must install Adobe Acrobat Reader on your computer before you can view the book on the CD-ROM. The

CD-ROM includes this program for your convenience. Acrobat Reader allows you to view Portable Document Format (PDF) files, which can display books and magazines on your screen exactly as they appear in printed form.

To view the content of this book using Acrobat Reader, display the contents of the CD-ROM. Double-click the eBook folder to display the contents of the folder. In the window that appears, double-click the icon for the chapter of the book you want to review.

USING THE E-VERSION OF THIS BOOK

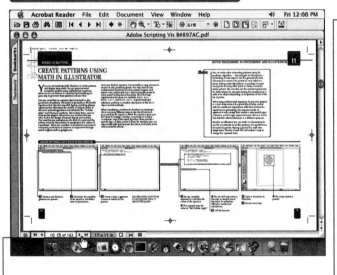

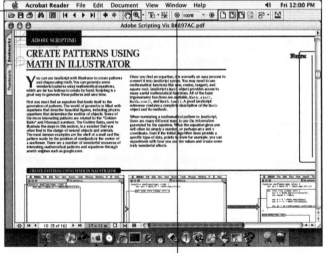

FLIP THROUGH PAGES

1 Click one of these options to flip through the pages of a section.

|◀ First page

◀ Previous page

▶ Next page

▶| Last page

ZOOM IN

1 Click 🔍 to magnify an area of the page.

2 Click the area of the page you want to magnify.

■ Click one of these options to display the page at 100% magnification (🔲) or to fit the entire page inside the window (🔲).

Extra

To install Acrobat Reader, insert the CD-ROM into a drive. In the screen that appears, click Software. Click Acrobat Reader and then follow the instructions on your screen to install the program.

You can make searching the book more convenient by copying the PDF files to your computer. To do this, display the contents of the CD-ROM and then copy the Book folder from the CD-ROM to your hard drive. This allows you to easily access the contents of the book at any time.

Acrobat Reader is a popular and useful program. There are many files available on the Web that are designed to be viewed using Acrobat Reader. Look for files with the .pdf extension. For more information about Acrobat Reader, visit the Web site.

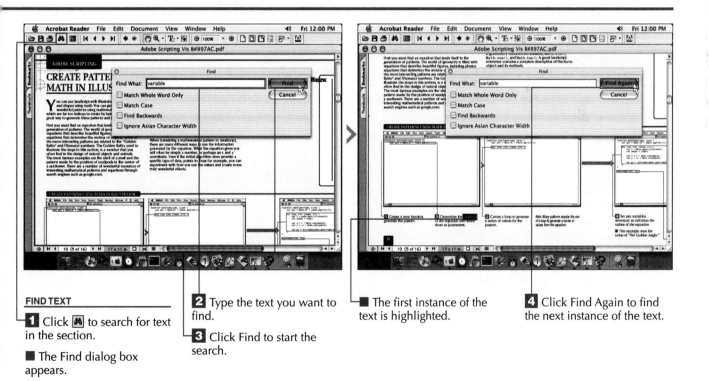

FIND TEXT

1 Click 🔍 to search for text in the section.

■ The Find dialog box appears.

2 Type the text you want to find.

3 Click Find to start the search.

■ The first instance of the text is highlighted.

4 Click Find Again to find the next instance of the text.

APPENDIX

WILEY PUBLISHING, INC.
END-USER LICENSE AGREEMENT

READ THIS. You should carefully read these terms and conditions before opening the software packet(s) included with *Adobe Scripting: Your visual blueprint for scripting in Photoshop and Illustrator*. This is a license agreement ("Agreement") between you and Wiley Publishing, Inc. ("WPI"). By opening the accompanying software packet(s), you acknowledge that you have read and accept the following terms and conditions. If you do not agree and do not want to be bound by such terms and conditions, promptly return the Book and the unopened software packet(s) to the place you obtained them from for a full refund.

1. License Grant. WPI grants to you (either an individual or entity) a nonexclusive license to use one copy of the enclosed software program(s) (collectively, the "Software") solely for your own personal or business purposes on a single computer (whether a standard computer or a workstation component of a multi-user network). The Software is in use on a computer when it is loaded into temporary memory (RAM) or installed into permanent memory (hard disc, CD-ROM, or other storage device). WPI reserves all rights not expressly granted herein.

2. Ownership. WPI is the owner of all right, title, and interest, including copyright, in and to the compilation of the Software recorded on the disc(s) or CD-ROM ("Software Media"). Copyright to the individual programs recorded on the Software Media is owned by the author, or other authorized copyright owner of each program. Ownership of the Software and all proprietary rights relating thereto remain with WPI and its licensers.

3. Restrictions on Use and Transfer.
(a) You may only (i) make one copy of the Software for backup or archival purposes, or (ii) transfer the Software to a single hard disc, provided that you keep the original for backup or archival purposes. You may not (i) rent or lease the Software, (ii) copy or reproduce the Software through a LAN or other network system or through any computer subscriber system or bulletin-board system, or (iii) modify, adapt, or create derivative works based on the Software.

(b) You may not reverse engineer, decompile, or disassemble the Software. You may transfer the Software and user documentation on a permanent basis, provided that the transferee agrees to accept the terms and conditions of this Agreement and you retain no copies. If the Software is an update or has been updated, any transfer must include the most recent update and all prior versions.

4. Restrictions on Use of Individual Programs. You must follow the individual requirements and restrictions detailed for each individual program in Appendix D of this Book. These limitations are also contained in the individual license agreements recorded on the Software Media. These limitations may include a requirement that after using the program for a specified period of time, the user must pay a registration fee or discontinue use. By opening the Software packet(s), you will be agreeing to abide by the licenses and restrictions for these individual programs that are detailed in Appendix D and on the Software Media. None of the material on this Software Media or listed in this Book may ever be redistributed, in original or modified form, for commercial purposes.

5. Limited Warranty.
(a) WPI warrants that the Software and Software Media are free from defects in materials and workmanship under

normal use for a period of sixty (60) days from the date of purchase of this Book. If WPI receives notification within the warranty period of defects in materials or workmanship, WPI will replace the defective Software Media.

(b)   WPI AND THE AUTHOR OF THE BOOK DISCLAIM ALL OTHER WARRANTIES, EXPRESS OR IMPLIED, INCLUDING WITHOUT LIMITATION IMPLIED WARRANTIES OF MERCHANTABILITY AND FITNESS FOR A PARTICULAR PURPOSE, WITH RESPECT TO THE SOFTWARE, THE PROGRAMS, THE SOURCE CODE CONTAINED THEREIN, AND/OR THE TECHNIQUES DESCRIBED IN THIS BOOK. WPI DOES NOT WARRANT THAT THE FUNCTIONS CONTAINED IN THE SOFTWARE WILL MEET YOUR REQUIREMENTS OR THAT THE OPERATION OF THE SOFTWARE WILL BE ERROR FREE.

(c)   This limited warranty gives you specific legal rights, and you may have other rights that vary from jurisdiction to jurisdiction.

6.   Remedies.
(a)   WPI's entire liability and your exclusive remedy for defects in materials and workmanship shall be limited to replacement of the Software Media, which may be returned to WPI with a copy of your receipt at the following address: Software Media Fulfillment Department, Attn.: *Adobe Scripting: Your visual blueprint for scripting in Photoshop and Illustrator*, Wiley Publishing, Inc., 10475 Crosspoint Blvd., Indianapolis, IN 46256, or call 1-800-762-2974. Please allow four to six weeks for delivery. This Limited Warranty is void if failure of the Software Media has resulted from accident, abuse or misapplication. Any replacement Software Media will be warranted for the remainder of the original warranty period or thirty (30) days, whichever is longer.

(b)   In no event shall WPI or the author be liable for any damages whatsoever (including without limitation damages for loss of business profits, business interruption, loss of business information, or any other pecuniary loss) arising from the use of or inability to use the Book or the Software, even if WPI has been advised of the possibility of such damages.

(c)   Because some jurisdictions do not allow the exclusion or limitation of liability for consequential or incidental damages, the above limitation or exclusion may not apply to you.

7.   U.S. Government Restricted Rights. Use, duplication, or disclosure of the Software for or on behalf of the United States of America, its agencies and/or instrumentalities (the "U.S. Government") is subject to restrictions as stated in paragraph (c)(1)(ii) of the Rights in Technical Data and Computer Software clause of DFARS 252.227-7013, or subparagraphs (c) (1) and (2) of the Commercial Computer Software - Restricted Rights clause at FAR 52.227-19, and in similar clauses in the NASA FAR supplement, as applicable.

8.   General. This Agreement constitutes the entire understanding of the parties and revokes and supersedes all prior agreements, oral or written, between them and may not be modified or amended except in a writing signed by both parties hereto that specifically refers to this Agreement. This Agreement shall take precedence over any other documents that may be in conflict herewith. If any one or more provisions contained in this Agreement are held by any court or tribunal to be invalid, illegal, or otherwise unenforceable, each and every other provision shall remain in full force and effect.

INDEX

Symbols

− (decrement) operator, 14–15
// in comments, 37
/ (division) operator, 12
/* in comments, 37
− (subtraction) operator, 12–13
+ (addition) operator, 12
++ (increment) operator, 14–15
= (assignment) operator, 15
== (comparison) operator, 15
* (multiplication) operator, 12

A

Acrobat Reader, installation, 266
actions, 3
Actions palette (Photoshop), 180–181
active document
    reference, 46
    save, 120–121
active layers (Photoshop), 60
add( ) method
    gradients, 84–85
    Illustrator documents, 44–45
    object creation, 42
    objects, 38
    path items, 68–69
    text string variables, 132–133
addition (+) operator, 12
Adobe Acrobat, CD-ROM bundle, 266
Adobe Photoshop Scripting Plug-In, installation, 266–267
alert( ) function
    communication with user, 36
    overview, 8
alerts, arrays, 23
anchor point (Illustrator), 68–69
AppleScript (Macintosh), 3
Application object, 38
    application methods, 190
    communication methods, 190
    methods, 190, 230–231
    properties, 190, 230
area text (Illustrator), 100–103
arguments, functions and, 26
arithmetic operators, 12
Array.length property, 23

arrays
    alerts, 23
    convert from string, 34–35
    definition, 18
    length property, 19
    loops and, 22–23
    multidimensional, 52
    point arrays, 40
    rectangle arrays, 40
art layers, 56–57, 60–61, 92–93
artLayers collection, 242
artLayers.add( ) method, 56
artworkKnockout property, common features, 221
assignment (=) operators, 14–15

B

batch processes, 151–155
BBEdit/BBEdit Lite, installation, 267
bind variables, 130–131
blendingMode property, common features, 221
BMPSaveOptions object, 252
Boolean variables, 10
braces ({ }) in JavaScript, 8
brackets ([ ]) in JavaScript, 8
break statement, 21
browse for scripts, 6

C

C, JavaScript comparison, 8
C++, JavaScript comparison, 8
call a function, 24
    batch processes and, 152
    recursive functions, 29
canvas, 48–49
capture dataset, 131
case sensitivity, variables and, 10
CD-ROM bundle
    Acrobat version, 266
    author's source code, 266
    e-version of book, 268–269
    license agreement, 270–271
    software installation, 266–267
    system requirements, 266
Character object
    methods, 200
    properties, 198–199

Adobe Scripting:
Your visual blueprint for scripting
in Photoshop and Illustrator

INDEX

Adobe Scripting:
Your visual blueprint for scripting
in Photoshop and Illustrator

INDEX

Adobe Scripting:
Your visual blueprint for scripting
in Photoshop and Illustrator

INDEX

Adobe Scripting:
Your visual blueprint for scripting
in Photoshop and Illustrator

O

object-oriented programming, 38
objects
    add( ) method, 38
    Application, 38, 190, 230–231
    artLayer, 242–247
    Character, 198
    color, 259–260
    create, 30
    Document, 191–193, 234–237
    DocumentInfo, 237–238
    EPSSaveOptions, 215
    export, create, 144–145
    export options, 215–220
    ExportOptionsFlash, 217
    ExportOptionsGIF, 218
    ExportOptionsJPEG, 218–219
    ExportOptionsPhotoshop, 219
    ExportOptionsPNG8, 220
    ExportOptionsPNG24, 219–220
    GroupItem, 196–197
    Illustrator hierarchy, 39
    IllustratorSaveOptions, 216
    IndexedConversionOptions, 241
    Layer, 194–195
    layer objects, 242–249
    layerSet, 248–249
    length property, 38
    Open Options, 215
    Paragraph, 200–203
    PathItem, 224–225
    PathPoint, 226
    Selection, 238–240
    TextArtItem, 203–206
    TextFace, 206
    textItem, 249–251
    TextLine, 207–209
    textPath, 210
    textRange, 211–212
    Words, 213–214
opacity property, common features, 221
open documents, batch process, 152–153

Open Options objects, 215
operators
    arithmetic, 12
    assignment (=) operators, 14–15
    comma operator, variable declaration, 11
    comparison (==), 15
    decrementing variables, 14–15
    incrementing variables, 14–15
    typeof, 11
orientation property, Illustrator text, 101

P

pageToOpen property, PDFOpenOptions object, 215
palettes
    Actions (Photoshop), 180–181
    Layers (Photoshop), 60
    Variables (Illustrator), 130–131
Paragraph object
    methods, 203
    properties, 200–202
paragraphs (Illustrator), 114–115
Paragraphs collection, 200
parameters
    function values, 26
    names, 26
    pass to functions, 26–27
parent property
    common features, 221
    Documents collection, 191
pass parameters, to functions, 26–27
paste( ) method, Photoshop clipboard, 54–55
path items
    create, 68–69
    drawing tools, 70
    points, 68–69
    position, 76–77
    rotate, 76–77
    scale, 76–77
    scripting uses, 2
    text flow between, 110–111
path text, 100–103
PathItem object, 224–225
PathItems collection, 223–224

INDEX

Adobe Scripting:
Your visual blueprint for scripting
in Photoshop and Illustrator

INDEX

Adobe Scripting:
Your visual blueprint for scripting
in Photoshop and Illustrator

INDEX

Adobe Scripting:
Your visual blueprint for scripting
in Photoshop and Illustrator

with these two-color Visual™ guides